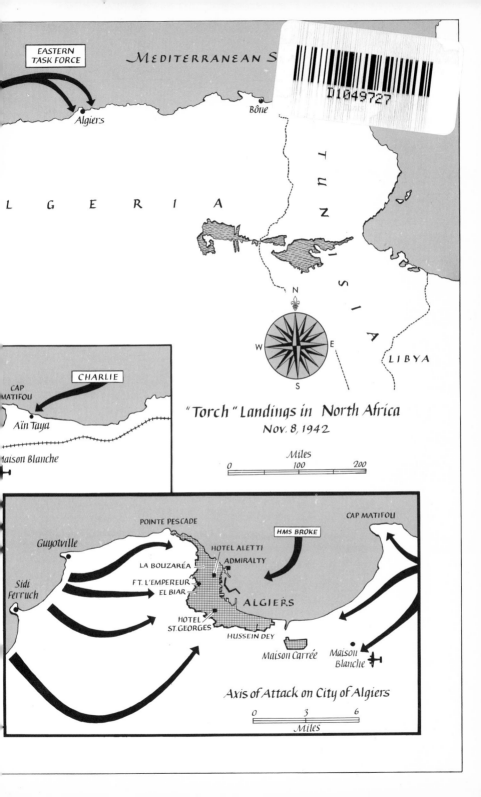

EASTERN
TASK FORCE

MEDITERRANEAN S

Algiers

Bône

D1049727

L G E R I A

T
U
N
I
S
I
A

LIBYA

N
W   E
S

CAP
MATIFOU

CHARLIE

Aïn Taya

Maison Blanche

"Torch" Landings in North Africa
Nov. 8, 1942

Miles
0   100   200

POINTE PESCADE

CAP MATIFOU

HMS BROKE

Guyotville

HOTEL ALETTI
ADMIRALTY

LA BOUZARÉA

Sidi
Ferruch

FT. L'EMPEREUR
EL BIAR

ALGIERS

HOTEL
ST.GEORGES

HUSSEIN DEY

Maison Carrée

Maison
Blanche

Axis of Attack on City of Algiers

0   3   6
Miles

THE
MURDER OF
ADMIRAL DARLAN

A Study in Conspiracy by

PETER TOMPKINS

SIMON AND SCHUSTER · NEW YORK

FIRST PRINTING

Library of Congress Catalog Card Number: 65-11983
Manufactured in the United States of America
By The Book Press, Brattleboro, Vermont
Designed by Eve Metz

THE AUTHOR AND THE PUBLISHERS ARE GRATEFUL FOR PERMIS-
SION TO INCLUDE IN THIS BOOK MATERIAL FROM THE FOLLOWING
SOURCES:

Dodd, Mead & Company for material from *Adventure in Diplomacy: Our French Dilemma* by Kenneth W. Pendar, copyright 1945 by Kenneth Pendar.

Doubleday & Company, Inc. for selections from *Crusade in Europe* by Dwight D. Eisenhower, copyright 1948; and from *Diplomat Among Warriors* by Robert D. Murphy, copyright © 1964.

Éditions Médicis for material from *La Vérité sur l'armistice* by Albert Kammerer, 1945.

Harper & Brothers for selections from *The Time for Decision* by Sumner Welles, 1944; and from *Calculated Risk* by Mark W. Clark, 1950.

Houghton Mifflin Company for material from *Memoirs of the Second World War* by Sir Winston S. Churchill.

Alfred A. Knopf for material from *Our Vichy Gamble* by William L. Langer, 1947.

Librairie Académique Perrin for material from *L'Amiral Darlan parle* by Alain Darlan.

McGraw-Hill Book Company for material from *I Was There* by William D. Leahy, copyright 1950.

Charles Scribner's Sons for material from *The Secret History of the War* by Waverley Root.

Simon and Schuster, Inc. for selections from *My Three Years with Eisenhower* by Harry C. Butcher, 1946; and from *The Complete War Memoirs of Charles de Gaulle*.

Paul Winkler for material from his book, *The Thousand-Year Conspiracy: Secret Germany Behind the Mask*, published by Charles Scribner's Sons.

For my wife:
without whom this book
would never have been written—
let alone typed.

CONTENTS

FOREWORD

by Charles Collingwood

It has always been difficult to understand why the North African phase of the Second World War has been so neglected by historians. From the military point of view it was a rehearsal for the successful landings in Europe two years later. From a political point of view it was a rehearsal for all the tribulations of the Western Alliance in the postwar period. The North African drama assembled in its cast the three men who fifteen years later were to lead the greatest Western Powers—Eisenhower, Macmillan and de Gaulle—each at a crucial point in his career.

They found themselves involved in an intrigue of Byzantine complexity. What was at stake was nothing less than the future of France. The Allied leaders understood this only dimly. The French understood it very well and, according to their prejudices, ambitions and delusions, sought to determine the outcome. There ensued a confrontation between the pseudo-Machiavellian American diplomacy of the Roosevelt era and the baroque machinations of prewar French politics. As might be expected in such a contest, American policy did not carry the day. Nor, for that matter, were the most dangerous of the French plotters successful. In the end, Charles de Gaulle came to power among the French in North Africa. It was already in 1942 a gross misreading of the realities of the situation to think he would not. But his triumph was no thanks to us, and de Gaulle has never forgotten it, nor, one suspects, forgiven it.

The central figure in the episode Peter Tompkins recounts is Admiral Jean Darlan. He bore the burden of the hate of some of the participants and the hopes of the others. Darlan is one of the great "might-have-beens" of history. When France fell, both

Churchill and Roosevelt wanted Darlan to become the leader of Frenchmen who would still fight against Germany. As Churchill wrote in his memoirs:

". . . how vain are human calculations of self-interest. Rarely has there been a more convincing example. Admiral Darlan had but to sail in any one of his ships to any port outside France to become the master of all French interests outside German control. He would not have come like General de Gaulle with only an unconquerable heart and a few kindred spirits. . . . The whole French Empire would have rallied to him. Nothing could have prevented him from being the liberator of France. The fame and power which he so ardently desired were in his grasp."

Darlan did join the Allies: only two years later in 1942. His mistake was the unforgivable one of bad timing. In his case it was also fatal.

But this is getting ahead of Peter Tompkins' story. As an agent of the United States government, he was an eyewitness to much of the melodrama in Algiers in 1942–43. From what he saw then and what he has since laboriously reconstructed, he has pieced together the whole lurid and implausible tale. It is as exciting as a detective story. It involves murder in high places, plots, counterplots, spies and, every now and then, honest men. Everyone had a motive and many a false trail was laid. Above all, if you look back on it, the ending is inevitable. That is something that good history shares with good detective stories.

Much of all this has never been told before. Those of us who were there could only report part of what was going on. It was felt that any clear account would embarrass governments, as well it might. Since then few of the chief participants have been anxious to reveal their roles, and the tongues of some of the principal witnesses have been stilled by death—usually under violent circumstances.

This, then, is the most complete account yet assembled of one of the most bizarre and significant episodes of the Second World War.

New York City, 1964

AUTHOR'S PREFACE

THE BLAST OF FOGHORN, the scream of sea gull, the smell of steam and bilge and railing polish, were all familiarly nostalgic of a voyage to the East.

Only this time, there was the added excitement of barrage balloons, corvettes, and the silhouettes of other transports.

One of the greatest armadas of all time—nearly 800 warships and troopships—was being launched on what the United States Army's Chief of Operations called the most complex operation in military history: the invasion of North Africa.

"No government," remarked General Dwight D. Eisenhower, in command of this Allied venture, "ever attempted to carry out an overseas expedition involving a journey of thousands of miles from its bases and terminating in a major attack."

To add to the gamble, some 40 German and Italian U-boats were known to be lying in ambush round the Bay of Biscay. No mean threat: Of the most recent convoy to go our way, through the Strait of Gibraltar en route to Malta, a bare quarter of the ships had arrived in port, there to be bombed by a thousand planes. The last such convoy in which I had traveled, as a war correspondent the year before during the evacuation of Crete, had offered me the gruesome spectacle of ship after ship blown skyward or submerged with an appalling loss of life. Yet now—a bright sunny morning in late October of 1942—as our converted P&O steamer moved slowly down the estuary of the Clyde, its camouflaged flanks whipped by a light sou'wester, I was whistling an Offenbach waltz. At twenty-three, in charge of half a dozen Psychological Warriors, I knew where we were going. As chief of even so tiny a mission, I had been privileged to attend briefings at Eisenhower's London headquarters, where our secret operation, first code-named Gymnast, then Semi-Gymnast, then Super-Gymnast, had finally blossomed into Torch. At Norfolk House I had been given access to "Most Secret" studies, neatly divided by British intelligence into sections dealing with the geographic, military, social and political aspects of the area to which we were going.

I knew that our Eastern Task Force was heading into the Mediterranean for Algiers, that the Center one had set out for Oran and that a Western Task Force, direct from the United States, was on its way across the Atlantic to the Moroccan port of Casablanca.

Six weeks earlier in New York, when I had first been recruited for the job, partly because of my knowledge of French, I had presumed we would be crossing the Channel to a beachhead in Continental Europe.

This had also been the idea of the United States Joint Chiefs of Staff, whose chairman, General George C. Marshall, was as eager to attack the Germans directly across the Channel as he was opposed to a "diversion" in the Mediterranean.

But Prime Minister Churchill had obtained President Roosevelt's consent to abandon all cross-Channel plans for 1942 in favor of the North African venture, and Roosevelt, in spite of the protests of his highest ranking advisors, had given the final directive for an offensive with Algeria and Morocco as targets. The purpose of our expedition, launched at a time when Allied fortunes were at their lowest, appeared sensible enough: to threaten Rommel in the rear at the very moment when Generals Alexander and Montgomery were mounting their Commonwealth attack at El Alamein, and, by our diversionary action, to relieve the pressure on the Russians.

In the long run the aim of our expedition was to clear the Germans and Italians entirely from North Africa—all the way from Suez to Gibraltar—so as to give Allied shipping a shorter supply route to the Middle East (and to Russia through the Persian Gulf), a saving to each cargo ship of some forty-five days at sea. Once this was accomplished, North Africa could develop into a base from which the Allies could strike at the "soft underbelly" of Europe through Italy, the south of France and the Balkans.

As we sailed past Gibraltar at midnight, the landmark looming dark and fateful against its somber background, we did not know that the United States Chiefs of Staff had been strongly averse to any large-scale operation *beyond* the Strait, fearing that if the Germans or the Spaniards were to seize the Rock, they could cut off and annihilate the entire Allied force within the Mediterranean. This had led the Joint Chiefs to insist on a large Western Task Force to secure a base on the Atlantic coast at Casablanca.

To the British, who considered the key to the whole operation to be control of Tunisia and the Straits of Sicily, the objective was to land *as far east* as air support would allow, and make a dash for Tunis and Bizerte. That these objectives were contradictory passed unnoticed; and we would have been amazed to learn that our own Supreme Commander—at that moment buried in the bowels of the Rock, in a damp, freshly excavated tunnel, surrounded by a mixed and untried staff, with what was to prove the most ineffective communications organization in modern history—had his heart set against the operation, which he described as "vague, the amount of resources unknown, the final objective indeterminate, and the only firm factor in the whole business our instructions to attack."

True, we were puzzled that the Axis had not already spotted and attacked our convoys—visible to their agents on either side of the Strait in Algeciras and Tangier—and could not decide whether to attribute this lack of Axis action to the brilliance of Allied cover operations, to stupidity on the part of the Axis, or to sabotage within their own intelligence. It was, as we later learned, a mixture of the three.

How fascinated we would have been had we known that despite Eisenhower's almost manic preoccupation with security, the blueprint for the whole invasion had already fallen into foreign hands, and that a few days earlier a special messenger from London flying the actual plans of the invasion, complete with D day, to the Commander of Gibraltar, General N. K. Mason Macfarlane, had been shot down and his body washed ashore in Cadiz Bay, there to be searched by Spanish police who had found the secret papers —only to return them to the British "apparently untouched and untampered with."

Secure from such details, we steamed toward our objective, along the hazy coast of Africa, over which a balmy sirocco was wafted from the Sahara, glancing up at the light strands of cirrus for the sudden appearance of the Luftwaffe, or down at the sporting dolphins for the wake of a U-boat torpedo, exhausting our ardor in a series of disciplining boat drills till, one bright morning, we found ourselves, still untouched by the Germans, in the broad blue crescent of Algiers Bay.

Before us, in a slight mist, lay the old pirate city of Algiers—a quarter million Europeans and half as many Moslems—its aspect as described by one Frenchman that of a reclining woman, white and naked, leaning on her elbow.

But for several hours they would not let us at her. Accustomed as I was to dash as I pleased in pursuit of my Muse, the torture of being paddocked, within scent of the story, was excruciating. Though I was no longer a correspondent, getting the news was as much my job as ever, overtly for the OWI and covertly for the OSS; and I could sense that in that exotic city, in which plot after plot had been hatching for months, lay the most tantalizing of prizes: the story of a lifetime.

Washington, D.C., 1964

IT IS THE BUSINESS OF DEMOCRATIC JOURNALISTS TO TRY TO TURN THE LIGHT OF DAY INTO THE DUSTY CORNERS OF SECRET DIPLOMACY, AND TO EXPOSE TO THE VIEW OF THE PEOPLE THE MACHINATIONS WHICH SEEK TO DISPOSE OF THEM, EVEN IN THE REPUBLICS, IN DEFIANCE OF THE PRINCIPLE WHICH STATES THAT THE PEOPLE SHOULD DECIDE THEIR OWN FATE.

SUCH JOURNALISTS ARE THEREFORE ENGAGED IN AN UNENDING WAR AGAINST SECRETIVE OFFICIALS. THEY SEEK TO EXPOSE WHAT THE OFFICIALS SEEK TO HIDE. IF THEY WIN, THE OFFICIALS OF THE FUTURE WILL BE OF A NEW STRIPE (OF WHOM WE HAVE SOME ALREADY), WHO WILL CARRY ON THEIR ACTIVITIES IN THE FULL VIEW OF THE PUBLIC, HIDING NOTHING FROM THEM.

IF THE KEEPERS OF THE SECRETS WIN, THERE WILL BE NO MORE JOURNALISTS IN THE FUTURE AT ALL, ONLY SCRIBES SETTING DOWN SLAVISHLY WHAT THEY ARE TOLD TO WRITE. WE HAVE SOME OF THESE ALREADY, TOO.

—WAVERLEY ROOT

PART ONE

GROUNDWORK

FOR INVASION

1

SINCE THE DAYS before Pearl Harbor, when the OWI and the OSS were still in a single egg called COI, beneath the wing of the United States Coordinator of Information, Colonel William "Wild Bill" Donovan, American agents had been spying in North Africa.

Official United States interest in the area had developed with the Fall of France.

When Hitler signed a lenient armistice with Marshal Henri Philippe Pétain so as to retain an amenable French government, he further appeased the aged French chief by leaving unoccupied not only that third of Metropolitan France which was to be known as Vichy, but all of France's vast and little-known African empire.

To investigate the resources of this mysterious domain, Commander Roscoe Hillenkoetter, an obscure American naval attaché to the French government,* made a quick trip through North and

* Later to become the first head of the CIA.

West Africa. There, in the summer of 1940, he found an estimated 125,000 combat-trained French soldiers still on active duty, plus another 200,000 in reserve. To Washington he cabled his opinion: "If France is going to fight again anywhere in this war, I believe North Africa will be the place."

The report reached President Roosevelt, who was so intrigued with the prospect that he summoned from Vichy the American Counselor of Embassy, Robert D. Murphy, and told him to obtain permission for another careful survey of the area.

"If you learn anything in Africa of special interest," added the President, "don't bother going through State Department channels."

So the plotting began.

Robert Sherwood, the President's speech writer (and later head of the Overseas Branch of the OWI), liked to say that as early as August of 1940 President Roosevelt had sketched in the idea of an Allied attack on North Africa. One hot evening in the White House study, the President—always fascinated, as was Churchill, by what his Chiefs of Staff considered to be eccentric military operations—had drawn a map marking the coastal defense of the Eastern Seaboard of the United States to illustrate to his aide, Harry Hopkins, that we could defend only about 1½ per cent of the coastline, and that an enemy could land at innumerable points.

The moral was that *we* should land first on enemy shores: "On the northwest coast of Africa, for instance," suggested the President.

In December of 1940, when Murphy flew to Algiers and Dakar on his secret Presidential assignment, the United States was still neutral and a year away from entering the war. Murphy's task was primarily to find out more precisely how the French felt about their ambiguous position.

Soon enough he learned that the forces about which Hillenkoetter had reported were convinced they could hold the area against any threat, including that of the Axis, providing the United States would supply them with military equipment, petroleum, and enough consumer goods to pacify the native population.

The main trump counted on by the French for eventual anti-

Nazi action in Africa was the newly appointed Delegate of France,
a relic of the Victorian era, sent by Pétain to wield powers over all
of North and West Africa similar to those of an ancient Roman pro-
consul: General Maxime Weygand, then in his seventy-fourth year.

Staunchly royalist, this diminutive *generalissime* was described
by our Ambassador to Vichy, Admiral William D. Leahy, as "a religious fanatic." Built like a jockey, Weygand, after fifty-seven years
in the army, was still so proud of his second lieutenant's figure that
he would vault a conference table to reach his place at the head
of it.

So important did President Roosevelt consider this potential
French leader that he transferred Murphy to Algiers to be in constant touch with him there.

Murphy, in his middle forties, born in Milwaukee of a South
German mother and an Irish father who worked on the railroads,
had spent twenty years of his career in the United States consular
service before being raised to Counselor of Embassy in Paris by
our Ambassador to France, William Bullitt. Described by Langer
as "perhaps the most competent man in the Paris Embassy with the
exception of the Ambassador, but handicapped by his own personality in dealing with the subtle intrigues of French politicians,
with whom he was somewhat out of his depth," Murphy was
summed up by General Charles de Gaulle, in his memoirs, as
"skillful and determined, long familiar with the best society and
apparently inclined to believe that France consisted of the people
he dined with in town."

With Weygand Murphy got along so well that by the spring of
1941 they had signed an historic accord by which the United States
was to export to Africa (in defiance of the British blockade)
shiploads of heavily rationed staples such as tea, sugar, cotton
goods and fuel oil. Overtly to obtain the good will of the Arab
population (which outnumbered the French ten to one), covertly
the purpose of the accord was to allow for the entry into Africa of
a dozen United States "control officers" charged with seeing that
the staples were not passed on to the Germans.

Though they were thinly disguised as United States vice-consuls (with the special privilege of traveling about North Africa with sealed diplomatic pouches), it was understood by everyone "from Pétain and Weygand down," according to Murphy, "that these Americans really would be intelligence officers."

To the Axis armistice commission in North Africa this was no mystery at all. German reaction to the influx of Americans (summed up in a report to Berlin intercepted by French security and shown to Murphy) was mordantly acid: "We can only congratulate ourselves on the selection of this group of agents, who will give us no trouble. . . . They are totally lacking in method, organization and discipline, the danger presented by their arrival in North Africa may be considered nil."

In this opinion, even the American "vice-consuls" were at first happy to concur. "We flew over," wrote Kenneth Pendar, a young archeologist from Harvard, "to drop like so many Alices into the African wonderland."

But despite their general dilettantism—one had been a wine merchant in Marseilles, another a Coca-Cola salesman from Mississippi, and a third was best described as "an ornament of Harry's Bar in Paris"—two at least had attended Saint-Cyr and served in the French Foreign Legion. And despite the fact that they were to receive little help and no sympathy from the regular Foreign Service personnel, who considered their activities altogether improper and hardly suited to "gentlemen," Murphy's "vice-consuls" were to accomplish some very effective sleuthing.

To remedy our appalling lack of intelligence personnel, President Roosevelt issued an executive order on July 11, 1941, officially creating the office of Coordinator of Information, naming as Coordinator William J. Donovan, a New York lawyer prominent in Republican politics who had earned a Congressional Medal of Honor in World War I at the head of the famed Rainbow Division.

Recently back from a fact-finding tour of Europe, the Balkans, and Africa, Donovan had already acted as an observer during the Italian war against Ethiopia in 1935 and again in Spain during its civil war, and was well prepared to assume the "ungentlemanly" task of developing "Secret Intelligence" and "Special Operations" with which to subvert governments, sabotage industry, smuggle "bodies" and explosives, set up clandestine radio networks, organize parachute drops and submarine voyages, falsify documents, develop secret inks and poisoned pills, and perform those tasks which the regular Foreign Service would not or could not carry out effectively.

As Chief of Special Operations for North Africa, Donovan appointed in October of 1941 a tall, heavyset American of Swedish origin, Lieutenant Colonel Otto Solborg.

Solborg's qualifications for the job were that he had been in the Regular Army, which he quit in 1919 to become a businessman, that he had lived twenty years in Europe, with headquarters in Paris, and that he had connections all over the world, especially in the steel business. As a base of operations, Solborg chose Lisbon. The advantages of the Portuguese capital were that it was a neutral and international port which for centuries had been in the British sphere of influence, and that in its cosmopolitan hotels, narrow back streets and noisy cafés there pullulated agents and double agents of all sorts and all nations.

Under cover of the United States military attaché's office Solborg was to recruit agents, establish a network of secret radio transmitters along the coast of North Africa, and make contacts with friendly elements in the French North African Army, Navy and administration, as well as with the native chiefs.

Within North Africa, but safely in the neutral enclave of Tangier just across the Straits from Gibraltar, the man directly in charge of these clandestine operations was to be a Marine lieutenant colonel, William A. Eddy, who had grown up in the Middle East, spoke fluent Arabic and French, and had been partly disabled from wounds in World War I. For cover he too was assigned the title of United States naval attaché.

As North Africa had been declared, on the highest level, an area primarily of American interest, British Secret Intelligence and Special Operations were technically subordinated to Lieutenant Colonel Eddy, who was to keep in close touch with his British deputy in Gibraltar, Colonel Brien Clarke.

Though Eddy could report directly to his COI superiors in London and Washington, the person to whom he was responsible in the field, and under whom he had to coordinate his activities in the area, was Robert Murphy.

So, while Murphy flirted with Weygand, Solborg and Eddy began to arrange more secret assignations with the lower-level echelons of the military and administrative organizations in North Africa, hoping to find some stalwart resistance to Vichy and the Germans.

But resistance to the Germans, in the dark days of 1941, was a poor prospect for those already defeated or subjugated, and not much better for those still fighting. To the British, disaster had followed on disaster: in Greece and Crete, and especially in the Libyan Desert where they had suffered a defeat as crucial as Dunkirk. The Germans (with the permission of Vichy's Premier, Admiral Jean François Darlan) then ferried troops across French Syria to organize a successful revolt in Iraq. Rommel was at the gates of Cairo (also with Darlan's connivance in letting him use the ports of Tunisia), and it looked as if the entire Middle East might fall to the Germans.

Meanwhile all of French North and West Africa had fallen firmly under Vichy control. Hundreds of officials suspected of being Gaullist or even vaguely pro-British had been removed and replaced by "reliable" collaborators.

For a picture of the fascist regime set up by Vichy in an Africa nominally under Weygand, the one painted by William L. Langer, an official of the U.S. State Department, is clear enough: "By the beginning of 1941," says Langer, "the elite of Vichy henchmen had been organized in the Service d'Ordre Légionnaire (SOL), only to be reinforced a little later by the formation of Jacques Doriot's Parti Populaire Français (PPF).* These were the shock troops of French Fascism, the rowdies who initiated the anti-

---

* Doriot, a former Communist deputy to Parliament, having been removed as mayor of Saint-Denis for corruption and gangster methods, shifted to organizing the fascist PPF just before the war.

Semitic terror in North Africa, and worked in conjunction with Nazi agents and spies."

Langer also gives a revealing glimpse behind the scenes at the clique of Vichy industrialists and financiers who were manipulating these fascist gangs.

"Mention," says he, "must be made of the *Comités d'Organiza-tion,* or *Groupements,* which exercised complete control of the economic life of the country. These graft-ridden bodies were the tools of the Vichy collaborationists, the chief financial support of the SOL and the PPF, and the willing helpers of the German armistice commission in its systematic looting of the country."

Yet in all this national decay, there were incidents of resistance. Solborg, Eddy, and Murphy's vice-consuls soon discovered that not all of Weygand's officers and officials were wedded to Vichy. Some had even managed to lay the groundwork for a resistance movement, the nuclei of which had been in the process of development since the Fall of France.

The earliest such group, as might be expected, was Gaullist. One of the first avowed Gaullist operators in North Africa was a young Basque police officer with a lively intelligence, André Achiary. As Vichy's security officer in charge of counterespionage for the whole Algerian territory, he was in an ideal position to conspire.

By means of a clandestine transmitter (lost by three Gaullist agents who had been infiltrated into North Africa from London) which Achiary recovered and installed first in his office and then in his bedroom, he was able to make contact with British intelligence in Gibraltar.

Spreading his network, he organized cells in the port of Oran and in the coastal town of Cherchel. In Oran, Achiary's main contact was a dashing figure: Henri d'Astier de la Vigerie, a forty-year-old nephew of Cardinal d'Astier. Tall and thin, with black feline eyes and the delicate bronzed features of a Spanish aristocrat, d'Astier radiated charm. Though Achiary was a staunch republican and d'Astier an avowed royalist, both were Gaullist from the start, and gradually they joined with others of equally varied political hues to plot the re-entry of France into the war.

Meanwhile anti-German military members of Weygand's staff had secretly decided to see if they could negotiate with the United States to equip a clandestine military force in North Africa. These French officers had managed to hide much of their equipment from the Germans, burying in caves and barns of remote farms the necessary trucks, tanks, field guns and machine guns. But they had only enough fuel and ammunition to face an enemy for two or three days; and what they had was sadly antiquated.

They therefore decided to get in touch with Robert Murphy; and to add verisimilitude to the cover story that their meeting was just another of Murphy's social outings, several ladies, some with titles, were invited to join the plotters at the Hotel Alexandra in the residential heights above the city.

But this first shady deal, hatched in the hot Algerian atmosphere before the professionals in "Secret Operations"—Eddy and Solborg—had arrived on the scene, nearly ended in disaster. The French military expert who had drawn up the list of required material was a young army captain on the Governor General's staff by the name of André Beaufre. Married to the daughter of an English baronet, he lived at that time in an exotic section of the Arab quarter high on a hill in *Mustapha Supérieur,* in one of Algiers' oldest villas, the Dar Mahieddine.

Already in April of 1941 Beaufre had outlined such a plan to Ambassador Leahy in Vichy, and it was a French intelligence major named Loustaunau-Lacau who, disguised as a merchant of wines, brought from Vichy the necessary secret documentation.*

In Algiers Loustaunau-Lacau was almost immediately betrayed by a friend, and the secret meeting of the conspirators was raided by the police.

---

* As an indication of the complexity of French underground politics and the pro- and anti-de Gaulle struggle which was already developing, Loustaunau-Lacau, as he admits in his memoirs, had received from Pétain 300,000 francs to start a resistance movement in competition to de Gaulle. An old hand at conspiracy (he had run an anti-left-wing network in the Regular French Army), Loustaunau-Lacau had also just made a trip to Lisbon where he had arranged with British intelligence to organize a network to gather military information in the unoccupied zone.

Ironically, this contretemps might have been fatal to the budding North Africa conspiracy had it not been for the quick thinking of a clandestine Gaullist.

Searched by the police, Beaufre was discovered to be in possession of some cryptic notes, one of which turned out to be the code in which he corresponded with what were presumed to be his accomplices in Metropolitan France. Among them appeared the name of M. Jacques Lemaigre-Dubreuil, recent owner of Dar Mahieddine.

But the interrogation of the plotters was assigned to none other than the Chief of Security—André Achiary. In the course of being questioned, Beaufre realized he was getting more information than he was giving. By the end of the interrogation both men were smiling. Instead of being weakened, the links of the conspiratorial chain had been strengthened.

Though Achiary could not prevent Beaufre from being sent back to non-occupied France to stand trial before a military tribunal in Clermont-Ferrand (where he was found guilty of conspiracy and imprisoned), he did manage to destroy most of the compromising documents which had been seized.

Achiary also managed to let Loustaunau-Lacau, who still had his false papers as a wine merchant, slip aboard a boat and leave that day for France. But to cover himself with his superiors in Vichy, Achiary requested a police report on the mysterious Lemaigre-Dubreuil. This suspect (who was, in fact, the real leader of the conspiracy) was arrested and questioned, but, thanks partly to the subtlety of Achiary's report, which contained nothing damaging, he was quickly released. According to the Vichy police report, Lemaigre-Dubreuil was a French industrialist working with the Germans, who had close connections not only with the Vichy Minister of the Interior, Pierre Pucheu, but with the Germans in occupied France, and was known to express pro-German sentiments in public.

Lemaigre-Dubreuil, who before the war had become head of one of the largest oil concerns in France, Le Sueur et Cie. (by marrying into the family), had become *persona grata* with the Germans after the Fall of France by reopening his peanut oil factory in Dunkirk to supply their needs.

Described by one of his compatriots as "sure of himself, speaking loudly, his angora hat at a tilt, and displaying an innate taste for being observed," Lemaigre-Dubreuil moved about freely "disguising his conspiracy, like Ali Baba, in so many barrels of oil."

In a book which he later wrote, under his wartime code name of "Robinson Crusoe," Lemaigre thus explained his actions: "Certain Frenchmen considered that Europe would be dominated for a thousand years by a Germany whose military power seemed colossal, and were prepared to make their peace with the conqueror, in fact soon to collaborate with him."

"Others"—and it was among these that Lemaigre clearly wished the reader to class him—"gritted their teeth and longed for revenge."

To Robert Murphy, who had known him since his days in Vichy, Lemaigre-Dubreuil was "a sincere and patriotic Frenchman who was double-crossing the Germans and his Vichy connections only so as to prepare the way for France's revival."

Whatever his intentions, a series of "coincidences" was to be enormously helpful to Lemaigre.

First, the Governor General of French West Africa, Pierre Boisson, requested from Vichy that some French industrialist construct in Dakar a factory for extracting peanut oil. Le Sueur was awarded the contract. Lemaigre-Dubreuil, as its director, was thus enabled to travel freely to West Africa at a time when permits, fuel and travel priorities were impossibly scarce.

The factory in Dakar led to plans for another in Casablanca, and still another in Algiers. Lemaigre-Dubreuil was enabled to travel not only from Occupied France to Vichy, but to any part of France's North and West African empire.

Lemaigre too had counted on General Weygand to head the conspiracy in Africa; but when Weygand was deposed on orders from the Germans and—without a whimper—went into retirement in October of 1941, someone else had to be found to take the lead.*

With Weygand gone, Lemaigre immediately flew to Algiers to ask Achiary if he knew of someone who could reconstitute the armament program worked out by Beaufre, who was still in jail.

Achiary suggested Lieutenant Colonel Louis G. M. Jousse, a tall good-looking officer at Headquarters in Algiers whom he secretly knew to be both a Gaullist and a republican.

To work out the details with Jousse, Lemaigre said he would bring from France a reliable man of his own. There now appeared on the scene a character even more amazing than "Robinson Crusoe"—his "man Friday." A thin little man in his forties, with a livid complexion and pale gray staring eyes, Jean Rigault had for years been in the thick of political intrigue.

Disguised as the personal secretary of Lemaigre, for whom he handled a very complicated business empire, Rigault had even managed his master's prewar right-wing paper, *Le Jour Écho*.

On Christmas Day of 1941 Jousse finished drafting a note which Rigault delivered to Murphy.

In the note Jousse listed the equipment which he believed necessary to equip a French resistance movement in North Africa. Even to Murphy's unmilitary mind it looked like enough for a whole Army of Liberation. Among the requested items was equipment for six motorized and two armored divisions, plus 300 fighter planes complete with ground crews. The note specified precise dates, quantities and localities for smuggling this armament into Morocco, Algeria and Tunisia.

* The details of Weygand's removal were suitably melodramatic. Partly because of his openly anti-German attitude, partly because of articles in the Allied press which were building up Weygand as a pro-Allied hero, and partly because Vichy Foreign Minister Pierre Laval disliked him and was jealous of his power and his close ties with Pétain, the Germans became suspicious of Weygand, but lacked sufficient evidence with which to force Pétain to dismiss him. They therefore sent General Charles Huntziger to North Africa to collect a dossier on Weygand's anti-German activities. To save Weygand, Darlan ordered Huntziger's plane to be sabotaged on its way back from North Africa. The plane duly crashed and Huntziger was killed, but the report on Weygand was retrieved by unsuspecting gendarmes and could not be hidden from the Germans.

Whether to stall, or because he really considered it vital, Murphy pointed out that no formal engagement by the United States could be undertaken until the French had named a leader for this force.

President Roosevelt (much more than nominally in charge of our foreign affairs) still hoped, like Murphy, for General Weygand: so much so that two days later, on December 27, a letter from the President was delivered to Weygand at his retreat near Grasse by Douglas MacArthur II—a nephew of the commander in the Pacific, then an attaché at the American Embassy in Vichy.

The President proposed to equip the six or eight French divisions in North Africa, on condition that Weygand undertook to come back and command them.

Weygand refused. He was too old, said he, to become a "rebel."

Undaunted, and no doubt fired by the prospect of acquiring for themselves such power, "Robinson Crusoe" and his "man Friday" stepped into the breach. Lemaigre-Dubreuil sent word to the general that he and his conspirators were prepared to take the lead in organizing resistance in North Africa, if the general himself would not cooperate. To put this plan into effect, "Crusoe" and "Friday" formed a cabal made up of five incongruous characters, which came to be known as "the Five."

First among the new recruits was Henri d'Astier de la Vigerie, with the code name of "Uncle Charlie," largely responsible for the plotting in Oran.

Next came Colonel A. S. van Ecke, a great, brusque, redheaded Dutchman of fifty with a barrel chest and a rugged voice, known as "Robin Hood," who had spent twenty years in the Foreign Legion. In charge of Pétain's youth movement in North Africa, the Chantiers de la Jeunesse, Van Ecke had a large reservoir of ardent and willing young recruits for any cause which meant action; and the fact that he could dispatch his boys about the country in their green berets and golf knickers, properly provided with official travel orders, was an incomparable asset to the conspiracy, operating, as it had to, in a vast territory with a single rail line, scarcity of gasoline and strictly controlled air travel.

Finally there was added a small man with a paunchy figure, long pointed nose and bald head, Jacques Tarbé de Saint-Hardouin.

A career diplomat and specialist in financial and economic matters —who had been *Chef de Cabinet* to the former rightist Premier of France, Pierre Étienne Flandin—he was essential to the conspiracy in that he could spend a good deal of time with Robert Murphy without causing suspicion. With his narrow eyes and gourmand's mouth, he was at his ease in the diplomatic world of expensive restaurants and select clubs; he also had the asset of a pretty and elegant young Turkish wife who ran a salon in which to entertain the *grand monde* of North Africa.

These were "the Five." Lemaigre traveled to and from France, Saint-Hardouin stuck close to Murphy, Van Ecke issued false passes, d'Astier set about spreading the plot and recruiting adherents, and Rigault kept the conspirators' archives, which, for safety, he consigned to a young army chaplain, the Abbé Louis Pierre Marie Cordier, an ascetic thirty-year-old Jesuit who acted as d'Astier's secretary and confessor, and who, for extra safety, hid them in the Convent of the Sisters of Notre Dame d'Afrique.

In a letter to our then Undersecretary of State, Sumner Welles, Murphy summed up the ideas of this little group of conspirators: "In essence, their purpose is the establishment in French Africa of a provisional government operating independently of Metropolitan France. They are searching and hope to find shortly a military leader."

All through the early spring of 1942 a great number of French officers in charge of all sorts of units in various regions of North Africa were approached by the conspirators. Some promised wholeheartedly to help; others offered only passive complicity.

Among the immediate enthusiasts were some major figures. In Morocco the Commander of the Casablanca Division, Brigadier General Émile Marie Béthouart was solicited by Van Ecke one hot afternoon, beneath the equestrian statue of Lyautey, and accepted immediately. By April 15 Rigault was able to discuss with him details for a plot in Morocco.

At the other end of Africa, in the vital port of Bône, nearest the Tunisian border, Colonel Lorber, in command of the local subdivision, and a friend of Saint-Hardouin, was instantly agreeable. "What a pity," he murmured, "that General Giraud isn't with us."

An odd remark, considering that three days later Giraud was to make a sensational escape from a German prison camp.

Yet while all this good work was going on, Murphy appears to have been less optimistic. As long as his friend Weygand had been in charge of all of French Africa, he had felt there was a chance of persuading a large number of French officers to come over to the Allied side. Now that the separate areas of Tunisia, Algeria, Morocco and West Africa had been placed under separate military and political commanders, Murphy was afraid the resistance would be limited to scattered elements.

Also, though four months had passed, there was still no reply from Washington about Jousse's note on military requirements.

What the North African conspirators did not realize was that in the early spring of 1942 Washington was having troubles of its own. Japanese advances in the Pacific and Indian Oceans had become so threatening, and Allied losses at sea so terrific, that any hope of action in the European theater had been momentarily abandoned; it was all Washington could do to wage a holding fight and try to build up production and shipping, while training raw recruits into some sort of fighting force.

In Europe, Hitler was still at his zenith, and most Europeans were still convinced he would win the war. So much so that in Vichy France, Pétain put Pierre Laval back in power, and our Ambassador, Leahy, cabled that the French were about to collaborate even more closely with the Germans.

To Admiral Leahy it was time "to consider a complete revision of American policy in regard to the Vichy Government": he asked to be recalled.

Harry Hopkins, in a salty cable to Roosevelt, supported this position by suggesting, "How about nailing that wood pussy Laval to your barn door?"

But from Murphy Roosevelt received equally urgent cables saying that *his* "contacts" begged the United States not to "slam the door in the French face now." Even Weygand managed to get a note to him to that effect.

In retrospect, this appears to have been the turning point in the entire drama that was to follow. Our whole Vichy policy lay in the balance. Then Murphy (and/or his "contacts") won out, and Roosevelt, disregarding Leahy's advice, answered Hopkins facetiously: "Your suggestion being studied but consensus of opinion is that odor is still too strong for family of nations."

Though Murphy received no precise authority from Washington to enter into an agreement with the conspirators, he was told he could go on talking to them and was to keep in close touch with Lieutenant Colonel Eddy in Tangier.

But by April of 1942, the equipment requested by the French, even if it could have been delivered, would, according to Lieutenant Colonel Jousse, no longer serve its original purpose.

Any intervention, said Jousse, designed merely as a *reaction* to a German move would now arrive too late. Once the Germans were in North Africa it would be infinitely harder to oust them. Allied convoys would take two to three weeks to arrive; and they could not sit around in their home ports, fully loaded, just waiting for the Germans to move.

What was needed now was *offensive* action. The Allies were the ones who must land in force, and bring the necessary equipment to the French.

For their part, the conspirators would undertake to see that the Americans got ashore without having to fight, and turn over to them key North African defenses and functioning port facilities.

Jousse estimated the necessary Allied landing force at seven motorized divisions, with 5 brigades of tanks (about 700 to 800 tanks); 120 antiaircraft batteries, half of which should be of small caliber for defending the landing zones. Also needed, to cover the landings, would be 500 fighter planes, 100 for each of five landing zones, complete with ground crews and fuel. All this with supplies and ammunition for a month.

Murphy cabled to Washington, urging the need for action and requesting a Regular Army officer to carry on discussions with French leaders in Algeria.

Meanwhile in Tangier, Colonel Eddy discovered that the British were already in contact with a resistance group in Morocco and that plans were under way to land supplies for them near Agadir and Fedala, to be consigned to the Office of Post & Telegraph in Casablanca, whose officials had been organized by two industrialists code-named Tweedledum and Tweedledee. Hurrying over to Gibraltar, Eddy talked the British out of the scheme and in favor of the American idea of much larger-scale aid to the French.

On April 13 Eddy also cabled Washington to ask when the United States would be able to furnish heavy material to Bathurst, Freetown or Liberia, where French vessels could pick up and transport it to Morocco without the knowledge of Axis agents. The cable specified a French request for 1,000 motorcycles, 500 sidecars, 50 105-mm howitzers with trucks and tractors, 150 105-mm antiaircraft guns, 300 37-mm antiaircraft guns, 240 M2A4 tanks, 300 M-3GRTT tanks, 150 scout cars and 150 jeeps.

All through April the situation continued to be tense, coming gradually to a crisis. All was ready, except for the material.

2

WHAT NO ONE in North Africa seemed to realize was that the United States Joint Chiefs of Staff had categorically rejected the idea of shipping war matériel to North Africa, despite a favorable opinion of the Joint Intelligence Committee.

"They were in accord," says an official report at the time, "with the policy of expanding funds judiciously for the purpose of initiating and maintaining guerilla opposition in that area."

One of the reasons, no doubt, was that at the beginning of March, 1942, there was a grand total in the European theater of 3,785 United States officers and men; there was no American heavy bomber unit, and not till May was there even one light bombardment squadron.

It is hard to say at what time Murphy learned of the decision

The Vichy Government, April 1942. In the center, wearing white gloves, Marshal Pétain. In the second row, Admiral Darlan stands at far left; beside him are Jean Ybarnégaray, minister for Pétain's fascist youth, and (wearing white tie) Pierre Laval. Others in group include General Weygand on Pétain's left and General Huntziger, ahead of Laval. [UPI PHOTO]

French Morocco,
November 8, 1942.
American troops going
ashore at Fedala,
preparatory to their
attack on Casablanca,
principal objective
of the Western
Task Force.

November 13, 1942.
General Eisenhower
forcefully insisting to
Admiral Darlan that
the French attack the
Germans in Tunisia.

[US ARMY PHOTO]

Algiers, November 13, 1942. Lieutenant General Dwight D. Eisenhower, Admiral Jean François Darlan, Major General Mark W. Clark, and Mr. Robert D. Murphy. Shortly after Eisenhower's agreement with Darlan to accept him as French "Head of State" on condition Darlan side with the Allies against the Germans.

[US ARMY PHOTO]

Admiral Darlan, consummating the accord of November 22, 1942 with Lieutenant General Mark W. Clark, in Algiers' Hotel St. Georges, under the aegis of Marshal Pétain, whose ubiquitous portrait still stands on the ornate Arab coffer at right. [US ARMY PHOTO]

Back in uniform, Darlan salutes the tomb of the unknown soldier in Algiers, December 1, 1942, in company of General Eisenhower and Admiral Sir Andrew Cunningham. To the right of Eisenhower stands his aide, Lieutenant Commander Harry C. Butcher; directly behind him (only mustache visible), General Henri Honoré Giraud.   [US ARMY PHOTO]

General Auguste Paul Noguès, Resident General of Morocco, with his ex-opponent, Major General George S. Patton, reviewing Moroccan troops at Rabat, capital of French Morocco, during a Moslem festival in December 1942.   [US ARMY PHOTO]

The Governor General of Algeria, Yves Chatel, and Mme. Chatel in the garden of their official residence, the Palais d'Eté, after he had publicly repudiated Vichy.   [US ARMY PHOTO]

The Count of Paris, son of the Duc de Guise, pretender to the throne of France, shown here as a volunteer in the Foreign Legion, 1940, seated on his comrades' shoulders. [LIBRARY OF CONGRESS]

"Robinson Crusoe" in America, December 25, 1942 (the day after Darlan's assassination). General Giraud's mission to the United States arrives in Washington, D. C., led by General Marie Emile Béthouart, to be greeted by the chief of U.S. Ground Forces, General Joseph T. McNarney. In the center of the photograph, hat in hand, stands Jacques Lemaigre-Dubreuil. [UPI PHOTO]

Farewell to Darlan. Mourners at the Cathedral in Algiers after Darlan's funeral service, December 26, 1942. In front row (left to right) Cunningham, Eisenhower, Giraud, Chatel, Noguès. Behind Cunningham stands Mark Clark, and behind him, Major General Walter Bedell Smith.

[US ARMY PHOTO]

Casablanca, January 1943. Posed picture on the lawn of the presidential villa at Anfa, French Morocco, for the "wedding" of Giraud to de Gaulle, sponsored by Roosevelt and Churchill.

The famous handshake. "The four actors put on their smiles. The agreed-upon gestures were made . . . America would be satisfied, on such evidence, that the French question had found its *deus ex machina* in the person of the President."—Charles de Gaulle: *War Memoirs* [US ARMY PHOTO]

A reluctant five-star General Giraud greets a condescending two-star General Charles de Gaulle, now to be his co-equal as head of the French Committee of National Liberation. Blida Airfield, Algiers, May 29, 1943. [US ARMY PHOTO]

of the Joint Chiefs; he continued for some weeks to send messages begging for action.

On April 18 Murphy cabled Secretary of State Cordell Hull: "Practically a year has elapsed without to my knowledge the offer as practical encouragement of as much as a cap pistol to our friends in this area."

Exasperated by what they considered American dilatoriness, the Five addressed a letter to Murphy on May 1, reminding him that for the past sixteen months they had been working clandestinely and asking the United States for support to bring French Africa back into the war, but that so far no answer of any sort had been received.

If, said they, by May 20 no answer was forthcoming, regretfully they would cease from any further effort at Franco-American cooperation, and turn to the British.

At the same time the Five stipulated that if Murphy, as Mr. Roosevelt's representative, wished to work with them, he must formally declare that it would be with their group alone "so as to avoid disordered activities which might be harmful to French interests." At this Murphy smiled and made a joke about jealous women; "but the somber look on the faces of his interlocutors"— so recounted one of the Five—"caused him to accept this sequestration with the coquetry of a Turkish lady."

To Hull, Murphy cabled the warning that "our long continued reticence is arousing suspicions on the part of the friendliest elements regarding our motives and they have returned to me the funds advanced by COI."

As a result of all this, Lemaigre wrote later, and "afraid we would become discouraged by all the delays and turn to the British," President Roosevelt dispatched a special delegate to Robert Murphy to be in touch with the French group in Algeria. At least this is what Lemaigre deduced.

The messenger turned out to be the OSS's Colonel Solborg, who brought along, says Lemaigre, a formal promise that the United States would handle the North African operation.

According to Solborg, what was holding up matters in the

United States was the lack of an acceptable military leader designated by the French to head the resistance movement in North
Africa.

What Solborg did not tell Lemaigre was that he had become impatient at the endless delays which were beginning to cause bad
blood among the French, and had decided, on his own initiative
and without authority from Washington, to get the operations
moving.

"His great idea," says Langer, "was that a prominent leader
must be found for the French in North Africa." Lemaigre too took
matters into his own hands—if, indeed, he had not had them
there all along. For who should appear, as if by magic, but the
very man to fill the role so earnestly requested by the United States
as a pledge for its aid.

From the "escape-proof" hilltop fortress of Koenigstein (near
the German-Czech frontier in what is known as Swiss Saxony,
where the Germans held about a hundred French generals), Henri
Giraud, imprisoned since his capture near Sedan in 1940, now
made an incredible escape.

In his sixties, over six feet three, and with a game leg, this five-
star general had already escaped from a German camp in World
War I when he had avoided German dragnets in Belgium by disguising himself first as a woman and then as a circus performer,
finally to be aided to freedom by none other than nurse Edith
Cavell.

This second and even more dramatic escape (made with the
help of a wire-filled rope reportedly smuggled to him in several cans
of ham, and partly woven by him over a period of months from
tattered linen) seemed handmade to arouse popular imagination;
also to raise the eyebrows of professionals as to the extent to which
his departure may or may not have been abetted by his jailers.

In any case Lemaigre, having flown to France, quickly managed
to arrange a meeting with Giraud in the Château de Froments, a
magnificent dwelling conveniently placed at Giraud's disposal by
an industrialist from Lyon.

There, on May 19, the very last day before the expiration of the deadline set by the Five with Murphy, Lemaigre found Giraud in "the bourgeois sitting room of a shuttered apartment."

"From the general's first words," says Lemaigre, "all was fixed. Giraud decided to act. In fact he was already in possession of a long-matured, strategic plan for bringing France back into the war against Germany."

Giraud's plan was to use the Metropolitan French Armistice Army of about 100,000 men as the nucleus around which to organize uprisings not only in France but throughout German-occupied countries and, hopefully, in Germany itself.

Immediately Lemaigre tried to sway Giraud to his own idea of a North African uprising aided by the Allies. But all he obtained from Giraud was permission to send along two members of the Five who could brief the general on North African military details and their degree of preparation.

So, at the beginning of June, Rigault and Van Ecke left for Lyon and after exposing their plans in detail succeeded in persuading Giraud to make room in his scheme for the North African venture. His basic view, however, was unchanged: the affair would not work without a landing in France. To coordinate his efforts with the Algiers conspirators Giraud agreed on a system of couriers, special ciphers, and, more important, he gave them letters of introduction to several officers in North Africa who he believed would rally to the cause. As his representative in North Africa Giraud named General Charles Emmanuel Mast, a thin little man to be code-named "Flagpole," who had arrived in Algiers in April to become Chief of Staff of the XIX Corps stationed in Algeria. By coincidence Mast had also been a companion of Giraud's in the fortress of Koenigstein from which the Germans had released him on parole.

It had been through Mast, says one source, that Giraud's escape was organized by the Deuxième Bureau of the French Armistice Army with a group of officers, all of whom were later to become involved in the North African conspiracy.

By an even odder coincidence, at the very moment General Mast was named by Giraud as his representative in North Africa, Vichy promoted Mast to command of the Algiers Division. Immediately Mast requested and obtained as a subordinate commander for the Algiers garrison Colonel Jousse. This brought under the eyes of the conspirators all of the official military paper work of the region, including the most secret and most recent reports, and gave them the necessary letterheads and seals with which to issue orders. With one stroke the conspirators had the possibility of confirming from official sources all the military data painfully accumulated by Murphy's minions over the past years. It also gave them the exact emplacement of each and every gun in North Africa, its power, angle of fire, and made the communications network available to them.

Directly senior to Mast in Algiers there were only two officers who needed to be brought into the plot or neutralized at the time of action: General Louis Koeltz, in command of the XIX Corps, and General Alphonse Juin, Commander in Chief of all French forces in Africa.

Lemaigre then got in touch with Solborg in Casablanca and, "having gotten him to swear on his honor, and in writing" that the information would go only to President Roosevelt and to General Marshall, "revealed to him the fateful name of the figure who was to lead France back into the war: Henri Honoré Giraud."

All this precaution, explained Lemaigre, was to avoid a repetition of what had happened in the case of Weygand, whose candidacy had been compromised "by premature and laudatory stories in the American press which had angered the Germans."

But why, when the Allies already had a leader for French forces, in the person of General de Gaulle, did Lemaigre have to go to such lengths to produce a Giraud?

Even Lemaigre formulated the query rhetorically, then gave his own answer: "The African Army on the whole disliked the British. Too much blood had been shed fighting them at Mers-el-Kebir, in Syria and at Dakar. All of this may have been necessary for the British, but it was humiliating and costly to France."

None too subtly, Lemaigre was insinuating that de Gaulle was a British puppet.

"However," added Lemaigre, speaking of the North African Army, "all these Frenchmen were quite pro-American."

His suggestion—though it was given ex post facto—was to start the operation with Giraud and the Americans, and, once in control of the situation in North Africa, get Giraud and de Gaulle to come to terms. "In any case," says Lemaigre, assuming an unaccustomed naïveté, "that is what the Five believed."

True or not, this became the line of the State Department's policy, and subsequently the basis of all American policy. In his *Crusade in Europe* Eisenhower shows how this point of view percolated all the way down to his London headquarters in Norfolk House: ". . . a constant stream of information came to us from consuls and other officials whom our State Department maintained in Africa throughout the war. All of this information was to the effect that in the regular officer corps of the French Army de Gaulle was, at that time, considered a disloyal soldier."

To this Eisenhower, also writing after the fact, immediately added: "His standing with the resistance elements of the civil population was vastly different. But at that moment resistance elements, particularly in Africa, were inarticulate and ineffective—and we had to win over the armed services as a first objective."

Some time later, when asked why he had made the choice of Giraud, Lemaigre was more revealing: "I chose him," said Lemaigre, "from his photograph. Giraud is the typical type of French general. *Des feuilles de chêne, aux belles moustaches,* just as they cast them in Hollywood. He was bound to be agreeable to the Americans!"

He was right! Colonel Solborg not only bought Giraud but resold him at a higher value. True, Solborg was diplomatic enough to go to London and confer with de Gaulle and other French leaders. However, according to a telegram from H. Freeman Matthews, then at our Embassy in London (and later Eisenhower's political adviser in Gibraltar), Solborg, having reported adversely to General Donovan on de Gaulle himself, improved the chances of his own candidate by adding that he had "sounded out de Gaulle regarding Giraud and had found that the Free French leader was enthusiastic."

Then, early in June, Solborg made a costly mistake. Posing as an official representative of the United States government, Solborg traveled on his own initiative to Algiers for further conferences with Murphy, Lemaigre and other French underground leaders. Detailed plans were worked out for Solborg to take back to Washington, while Lemaigre was to take copies to Giraud for approval.

"The substance of the plan," as Solborg cabled it to Donovan in Washington, "was that Giraud assume command of French forces in North Africa to receive our task force without opposition whenever the opportunity arrives."

Armed with this plan, Lemaigre set off for France during the second half of June. But by way of precaution, says Langer, "he first went to Paris to sound out Laval."

Though this extraordinary move is best explained in the light of subsequent events, Marcel Aboulker, in his book *Alger et ses complots,* maintains Lemaigre would all along have preferred a "legal" Algerian dissidence, under the aegis of Pétain. Aboulker quotes Lemaigre as saying, "I often proposed this to Pierre Laval. And it was only when I lost all hope of getting any legal action from a government whose internal policy I nevertheless approved, that I decided to approach the problem illegally."

Gabriel Esquer, in his book *The 8th of November,* was even more specific. He writes that Laval and Lemaigre were hoping for a negotiated peace between Germany and the Allies; both agreed that for France to make her views felt during such negotiations she would need a strong army furnished with modern equipment. It was Laval's conviction that as head of the French government he could obtain such armament from the Germans. Lemaigre insisted that the Germans, knowing the French might turn these weapons against them, would not provide them. The Allies would.

According to Esquer, Laval had therefore agreed that if France could not obtain the weapons from the Germans, someone would have to turn to the Allies—and he authorized Lemaigre to discuss the matter with the Americans.

By the time Lemaigre returned from his mission to Giraud (and Laval), Solborg was already on his way back to Washington where he proposed to report in person to both Donovan and Marshall. But Donovan, furious at Solborg's failure to obey his orders not to go to North Africa in person, would not even receive him. Donovan "cold-shouldered all his reports, dropped him from the rolls of the OSS and refused to pursue the matter."

In Tangier, Solborg's OSS colleague, Colonel Eddy, also had an unpleasant surprise. Two weeks earlier more than 300 French resistants, some army, some navy, some air force, had been arrested in Morocco for belonging to a secret organization.

Fascist strong-arm squads were now rampant; the PPF had been organized to break up all political demonstrations, and, according to Eddy's report, "to act as key men at strategic points in the event of an American invasion of the territory."

From Algiers Murphy kept cabling Solborg for news of what was happening in America to their plan. Failing to get any answer, he became worried and decided to go to Washington himself. Luckily Colonel Eddy, on a quick trip to London, managed to set things straight with General George V. Strong, Assistant Chief of Staff of G-2, who was anxious to check the authenticity of Solborg's reports about the situation in North Africa.

Much impressed by what he heard from Eddy, Strong was prepared to put faith in these reports, and brought the entire situation to the attention of Eisenhower's staff.

What neither Murphy nor Eddy could know was that on July 23 Roosevelt and Churchill had top-secretly decided to launch an expeditionary force to North Africa as soon as possible after October 30 of that same year—1942.

On August 17 Eddy's concrete recommendations about French cooperation for such an expedition were submitted to the Joint Chiefs of Staff, and although they were approved in general, the item about staff talks with French leaders was disapproved "as the danger of information leaking out by staff talks with separatists appears too great."

This was to prove a severe blow to any successful plotting. But when Murphy reached Washington on August 30, he had the pleasant surprise of being called in for conference with General Marshall, Admiral Leahy and Admiral Ernest Joseph King, and the even greater surprise of being invited to Hyde Park to see the President. It was then that he first learned that an expeditionary force was to be sent to North Africa. However, the President ordered him to discuss the plans with no one at the State Department. So that he could meet Eisenhower, it was decided to fly Murphy to London in the utmost secrecy, masquerading as a Lieutenant Colonel McGowan. "No one," said Marshall, "ever pays attention to a lieutenant colonel."

Commander Harry C. Butcher, Eisenhower's aide, met "Mc-Gowan" at a blacked-out London station and drove him directly to the secret hide-out of the Commander in Chief of Torch—by a golf course on the outskirts of London.

Murphy brought along a draft directive from the President which appointed him "Adviser on Civil Affairs." But this title gave Eisenhower some qualms, as it appeared to give Murphy political authority independent of that of the military. To avoid the impression of a divided authority the President agreed that Murphy should act *under* the commanding general.

For any real collaboration a great deal now depended on the evaluation by Eisenhower (and the British) of Murphy's military knowledge, so they could decide—in Butcher's words in *My Three Years with Eisenhower*—"how much, if any, of their actual plans of where, when, and how, they could impart to him."

Though Butcher's first appraisal of Murphy turned out to be extraordinarily perceptive—"the Murphy I saw was tall, slightly stoop-shouldered, and talked more like an American businessman canvassing the ins and outs of a prospective merger than either a diplomat or a soldier"—any military reticence toward his personal representative was hardly what the President had envisaged.

Still, the lieutenant colonel in "McGowan" must somehow have appealed to the lieutenant colonel in Eisenhower (then his actual rank), because, says Butcher, Murphy's grasp of "matters of mili-

tary significance" and "his judgment and discretion" gained Eisenhower's "utmost confidence."

This reciprocal confidence was to be more apparent than real.
From the questions that were asked him about North Africa Murphy realized "that Eisenhower and some of his officers had mental
pictures of primitive country, collections of mud huts set deep in
jungle." Even worse, the military kept from Murphy the secret of
the limited landing forces at their disposal so as to use him as a
smoke screen for a bluff.

"Eisenhower," says Butcher, "authorized Murphy to tell his
French friends that there would be an initial force of 150,000
men in the North African expedition, and a build-up to half a
million men as rapidly as port facilities would permit."

At the same time, Murphy—who had been authorized by the
President's draft directive to give advance notice of D day to
reliable friends and to identify for them the appropriate beaches
—was persuaded by Eisenhower to hold back even the approxi-
mate date.

As a result, Murphy became so obsessed with the danger of
breaking security that he proposed to tell his French friends that
the date contemplated for the landings was to be early in 1943,
exculpating himself on the untenable premise that "it would then
be simple to move forward the date later on, and cite Axis provo-
cation, or some reason, for the change."

Back in Casablanca, Murphy met his co-conspirator Lemaigre-
Dubreuil, who had been on a trip to Dakar to sound out Governor
General Boisson.

Brimming with good spirits, Murphy told Lemaigre of his conversations with F.D.R., of the aid the United States would make
available for the North African operation, dropping hints of an
expeditionary force of 500,000 men, 2,000 planes, 100 transports
protected by battleships and aircraft carriers—but not a word
about the imminence of the operation.

The two conspirators flew back to Algiers in a plane filled with

German armistice commission personnel, toasting each other with champagne.

For Lemaigre the problem was how to persuade Giraud, who still insisted on simultaneous landings in France and Africa in the spring of 1943, to abandon the operation in France and take command of the one in North Africa.

Earlier, when Giraud had realized the Allies were not paying attention to his plans, he had become furious and had given Rigault orders for the conspirators to refuse any further collaboration with the Americans if they insisted on acting unilaterally.

These orders Rigault was careful not to pass on to either Mast or Béthouart in North Africa, but the situation was tense; with only three weeks before D day, Murphy had to maneuver delicately. He was, however, fully charged by the President with freely handling the *political* negotiations preparatory to the landings. With this advantage Murphy decided to embark upon a series of political talks with the Five, mostly in the quiet back room of a black-market restaurant on the heights of El Biar, not far from Dar Mahieddine.

These talks, which took place on October 15, 18 and 19, resulted in the drafting of an official accord in the form of letters to be exchanged between Murphy and Giraud. In return for French help during the eventual landings, the United States government was pledged by Murphy, in the name of Roosevelt, to the principle of restoring France to full sovereignty and territorial integrity, both metropolitan and colonial, as of 1939. Furthermore, the United States agreed to come to North Africa only at French request, to allow the French to select D day, to treat France as an ally, to leave intact the internal administration of the territories momentarily occupied by its troops, and to equip France's new army.

This last stipulation was, of course, just what Lemaigre and Laval had been looking for, and would put any Frenchman who could secure its implementation in a position of considerable power, not only in North Africa but eventually in France.

To Lemaigre such power was essential. To obtain it he would have to work through Giraud. To persuade Giraud he would have to produce details of the specific military forces involved. To obtain such details a military conference would have to be held between staff officers of Generals Eisenhower and Giraud.

Eisenhower agreed, and would have liked to take part himself, but instead selected his trusted West Point classmate and deputy commander, Major General Mark W. Clark. Giraud nominated as his deputy General Mast.

The problem was to find a place for this meeting.

3

IN ALGIERS, during the third week of October, one of Murphy's "vice-consuls," Ridgway B. Knight, who had been a wine salesman in France before the war, sounded out the conspirators about finding a villa somewhere along the Algerian coast, suitable for a clandestine meeting.

The house, said Knight, must be spacious enough for several overnight guests, be well isolated, be surrounded by a thick garden, and—most important—must have access to a private beach.

No easy assignment, considering the strict Vichy police measures and the constant scrutiny of the Axis armistice commission; the only solution seemed to be to find some conspirator who either owned such a property or had a friend who did.

As usual Rigault and d'Astier set to work and soon heard from one of their men of what sounded like a suitable villa in the coastal town of Cherchel, the ancient Roman city of Caesarea, some 75 miles west of Algiers. The villa belonged to a rich *colon* whose son-in-law, one Jacques Tissier, had the use of it.

Driving out to see the place, Rigault and d'Astier found it about 17 kilometers beyond Cherchel on the way to Gouraya, by the mouth of a small stream called Oued Messelmoun.

Hung above the Mediterranean, with about four kilometers of private coastline where the water was deep enough for a submarine to approach submerged, and with a discreet copse of pines to hide both the house and its private beach from the inland road, the property, which had once been a smuggler's haven, seemed ideal for their purpose.

The villa itself, a large square house built in the colonial style of the turn of the century, with a red tiled roof and walls of stucco, mostly covered by a heavy coiled mass of wisteria and bougainvillea, had a terraced garden which gave onto the private beach, smooth and pebbly between two rocky promontories.

Heading through a Spanish patio, "its air sweet with the fragrance of lemons," Rigault and d'Astier found a house full of unused rooms crammed with bourgeois furniture, the ceilings splotched with yellow from the dampness, but big enough for a conference, and with enough beds for the expected guests.

There was only one problem. The entire coastline, including the four kilometers of private beach, appeared to be rigorously patrolled by a coast guard.

Fortunately, their fellow conspirators in Cherchel had recruited among their adherents the very coast-guard officer in charge of that particular stretch of beach, a Lieutenant Le Nen, who, with a midshipman named Michel and two native *douair* coastguardsmen, agreed to patrol the area, in defense not of Vichy but of the conspirators.

All seemed in order for Murphy and Mast to receive the secret Allied mission.

To make sure the submarine could spot the house and know that it was safe to come ashore, Murphy informed London that a white light would be hung in an upstairs window.

On October 19 the Allied party—with Clark in the stock disguise of a lieutenant colonel—left London for Gibraltar. There, for extra security's sake, they were transferred by curtained vehicle to a waiting British submarine, H.M.S. *Seraph,* under the command of a twenty-nine-year-old Royal Navy lieutenant, N. L. A. Jewell, who for weeks had been studying the North African coast through his periscope.

That same starry night, heading past Europa Point, while Clark and his companions settled down to a constricted routine of bridge, the *Seraph* nosed toward the African coast and a rendezvous point 500 miles to the west, recognizable from the sea by a nearby sugarloaf hill, where it was due on the night of October 21.

In Algiers, late that afternoon, Robert Murphy and Ridgway Knight, who was to act as interpreter for the meeting, climbed into the Consulate's old gray Studebaker and headed for Cherchel to find young Tissier, who was to act as their host.

Murphy's Studebaker was followed shortly by a Peugeot with Colonel Jousse, Rigault, and d'Astier, who for the occasion was accompanied by a young medical student, José Aboulker, who had organized a large number of secret insurgents.

General Mast, who could hardly arrive at such an hour in an official divisional vehicle, was to come in the morning, shortly after six, accompanied by other senior French officers.

At 11 P.M. sharp, Knight and Tissier hung an unshaded light bulb four feet from the ceiling of a top-floor room whose handy mansard roof hid the glare from any angle but straight out to sea.

At midnight Ridgway Knight went down to the beach to patrol, staring out at the calm Mediterranean on which a faint, pale moon was reflected.

Though he reported that he saw a shadow on the waters, nothing approached the coast. Toward six in the morning, when the sky clouded over and waves began to pound against the beach, Knight called off the vigil, aware that by daylight the submarine could no longer surface.

Despondently the conspirators returned to Algiers. The next rendezvous, as they understood it, was to be on the night of the 23rd; so they dispersed and went about their normal affairs.

The submarine, delayed en route—by, of all things, compulsory boat drills—had arrived on the spot at 4 A.M. The friendly signal was sighted, but Lieutenant Jewell decided it would be impossible to get a party safely ashore before daylight.

Radioing Gibraltar to organize a reception for that same night, he prepared to have the *Seraph* lie submerged off the coast all day.

The message, duly forwarded to Murphy by secret OSS radio,

caused some confusion in Algiers. To begin with, the transmitter was in the house of an agent in the port area, and if Murphy wished to send a message, a typewriter cover had to be hung from the office balcony so that a messenger, cycling by, could pick up the signal.

By this quaint method Murphy answered Gibraltar that all was in order. But in Algiers it meant a mad scramble to obtain the necessary transport and gasoline for another 150-mile round trip, and to realert (usually by personal messenger) all the French participants, one of whom, Commander Barjot, could no longer be found.

By evening, Murphy, Knight, Tissier, and a young businessman called Bernard Karsenty—who had been recruited as liaison officer, cook and general caretaker—drove back to the villa, arousing the curiosity of the inhabitants of the quiet fishing village of Cherchel.

Worse still, as the caravan pulled up in the driveway, they found the villa guarded by an Arab night watchman whom Tissier had not expected. In the nervousness of the moment Tissier pulled out a 50-franc note and told the Arab to go away and say nothing of what he had seen.

From the trunk of the car the conspirators unloaded hampers of food and wine. Once more Knight lighted the signal, then went down to the beach to stand watch.

It was a calm autumn night, with a thin crescent of moon that appeared intermittently from behind a light bank of cumulus. The only sound came from the dogs of a nearby Arab *douair,* howling at the moon. Just after midnight, on the calm surface of the sea appeared a low silhouette, which turned out to be a collapsible kayak. From it stepped a United States businessman serving as a colonel in Allied Force Headquarters G-1, Julius C. Holmes, who spoke excellent French; he was accompanied by a young British commando officer, an expert on navigation, armed with dagger, Sten gun, flashlight, infrared projector, and carrying a small walkie-talkie with which to signal the submarine.

In quick succession there arrived a second kayak in which

Brigadier General Lyman L. Lemnitzer, head of AFHQ's Plans Section, carrying a heavily weighted tube with secret documents, was paddled to shore by another young British commando, an expert on small boats. A third kayak carried Colonel A. M. Hamblen, shipping and supply expert, navigated by the United States Navy's liaison officer to AFHQ, Captain Jerauld Wright.

Murphy, once more "radiant," appeared on the beach to do the honors, introducing his guests.

Last ashore, because his boat had been overturned by the British commando in charge of the landings, came Major General Mark W. Clark, brandishing a carbine, which caused Colonel Jousse his first doubts about the whole operation as he mumbled to one of his compatriots, "A general with a rifle! What sort of army is this?"

Murphy greeted Clark with "Welcome to North Africa." Clark responded with "I'm damn glad we made it."

Brief introductions completed, and while the kayaks were being dragged ashore and carefully hidden under branches in a handy olive grove, the senior officers climbed through the garden to the villa.

After a warming highball they retired to several darkened rooms, where, in Victorian canopied beds which Clark described as "unkempt and much-used," they stretched out for a few hours' sleep.

At six in the morning the other members of the French team arrived by car, including, as Giraud's deputy, General Mast. To represent the Navy, they had recovered Commander Barjot (later Admiral and Chief of Staff of the French Navy); for the Air Force, they had Major D'Artois; and for the Chantiers de la Jeunesse, Colonel van Ecke.

By now a bright autumnal sun was causing a slight mist to form round the trees in the garden, sucking up the morning dew. Beneath the calm, murmuring sea, the submarine was once more submerged.

The French team, which had arrived in civilian clothes, but carrying neat little suitcases, now reappeared from various bedrooms, fully and properly uniformed. Coffee was served. Clark,

Murphy and Mast had a breakfast of bread, jam and sardines; then the conference started.

A good deal of information had been accumulated at the Consulate to transmit to the American military. Clark and Lemnitzer conferred with Murphy and Mast, while the other officers paired off to go over pertinent details with their opposite numbers: Barjot for the Navy; D'Artois for the Air Force. Clark's first task was to inform General Mast that the prospective landings would not be strictly American—though, of course, de Gaulle's Free French would still be excluded. Clark was to explain to Mast that because of the urgent demand for American naval forces in the Pacific, British air and naval forces would be required in the Mediterranean and, shortly after the landings, British ground troops to move eastward toward Tunisia.

To this Mast made no objection. He produced a detailed study of airfields, arsenals, batteries, and other key points, as well as a plan for the invasion which, according to Holmes, "surprisingly enough was almost identical with ours."

The major remaining problem was the threat of reaction by Mast's senior officers: Koeltz, in command of the XIX Corps, and Juin, in command of all North African forces, neither of whom had yet expressed any sympathy for the conspirators or the Allies. To prevent these officers from going over the heads of the conspirators and countering their orders to help the Allies, it had been decided that on the night of the landings, all such unfriendly senior officers would be arrested and held under house surveillance so as to neutralize them long enough for the Americans to get ashore and take possession of the area.

At the same time the conspirators were to cut the military communications network throughout the city so as to isolate and neutralize certain deadly coastal batteries manned by Darlan's naval personnel. In a word, they were to turn over to the Allies the city of Algiers.

The personnel for these operations was to be provided from

Colonel van Ecke's Chantiers de la Jeunesse as well as from volunteer action squads under the command of d'Astier de la Vigerie and other leaders already long attached to the plot, such as José Aboulker, a tall young man with intense blue eyes who had been charged by d'Astier with "federating" the various civilian organizations.

Important to the success of the entire operation was control of the Algiers airfields at Blida and Maison Blanche (as well as those in Oran and Morocco), to avoid any French Air Force reaction, and to provide landing fields for Allied fighters lined up at Gibraltar with a gasoline tank capacity for only a one-way trip; these planes were needed as extra cover to support the limited number of fighters which could be flown from the decks of the scant Allied supply of aircraft carriers. The French pleaded with the Americans to land as far east as Bône so that Allied armor could move quickly across the Tunisian frontier to seize Bizerte and Tunis before the Germans could get there. Thanks to Colonel Lorber, said the conspirators, the town and port of Bône could be delivered to the Allies without a shot; furthermore, they insisted that it was an operation which could guarantee the prize of Tunisia with very little effort. But Clark and his colleagues were not at liberty to discuss the Bône situation.

When Mast asked how large an American effort the French could expect, Clark—by his own admission—"tried to keep a poker face while saying that half a million Allied troops could come in, and . . . that we could put 2,000 planes in the air as well as plenty of United States Navy."

Nevertheless some good work was done in the course of the morning: signals were agreed upon for the Algiers area, the French arranged to have parties on the beaches where the Americans would land; code words, light signals, times, and places were agreed upon.

Among the more astute plans was an arrangement for Allied landings on the tiny headland of Pointe Pescade almost within

Algiers, from which troops could bypass the coastal defenses and enter the heart of the city.

Innocently, the French urged the Americans to act as soon as possible; and Mast reminded Clark of the importance of the agreement already reached that the date of D day not be fixed without prior approval from Giraud.

Little did Mast suspect that D day had long been settled and that the convoys were actually on their way.

In the afternoon, the question was raised of a post-landing re-equipment of French forces. Mast had estimated that the personnel for as many as eight French infantry divisions and two armored ones, plus separate tank, artillery and service units, could be provided in North Africa within a month.

After examining this proposition in some detail, Clark came to what was to prove the thorniest of technical questions: Who was to exercise supreme command of the joint Allied forces?

Clark hedged the question, but said it was the desire of the Allies to turn over control of North Africa to the French as soon as the situation permitted. He did, however, make it clear that a landing in the south of France, on which Giraud insisted, could come only *after* a successful North African venture.

In the course of the afternoon a résumé of the situation was worked out to be forwarded to Giraud in Eisenhower's name. Were Giraud to agree to come to Algiers and call on all Frenchmen to join him in a renewal of the war against Germany, the Allies would send a submarine from Gibraltar to pick him up off the coast of France.

Clark said he hoped to have an answer from Giraud by October 28.

The tragedy, of course, was that Clark and Holmes—who knew that the Allied plans were definitely fixed—could not help but give the appearance of having little confidence in the French sense of security. Knowing that the plans for the landing could not now be altered, they did not seem to listen carefully to the Frenchmen's suggestions, which were eminently sensible.

As Saint-Hardoin was bitterly to remark, "The French aid could have been infinitely more effective if the General had only told us the truth and had put some trust in the persons he was dealing with at Cherchel. . . . But he did not trust our collaboration, or, at the very least, wanted the direction and the glory of the operation to be solely in American hands."

Then there was to occur an incident which was even further to diminish Clark's trust in the French: Tissier's bribe to the Arab night watchman backfired.

Suspicious of such unusual generosity, the Arab decided either out of sense of duty or in the prospect of another 50 francs from the police, to go to the Commissariat in Cherchel.

Luckily the *Commissaire* was out. Even more luckily, the communal secretary, a Mr. Crabos, to whom the Arab watchman told his story, was a fellow conspirator, though he did not know about the secret meeting.

Dutifully noting the Arab's deposition about the unusual activity *chez* Tissier, Crabos said he would make an investigation, then cautiously phoned the head of the local conspirators. Informed that he was away for two days on a "hunting" expedition, Crabos realized that something important must be happening at the villa; making light of the matter, he reassured the watchman, telling him not to worry. But the Arab was stubborn. He wanted to tell his story to the *Commissaire*.

When the *Commissaire* arrived, he became very excited and wheeled out his motorcycle to go inspect the villa.

Luckily for the conspirators, Michel, one of the friendly coast-guardsmen, appeared on the scene at that very moment and queried his chief: "*Monsieur le commissaire,* where are you going in such a state of excitement?"

"I have good reason" was the answer. "I'm going to Tissier's to investigate. Something fishy goes on. Maybe Gaullists!"

Realizing the danger, Michel made a pretense of doing his duty. "But that is my affair, *monsieur le commissaire.* I will go imme-diately."

Cleverly immobilizing his own motorcycle, Michel took that of the *Commissaire,* only to sabotage it too on the way to the next police station, along the coast at Gouraya, where he requisitioned a third and last motorcycle. Having thus deprived the entire local seaboard of transport, he phoned the conspirators to warn them that a raid by the police might be imminent.

At these words—so General Clark described the scene—the French officers at the villa rose from their seats and were next seen in full flight for the woods, tearing off their uniforms as they went.

"One would have thought," said Clark, "that fifty dead skunks had been thrown on the table at the speed with which most of our French friends disappeared."

Not unhurriedly, Clark and the other Allied officers collected their papers and headed through a trap door in the patio down to a musty wine cellar.

D'Astier, sensibly emphasizing the pointlessness of his being caught on the scene, headed back for Algiers, while Knight and Murphy, having cleared the extra plates, spread some bottles round the room, emptied the money in their pockets onto the table, then pretended to be engaged in a solemn bout of poker dice with Tissier.

Meanwhile Clark and his companions could hear through the thin floorboards what was going on upstairs. For an hour in the dark they waited in suspense, then heard footsteps above. One of the commandos, his allergy restimulated by the damp musty air, was seized with a coughing fit. In the darkness he sputtered, then finally whispered, "General, I'm afraid I'll choke." "I'm afraid you *won't,*" answered Clark, forcibly inserting in the commando's mouth the gum he had been chewing since morning. Unaccustomed to the habit, the commando protested that the gum was tasteless. But it stopped his coughing.

Upstairs Tissier explained to the police that the American Consul General was in Cherchel to look for some black-market chicken. Not entirely convinced, the police decided to leave; but when Clark came out from the cellar he was determined—despite the fact that the conference with the French was only half finished, and that plans for Oran and Morocco were still to be discussed—to move off as soon as possible. By now a stiff breeze had risen and was piling huge breakers onto the once-tranquil beach.

For several hours Clark and his companions hid in the woods by the house "like the plainsmen in covered wagon days, with sentries, armed with carbines, lying down at all sides." Several times the police came back but perhaps because of the dark did not search the grounds.

Finally about 3:30 A.M., cold and nervous, Clark decided to try to launch the boats despite the whitecaps.

Several attempts were made, but as each time the waves capsized the unsteady craft, it was decided to hide out again in the olive grove and wait for the wind to die down.

Two hours passed, leaving only an hour and a half before dawn, at which time it would no longer be possible to leave.

Clark insisted that he must get away. Were the police to catch the Deputy Commander in Chief of Torch, the consequences, not only for himself and the conspirators but for the entire Allied expedition, might be disastrous. He refused to be taken prisoner. At the very worst he would seize, at gunpoint, the first boat in the nearest fishing village and make toward the submarine. Brandishing a bundle of thousand-franc notes, he approached the coast-guard lieutenant, Le Nen, and asked him to buy a boat of some sort, even a rowboat.

Le Nen shook his head. The slightest query about a boat would instantly incriminate him and all the others concerned.

Clark could but try the kayaks once more.

Carrying them down from the beach was a worse job than Knight had imagined. The boats were heavy, the path rough and strewn with gorse that tore at his legs with each trip.

This time, to launch the kayaks, it was decided that the departing officers should be seated in them while still on dry land and that Murphy, Knight, Karsenty and Le Nen with one of the coast-guardsmen, all stripped to their shorts, should try to carry the loaded boats into the water so as to launch them above the breakers.

Finally on the seventh attempt, after a supreme effort, General Clark reached the *Seraph,* which had dangerously approached to within a hundred yards of the coast.

Eventually the entire party was launched, and "Vice-Consul" Knight and Lieutenant Le Nen could at last stand naked and shivering on the beach, their teeth chattering, but smiling as they watched the small boats paddle away.

It was 4:15 A.M. with barely twenty minutes till dawn.

By the time the sun was up, Knight, who was suffering from a severe earache from his repeated dousings, was dressed and ready to step with Murphy into their gray Studebaker and head for Algiers.

On the beach, Le Nen and his coastguardsmen were carefully raking the sand smooth to eradicate all traces of the venture.

Later, at the police station, where Le Nen made his final report, he informed the *Commissaire,* with a slight wink, that he had found the United States Consul General drunk in the company of several *"petites femmes."*

Brow furrowed, the *Commissaire* debated what to do next. Le Nen waited anxiously for the final word. Then slowly the *Commissaire* raised his head and smiled. "Tell me," he asked, "were they pretty?"

In Algiers, Miss Hardy, Murphy's secretary, notebook and typewriter at hand, was waiting with Lemaigre-Dubreuil, Rigault, Saint-Hardoin, and d'Astier in the comfortable apartment of Vice-Consul Felix Cole, so as to record the results of the Cherchel conference for simultaneous dispatch to Washington and to General Giraud.

Three times during the night they had nearly started for Cherchel by car, but each time had been afraid that a trip so late in the night would attract unwanted attention.

The reason for their urgency was that Lemaigre had a plane reservation that morning to fly directly to meet Giraud near Lyon.

As the hours ticked by and the dawn came up with no sign of either Murphy or Knight, the conspirators realized that no precise report could be prepared in time for Lemaigre to take it with him;

hastily an "innocuous" code was devised for use over the regular French telegraph system to advise Lemaigre in France of any positive results of the meeting, and Lemaigre caught his plane.

At last, "white from mingled emotion and fatigue," Murphy and Knight arrived to tell the details of the meeting. A more formal report was then sent to Lemaigre and Giraud by Mme. Rigault, who left on the regular ferryboat from Algiers to Marseilles.

When Giraud first received the results of the Cherchel conference he still felt hesitant about rallying to the cause, believing that the decisive battle would have to be fought in France, and that any North African landings would be a waste of time. Yet he was impressed by the size of the prospective American aid.

After some reflection, on October 27, Giraud drew up a long note giving his accord in principle, but contingent upon a written text to be submitted by Murphy.

Now Eisenhower at last authorized Murphy to notify Giraud that the landings would take place early in November and that a submarine would be sent to pick him up.

This bit of news struck the French, who had been planning for much later landings, "like a thunderbolt," and Giraud answered that he could not possibly leave France before November 20.

So shocked were Lemaigre and the other members of the Five that the Americans could have been all through the parley at Cherchel at a time when the convoys were already at sea and never have taken them into their confidence, they seriously considered canceling their plans to help the Americans.

Mast argued so heatedly that Murphy cabled Eisenhower that unless the landings were delayed they were likely to turn into a terrible "catastrophe."

In Algiers, though the operations required the greatest care and attention, they might still be successful. Even in such cities as Bône, where the local commander was already secured to the plot, plans could be speeded up. But farther afield the problem seemed beyond any remedy in so short a time.

In the end, though almost à contre-coeur, Lemaigre decided to carry on with the plot and again took off for France on November

2nd to try to rally Giraud, who received him with "an avalanche of reproach."

Yet Giraud too, in the end, agreed to carry on and make the best of a bad situation. Designating a substitute leader to handle any eventual insurrection in France, he prepared to embark on the submarine—once more H.M.S. *Seraph*—which was to pick him up on the night of November 4 in the Gulf of Lions.

Now, at last, the stage seemed set for coordinated action between the French and the Americans, aimed at liberating North Africa and bringing French forces back into the war on the side of the Allies.

In Algiers, Giraud's representative, General Mast, promised that with four days' notice he could still guarantee that there would be little or no resistance from the ground and air forces of his Algerian command, and that naval resistance would cease shortly after successful landings.

On November 4th he was told to be prepared for action on the night of the 7th. This gave him only three days, but it would have to do.

What Clark had been specifically forbidden by Eisenhower to tell Mast at Cherchel, and what neither Giraud nor Lemaigre had been told, was that while the Americans were involved with Giraud and the Five, Murphy, at his superior's orders, had been dealing with a rival pretender—Admiral Jean François Darlan.

4

IN JUNE of 1941 Admiral Darlan had told Admiral Leahy, "If the United States is capable of landing at Marseilles 500,000 men, 3,000 tanks, and 3,000 planes, I, Darlan, will be ready to march with you."

Just before leaving Washington, Robert Murphy had been summoned by Admiral Leahy to see the President. Mr. Roosevelt wanted Darlan informed not only that the requisite conditions could be met, but that the United States was ready to furnish the armaments, supplies, and financial aid necessary to put France in the war again.

The President's overt motivation for this highly secret *démarche* appeared to be his belief that maintenance of the peace in the future would require "the re-establishment of France to her full sovereignty." To accomplish this end the government of the United States was therefore ready and willing to conclude "any sensible agreement to facilitate the re-placing of France in the hierarchy of nations."

The decision to deal with a man such as Darlan—an anti-British collaborator—was not, of course, caused by any sudden infatuation; it was the natural climax of a long-standing American policy to favor those forces in France which were represented at Vichy, coupled with aversion toward General de Gaulle.

William Langer, in his book *Our Vichy Gamble,* has denied that Darlan's arrival in Algiers at the time of the landings was pre-arranged, and has stated categorically that "neither is there any truth in the charge that secret arrangements had been made with him beforehand."

It is therefore worth looking at the evidence available to the public.

Hardly had Robert Murphy set foot in his Algiers office on October 11 when he was approached by "a representative of Admiral Darlan," who announced that the Commander in Chief of all French forces of land, sea, and air was being driven toward a choice between closer collaboration with the Germans and joining the Allies.

Was this coincidence? Or had word from Admiral Leahy already reached Vichy (through his direct radio contact with our Embassy in the Hotel Lutetia)? In either case, what was influencing Darlan, according to his own testimony, was news obtained by Vichy from both German and Japanese sources that the United States was planning an early assault on Dakar or Casablanca, or both.

Perhaps the most precise quotation of Admiral Darlan's advances to the Americans was recorded by his son Alain, who was used by his father as a political agent (disguised as a traveling salesman) for psychological intelligence in North Africa:

"Reports reach me indicating that you are about to undertake military operations against, or in, French possessions in Africa. You need us, we need you. But it is best for our plans to harmonize and synchronize, lest worse catastrophes befall us both."

By way of explanation, Alain writes, "It was because of his desire to augment the chances of France in harmonizing her efforts with those of the Allies that my father decided to enter into secret relations with the Americans during the summer and beginning of autumn of 1942."

These contacts, it seems, had been established for some time. Alain elaborates: "I do not know by what means my father was able to obtain these contacts, but I know that before my departure for Tunisia, in September 1942, he said to me: 'I hope soon, thanks to a direct line of communication, at last to be able to have more precise and surer information, from those interested, on the exact intentions of the Americans.' "

To this Alain adds, "Over and above the reports and information which my father received directly on the clandestine activities of the Americans, and in particular of Mr. R. Murphy, and his 'vice-consuls,' the Germans, who lived in fear of an Allied coup in Africa, communicated to him during the summer of 1942 the information they themselves were able to collect."

Alain is even specific as to names: "I know my father was kept informed (I believe it was through the regular service of counter-espionage of the Navy and the Army, and also by his personal agents) of the fact that the Americans were multiplying their contacts with certain French personalities, both in North Africa and France. . . . He mentioned several times certain names, among them that of M. Lemaigre-Dubreuil, in conversation during the first nine months of 1942."

Darlan, as will be seen, had a number of channels of communication with Murphy. An interesting one, in view of later developments, was a young Major Dorange on General Juin's staff. Immediately after Murphy's return from Washington, Dorange asked if it would be possible for him to visit the American Consulate without being detected.

On October 13—that is to say, two days before the first of Murphy's official agreements with the Five, and ten days before the Cherchel meeting—Dorange appeared in civilian clothes at the Consulate's back door for what one of Murphy's vice-consuls called "a feeler to test out the force of American intentions."

A journalist related to Dorange, Alain de Sérigny—who, with a colleague on the *Écho d'Alger,* René Richard, wrote a book on this series of events, based to a large extent on information derived directly from Dorange—states that the Murphy-Dorange conversations of October 13 resulted in a *pro memoria* which summed up their views as follows:

"The government of the United States wishes to deal only with the French government or with any person either officially or secretly delegated by it. The United States does not wish to make any gesture of hostility toward French territory, and will intervene only at French request, and under conditions fixed by France. Were the French to appeal for aid, the United States would be ready to bring, not only war material, but the aid of her armed forces."

In Vichy Darlan called in Captain Beaufort who handled the clandestine liaison between Lemaigre-Dubreuil and Metropolitan France and said to him, "I know what you are up to, and the contacts you have. I would like you to inform those who sent you that I am disposed to be the man they seek."

On October 17th, Murphy cabled to London and Washington the recommendation that an attempt be made to bring about "a cooperative relationship between Giraud and Darlan." This produced in the Allied capitals what the official United States Army historian described as "intense concern and lively activity."

Even Langer admits that in Washington Darlan's advances were not to be taken lightly and that "since the chief opposition to an American landing was expected from French naval forces, Darlan's assistance might be crucial."

Churchill summed up the situation in one sentence: "Kiss Darlan's stern if you have to, but get the French Navy."

More diplomatically phrased, the decision was made—although Giraud would be recognized as "our principal collaborator on the French side" and as Governor General of all French North Africa, responsible for civil and military affairs—to "negotiate with Darlan and to accept him in a military role which would be mutually agreeable."

This produced from the U.S. Army's official historian the candid remark: ". . . they agreed that one friendly French leader would be good but that two would be better, especially when one controlled the French fleet at Toulon."

Eisenhower, says Butcher, tried to "develop a formula for dealing with the nationalistic interests of the French leaders, particularly Giraud."

The solution he suggested, and which he not only put to the Prime Minister and to the British Chiefs but cabled to Washington, was that "once ashore, and with the French liberated and North Africa becoming a base for further Allied military operations, Darlan could be made Deputy Allied Commander in Chief in relief of Clark when he takes command of the American Fifth Army."

This wishful solution was given the blessings of the British Chiefs and, as Butcher says, "The PM congratulated him on his sagacity."

Even the King of England heard of the intrigue. George VI, says Butcher, in his diary for October 23rd, "knew the latest details of the Torch story. Wanted to know of Ike if he had heard from Clark and asked for Ike's opinion of the reliability of 'D,' and also of 'G.' " Eisenhower told Butcher later that he had "had to think quickly, as he hadn't been accustomed to using those initials for Darlan and Giraud."

On October 25th Butcher noted in his diary: "While the French Army seems to be friendly for this operation, the Navy is still a big question mark. We await news of McGowan's conference with Darlan's agent."

When Murphy, very gingerly, suggested to Mast that Darlan be brought into the Giraud ménage, he was told abruptly that Giraud alone could be dealt with, "that no negotiations whatsoever could be carried on with a rival who was not to be trusted and only wanted the opportunity for joining a successful operation."

Mast even went so far as to suggest that Giraud's prestige was so high that not only the North African Army would follow his standard, but the fleet as well. This opinion was based on Mast's and Giraud's plans for an operation sometime in the spring of 1943, by which time they hoped that public opinion would have swung away from Darlan and a German victory, in support of Giraud and an Allied one.

In fairness to Mast (and with no prejudice to his pro-Allied sentiments), it must be remembered that, as Giraud's deputy, he was to be second-in-command of any new French Army equipped by the Americans. Were Darlan and the other "legitimate" top officers, such as Juin, Koeltz and General Jean A. Mendigal, to be admitted into the fold, Mast would be relegated to a lower station in the official hierarchy.

The question of "legitimate" versus "dissident" support for the Americans was to play a vital role in the whole affair, and cause Murphy some sleepless nights.

Juin, for instance, as commander of French armed forces in North Africa, could, technically, have brought them all over to the Allies at the crucial moment; and Murphy was not unaware of Juin's penchant for the Allies. Saint-Hardouin had been told by Admiral Raymond Fenard: "Juin thinks as we do." The trouble with Juin was that he had been released from a German POW camp on parole, and Murphy was afraid this might prevent him from acting—at least until relieved of that commitment by a superior French officer.

Having made a legal engagement with Giraud (witnessed and initiated by F.D.R.), Murphy could hardly dally too openly with Darlan. Unable to induce his rival figureheads to agree, Murphy could only hope that one would triumph and the other disappear, or that, faced with a *fait accompli,* both would accommodate themselves to the situation.

On October 22, the very day on which Clark and Murphy began to negotiate with Giraud's representative at Cherchel, Admiral

Darlan set upon a curiously coincidental tour of North and West Africa—ostensibly to insure himself that all his defenses were ready to *prevent* a successful American attack.

This trip, carried out with every device of official Vichy propaganda, took him to the Moroccan capital of Rabat on October 24th, where Darlan reviewed French and Moroccan troops and had an audience with the Sultan, to whom he delivered a letter from Marshal Pétain.

The next day, accompanied by Resident General Auguste Noguès and the head of the local naval forces, Admiral François Michelier, Darlan reviewed more troops in Casablanca.

But the real purpose of his tour was to be revealed to one of Murphy's "vice-consuls," Kenneth Pendar, who, on a flying trip to Marrakech happened to run into an old friend and contact, Mehdi Glaoui*—son of the pro-Allied Pasha of Marrakech—who told Pendar that "he and his father, the Pasha, El Glaoui, had just entertained Noguès and Darlan, both of whom had come to Marrakech incognito and had been dressed in civilian clothes."

"Something is going on," added Mehdi Glaoui to Pendar. "Both men seemed so tense. I think they expect Allied action. What do you think?"

The next day Pendar ran into the Pasha himself. "El Glaoui," Pendar reported later, "put both hands on my shoulders and said earnestly, but with a smile, 'My friend, last night Admiral Darlan dined with me. I think we shall soon see the events which you and I have awaited so long.' "

On October 28th (the day Giraud was informed by Murphy that D day would be in early November) Darlan arrived back in Algiers and held a conference "on defense of the Empire" with Juin and other generals in command of the area.

The next day, after an ironic ceremony in which he reviewed the Algiers Division, commanded by General Mast, who was at that moment plotting to aid the Americans ashore, Darlan had lunch

---

* Killed fighting as our ally in Italy in 1944.

with General Juin at the latter's official residence, the Villa des Oliviers.

There they had a two hour tête-à-tête; for what transpired we have the testimony of the French Admiral Jules Docteur, who says, in his book, *Darlan—La Grande Énigme de la Guerre,* that they discussed in detail the October 13 arrangements between Murphy and Major Dorange.

On October 30th Darlan visited his son Alain in the Maillot Hospital, where he was suffering from an acute attack of polio contracted during his tour of Tunisia.

In the afternoon Darlan quit Algiers.

Having returned to Vichy, Darlan made an official speech in which he drew attention to the possibility of an Allied landing in Dakar—no mention was made of Casablanca, Oran or Algiers—and then went to his country home and burned a great number of secret and private papers.

There now enters upon the scene a young conspirator whose mysterious operations bear watching with attention. As a former Undersecretary of State for Air in the Vichy government, and now Inspector General of Air Defenses, he too had just returned on November 3rd from a quick trip to Morocco. His name was General Jean Marie Bergeret.

Though he was only a colonel during the Syrian fight against the British, and reputed to be thoroughly anti-Allied, French historians maintain that throughout the war he kept secretly in touch with British intelligence. In the course of the Pétain trial it was revealed that as early as October 30th Bergeret informed the marshal that the Allied landings were scheduled for November.*

* As early as July 25, 1940, Churchill, while publicly arranging a military agreement with de Gaulle, decided on a secret arrangement with Pétain. As he wrote to his Foreign Secretary, Mr. Eden: "I want to promote a kind of collusive conspiracy in the Vichy government whereby certain members of that government, perhaps with the consent of those who remain, will levant to North Africa in order to make a better bargain for France from the North African shore and from a position of independence."

On November 2nd Lemaigre-Dubreuil left Algiers for France to take Giraud the letter of agreement signed by Murphy as representative of President Roosevelt. That same day Murphy saw Juin and confirmed the agreement of October 13 about Allied landings, though he still gave Juin no indication of when they might take place, despite the fact that this might be his last chance to prevent the putting into action of resistance in North Africa.

On November 3rd Lemaigre sent a message to Algiers to inform the other conspirators that Giraud had agreed to come to North Africa immediately and that he, Lemaigre, would return as soon as possible.

That same day Darlan sent Colonel Chrétien, head of the counterespionage branch of the French intelligence service in Algeria, to see Murphy. There was a meeting on the 3rd or 4th at Guyotville in which Murphy once more "encouraged the Admiral's offer."

At this point, according to Admiral Docteur, a captain on Darlan's staff in Vichy went to General Bergeret and communicated to him the contents of a coded telegram from Lemaigre-Dubreuil, already back in Algiers: "Date advanced. Landings imminent."

This was the very day that Murphy finally decided to tell Mast and Lemaigre that D day was to be the night of the 7th to 8th.

Bergeret went straight to Marshal Pétain to emphasize to him in what an ambiguous situation the landings would place the military chiefs in North Africa, and to beg the marshal to transfer himself immediately to North Africa in order to "dictate to them, the military leaders, the attitude they should take, to avoid any drama."

The marshal, says Docteur, refused, saying that one did not defend France by quitting it, and that he did not wish "to abandon forty million Frenchmen."

That the marshal was informed is corroborated by Darlan's son Alain, who wrote: "I also know, because he told me, that Darlan kept the Marshal informed of all the important events and facts of which he learned during the months before the landings."

On November 4th Darlan also received an urgent message from

Admiral Fenard, his host in Algiers, advising him to return immediately because his son's condition had become grave. As proof of the truth of this message, Alain adds the macabre touch that his coffin was ordered.

However, the next day, Alain's health was remarkably improved.

In Vichy, on Thursday, November 5th, just two days before the landings, Admiral Darlan climbed aboard one of two planes reserved for Cabinet members and set off for Algiers—in the utmost secrecy. Because the second plane was being repaired, Darlan took the one reserved for Premier Laval, who intended to fly it to see Hitler the following week. In the circumstances, says Alain, "Laval did not hesitate to put the plane at the disposal of Darlan, asking only that it be returned no later than Tuesday, November 10th."

From this it is evident that Laval knew Darlan was heading for Algiers; Darlan knew that Laval was intending to see Hitler; and Pétain, whose position was home base, knew that the Allies were about to land in North Africa! The plot becomes transparent.

Darlan arrived in Algiers at 2:30 on the 5th, and it is worth quoting Alain precisely about the decision he then took:

"Despite the optimistic affirmations of the doctors, my father decided, after I got better on November 6, to stay on a few days and not leave till the morning of November 10th."

No mention of Darlan's having left Vichy was divulged to the press in France, and not a word was said of his arrival in Algiers.

On November 6th it was learned in Vichy that Allied convoys were gathering at Gibraltar. That afternoon General Bergeret boarded a plane with two French officers and headed for Algiers. At 7:30 that night he saw Darlan at the bedside of his son Alain and "informed him," so says Admiral Docteur, "of the imminence of the landings." Darlan, according to Docteur, answered that he did not think this was true, that he was taking his information from Roosevelt's representative, Mr. Murphy. The convoys would bypass North Africa, headed presumably for Malta.

Bergeret then drove back to Admiral Fenard's villa, where Darlan was staying; but—still according to Docteur—having no confidence in Fenard, he said nothing of all this until the pointed-

ness of Fenard's questions indicated to Bergeret that Fenard too
was in the know.

Thus not only Bergeret and Pétain but Darlan's host Fenard,
who had sent the cable which had summoned Darlan to Algiers, all
seemed to know the landings were aimed at North Africa, and in a
matter of days, if not hours.

That night, November 6, Bergeret and Darlan dined at the
Fenards'. After dinner, says Docteur, Bergeret insisted that Darlan
take the situation in hand. To which Darlan is said to have replied, "Go tomorrow to Bizerte and you will see if you cannot
observe the fighting off the coast of Sicily."

The next morning Colonel Rivet, head of the intelligence service
in Vichy, who had a contact by double agent with British intelligence, telegraphed Darlan in Algiers: *"Action importante contre
France va être incessament déclanchée."*

To this Darlan replied in the same vein: *"On a vu Murphy, pas
de danger immédiat."*

As for Giraud, he was at that very moment—the morning of
November 7—on the point of being drowned. The submarine which
had gone to fetch him (still with Lieutenant Jewell in command,
but technically under the United States Navy's Captain Jerauld
Wright, so as to persuade Giraud that only Americans were involved in the landings) had been delayed by bad weather and
prevented from surfacing on the night of the 4th to 5th off the
Côte d'Azur fishing village of Le Lavandou.

Despite Lemaigre's pleading with Giraud that he risked getting
to Algiers too late, Giraud insisted on going first to Gibraltar to
make sure of Murphy's promise that he would be in command of
the entire Allied forces.

Finally, on the night of the 5th to 6th, H.M.S. *Seraph* managed
to surface in the midst of a gale and pick up Giraud. He was
dressed in a neat herringbone suit and soft gray hat, and was accompanied by his son Bernard, a young aide named Viret, and our
old friend Captain Beaufre, conveniently released from a Vichy
prison just in time to join the party. With remarkable ease all of

them had managed to hide out in a seaside villa, avoid the tight surveillance of the local police as well as a special Gestapo dragnet, then, despite the jealous scene raised by a fisherman's wife who could not believe her husband was going out in such a gale, successfully commandeer a fishing smack with which to reach the submarine.

Safely aboard, they were to suffer an idiotic mishap. The radio went dead—making it possible to send, but not to receive.

A Catalina flying boat, dispatched to try to locate the *Seraph*, was lucky enough to spot it traveling on the surface.

There followed the complicated maneuver of transferring Giraud and his party from ship to plane. Buffeted by a still-choppy sea, Giraud missed his footing and was only just rescued by a quick-mitted crewman.

In Gibraltar, Eisenhower, as Commander in Chief of the operation, suddenly decided he did not care to speak to the aspirant French Commander.

Luckily Eisenhower was convinced by his civilian and military advisers that he had made "a mistake in deciding not to see Giraud, feeling the story that he has been detained in London will leave a lasting impression of deception."

To which Butcher adds the historic understatement of the campaign: "Time's a-wastin'."

It was.

PART TWO

THE COUP

5

IN ALGIERS, November 7, 1942, was a soft, warm day. The air was clear, the sea empty and calm. Along the winding rue Michelet, as it climbed from the port to the heights of El Biar, the sun, slightly green at that season, rippled the leaves of the plane trees, which were beginning to fall.

It was a typical Saturday.

Algerians, apart from a tiny number of conspirators, had no idea that D day was for the morrow, that H hour had been set for the middle of the night.

Even to the group leaders of the plot this explosive bit of news had been denied until Robert Murphy, sneaking off from the Consulate, turned up in the mirrored dressing rooms of a smart dressmaker's shop on the rue d'Isly called "Elysée-Couture." Run by a good-humored young co-plotter of Achiary's named Guy

Cohen (or Calvet for confusion), the shop had served for months as a secret meeting place and letter drop for the conspiracy.

There José Aboulker was alerted to prepare his teams for action within twenty-four hours.

As his own center for the action, Aboulker obtained the use of his father's apartment at 26 rue Michelet. From early morning of the 7th, individuals and groups of two or three had been climbing to the second floor to ring the bell beneath a plaque: DR. HENRI ABOULKER, OTO-RHINOLOGIE.

In the gilt and tapestried *salon* of this typically bourgeois apartment, furnished with the usual grand piano, the usual stack of *L'Illustration,* and an abundance of *objets d'art* donated by grateful patients, a surprising variety of conspirators congregated that day to organize their *coup,* including the doctor himself, then in his sixties, and his nephew Raphaël, in his thirties.

At 10 A.M. Henri d'Astier de la Vigerie arrived with a bundle of papers beneath his arm, followed shortly by Lemaigre and Saint-Hardouin.

Taking up a strategic position in the fumed-oak dining room, separated from the *salon* by a glass-paneled door, d'Astier spread on the dining room table a large map of Algiers.

With a pot of glue, several pencils, and a pair of scissors, he began a methodical piece of organization, selecting the targets for the night, and the groups to be assigned each target.

The object of the *coup* was peaceably to arrest the top military and administrative leaders of the area, and simultaneously occupy the nerve centers of the city, in an attempt to paralyze resistance to the landings: in the metaphor of one French historian, "to chloroform the city for the impending operation."

Cleverly, the rebels had hit upon the ruse of using the *official* French Army plan for defending the area against enemy landings, in order to place their own men among the guardians of the peace.

Partly because Colonel Jousse was in command of the garrison and could write official orders, and partly because Vichy had planned to maintain order with civilian volunteers recruited from the SOL—armed with rifles and identified by brassards on their sleeves—the scheme was not implausible.

Jousse issued armbands with black-and-white initials V.P. (for Volontaires de Place, a sort of home guard), properly stamped and with official seals. To each group of civilians, for verisimilitude, was assigned a rebel officer in uniform, furnished with "Secret" orders over Jousse's authentic signature and the seal of the Algiers headquarters, directing all concerned to let them pass on a confidential mission for the maintenance of internal security.

To be sure that the city was compliantly anesthetized, the rebels planned to cut all its nerve lines of communication.

Near the naval headquarters in the Hotel Saint-Georges, in the garden of a villa belonging to an Englishwoman, the conspirators had discovered the entrance to a tunnel through which they were able to explore a maze of subterranean passages dating from the time of the Barbary corsairs, or even earlier, which spread beneath the city. Via these passages the rebels traced the major telephone and cable lines.

One of the rebel leaders, a Parisian industrialist by the name of Pierre Alexandre, had drawn up a plan indicating the points at which the cables could be cut, reporting that beneath the Admiralty the cables were as thick as a man's arm, and so near the surface that sentries could be heard patrolling overhead.

Commissioner Bringard, a longtime associate of Achiary, proposed not only to cut the wires for regular phone service and the protected military network, but to take over intact the special police lines so as to give the rebels a means of their own with which to communicate. They could then, said Bringard, take control of the central Commissariat and order the peripheral stations to turn themselves over to the Volontaires de Place—in other words, to the rebels.

This might give them the added bonus of trapping military and official personnel, suspicious of what was going on but out of communication, who would gravitate to the nearest police station and fall into the hands of the rebels.

When the time came for action, to avoid giving the show away by unnecessary movement about town of suspicious-looking groups with arms, the rebel mobilization was to be carried out in a subtly staggered manner.

D'Astier had divided the city into five major sections, located the targets on his maps, assigned to each a number.

During the course of the morning, group leaders arrived at 26 rue Michelet to receive their orders and be assigned their targets and transports.

From across a side street, in a garage at Number 40, came the almost incessant sound of car engines being started and warmed.

"Lavaysse," remarked one of the conspirators, "hasn't worked that hard in all of two years."

Since early morning the Lavaysse brothers, owners of the garage, had been charging batteries, pumping tires, and turning over the engines of some thirty automobiles belonging to regular clients, who, for lack of gasoline, had not been able to drive their cars in months.

Now, thanks to the American Consulate, the rebels had managed to collect 3,000 liters of gas, 2,000 to be used for the night's operation, 1,000 to be reserved for Giraud's motorcade reception.

A trucking company, which had been bribed to provide seventy trucks, had finally produced six.

Assigned both target and transport, each group leader was to alert, during the course of the day, the cell heads of his own *apparat*.

The plotters were organized into classic cells of five, with only one member of each knowing the next link in the chain. The various cells were to be ready at prearranged addresses before dark. One hour before action, each group leader would go to the Lavaysse garage, pick up his transport, load it with the necessary number of weapons, and half an hour before H hour drive off to pick up his cell members at the prearranged addresses so as to move immediately on the targets.

In all nearly 800 conspirators were organized into cells. Many more from the Chantiers de la Jeunesse were not available that night because one whole class had just been disbanded and returned to their civilian homes, some of them many miles away.

During the course of the morning those of the conspirators who were in the know were electrified by an announcement, included in the special messages broadcast over the French program of the BBC: *"Allo Robert, Franklin arrive."*

Robert, of course, was Murphy; Franklin, the President. It was the signal to indicate that the invasion was on.

Off the master bedroom at 26 rue Michelet, "full of lacework and curly maple," a Mr. Browne, of the OSS, had installed in the bathroom a secret radio, by means of which he hoped to keep in touch with the Allied command in Gibraltar and the invasion fleet at sea.

During the course of the day messages were radioed directly to Béthouart in Morocco, and a courier was dispatched to Bône to warn Colonel Lorber that "he could expect his friends that night."

From Gibraltar a message had arrived that Giraud was due at Blida airfield shortly after dawn of the 8th, and that his plane could be recognized by a white cross and cockades plus three red flares.

To meet the Supreme Commander of the French, Lemaigre-Dubreuil secured a special order issued by Mast, and, for the occasion, donned his uniform as a captain in the reserve.

As an overall headquarters for Giraud, another apartment at 30 rue Michelet, belonging to Pierre Alexandre, had been prepared, and there Murphy was to hang his hat, there the United States Consul General in Algiers, Felix Cole, was to spend the night, as were "Vice-Consul" John Knox and his English fiancée Joan Tuyl.

Still another headquarters had been prepared on the top floor of 26 rue Michelet in the apartment of Colonel Jousse's brother-in-law, Jacques Brunel, son of the former mayor of Algiers.

By 5 P.M. Jousse was ready to give his final orders: The rallying of French North Africa to the Allies must be carried out, if possible without shedding a drop of blood. The rebels were *not* to shoot first.

Each Frenchman, said Jousse, even those who opposed them, would be needed to fight the Germans. Any traitors could be dealt with later by the courts.

As a final instruction, Colonel Jousse issued the password for the night, derived, it would seem, from some association with the Americans, and suitable for a nighttime rendezvous with their past and future allies—Challenge: "Whiskey." Answer: "Soda!"

At last evening fell, and there was nothing more for the conspirators to do but wait for the moment of action.

Robert Murphy spent most of the day at the Consulate burning compromising lists with the phone numbers and addresses of conspirators.

In the late afternoon he received a visit from "an old acquaintance from Paris and Vichy," a former French Premier, Pierre Étienne Flandin, who had recently arrived from Vichy.

Flandin, Murphy has reported, was in a state of great excitement and had come to warn him that the Axis was threatening to invade Tunisia. "If you Americans do not come here in full force within a month," he cried, "it will be too late."

Murphy says it was with some difficulty that he restrained himself from giving the veteran statesman any hint of the imminent Allied arrival.

However, as the very excuse which Murphy and Roosevelt were planning to use that night for landing in Africa was the threat of an Axis move against Tunisia, this visit of Flandin's seems curiously coincidental, especially in view of Flandin's subsequent behavior.

That night Murphy dined quietly in the flat of Felix Cole with Kenneth Pendar and a few others. At 10 P.M. after a final conference with General Mast in the apartment of Lemaigre's secretary, Murphy headed toward 26 rue Michelet to see how things were developing, and to see if any news had come in on the secret radio.

The city, with its subdued dimout, seemed surprisingly calm; on their way the American diplomats encountered the casual Saturday night crowds going home from one of the dreadful Axis-controlled movies that were the sole fare in occupied Europe and North Africa.

At the Aboulker apartment Murphy was to have his first official meeting with José's father Henri, president of the Radical Socialist party of Algiers and a *grand mutilé* who had lost a leg fighting the Germans in World War I. There were to be several such first meetings that night as old friends discovered each other in the plot.

Stretched out on one of the *canapés*, eyes closed, cigarette burning in his long thin fingers, Henri d'Astier was waiting for the moment of action. Others in the room nervously performed the mechanical operations of lighting cigarettes, pacing the floor, and drumming with their fingers.

Then the very scene they most dreaded was to be played before their eyes.

Too many visitors, too many cars stopping at the door, too many couriers coming and going from Number 26 had induced someone to telephone the police.

The chief of the political police of Algiers, who had been waiting for just such a tip, and had had a cell prepared for such suspects, set off on a personal inspection of Dr. Aboulker's.

The conspirators opened the door and, extemporizing on the situation, placed the Commissioner under house arrest. In the background Mr. Murphy smiled quietly, and Achiary was overheard to remark, *"Fini alors de faire la putain. . . ."*

Another incongruous flurry was caused by the appearance of the Abbé Cordier, charged with cutting the lines of the military Centrale Protegée, the main army telephone station.

An emergency had arisen. Someone had discovered that the night watchman possessed a fierce German shepherd.

"In celestial tones," says one eyewitness, "the young priest asked Dr. Aboulker for an ampule of poison with which to dispose of the creature."

This emergency was immediately followed by the unsettling discovery that General Mast's cook was a Japanese agent! Should they arrest her? They decided not to; the hour was too far advanced for the agent to be able to do much more harm.

By midnight most of Algiers had retired to bed.

Vice-Consuls Harry Woodruff, John Boyd and Laroux, the latter a career Foreign Service officer, unused to such assignments, set off for the landing beaches to act as guides.

The rest of the leaders, abroad on the streets in groups of no more than three, ran into isolated military men, who, as was the long-established custom between members of the SOL and uniformed officers, calmly exchanged salutes.

The first group arrived at the garage without incident. All was in order: uniforms, armbands, vehicles; each knew his orders, each knew his target. Only one item was lacking: weapons. For months the Allies had promised to provide the rebels with 800 Sten guns (psychologically impressive), 400 automatics, 400 defense grenades, 400 tear-gas grenades, 50 walkie-talkies.

General Clark had given his word at Cherchel to have the weapons landed at a point where the rebels could drive a truck to within 50 meters of the sea. The American Consulate had provided trucks and gas. But though the conspirators had waited on the nights of November 4, 5, and 6, the Americans never showed up.

Would they, the rebels now wondered, do the same again this night?

Luckily Colonel Jousse, as garrison commander, had managed to acquire from a secret army cache antiquated 1870 Lebel rifles which he had stored in the Lavaysse garage. The rebels were therefore armed, although they had scarcely any ammunition.

At three-minute intervals the cars moved off into the sleeping city, and the policemen, seeing the uniformed personnel seated by the drivers, looked at them and away.

Circumspectly the leaders collected their men and headed for the targets.

The key to the operation, of course, was control of the Central Police Commissariat.

As of 9 P.M., M. Esquerré, chief of the *Sûreté Départmentale,* had been named by General Mast as new Central Commissioner.

Mast's orders to Esquerré had been to arrange for the immediate installation of Volontaires de Place in every police station in the city for "the protection of public order" in view of a possible enemy landing!

Under the command of José Aboulker, a score of youths now headed for the Central Commissariat.

Only things did not go as planned.

Considered by d'Astier too young for the role, José was to have been supported by a full colonel in the air force, who, at the last moment, failed to turn up.

But there was no going back. A cooperative major volunteered; together they headed for the target and an unexpected bit of luck. The *Commissaire* on duty, though not one of the rebels, had already agreed with Esquerré to turn over the station.

From then on things worked more smoothly. The moment the military lines were cut, Aboulker and Cohen called through their private police lines to each *arrondissement,* giving orders for the installation of the V.P.s. Only one group, the first, hit a snag.

Because of the original delay at the central *arrondissement,* the group assigned to *arrondissement* Number 1 arrived at their station too soon, before any word could come through. Presenting General Mast's written order, the young conspirator in charge nervously waited to see what would happen. The police agent on duty could see in the faint light of the street the muzzles of the rifles of the V.P.s surrounding the buildings. Actually, there were fewer than twelve of them.

But the order seemed official enough and the agent was about to comply when the telephone rang.

Everyone looked on in silence. The agent answered.

It was the Central Commissariat confirming Mast's orders.

Everyone sighed.

Two of the rebels posted themselves beside the agent, two at the door, two more in the car outside, and the others set about acting as couriers between the Commissariat and Number 26 rue Michelet.

By 1:45 one group sent word that divisional headquarters at the Pelissier barracks was in rebel hands.

Then came less good news. For one reason or another many rebels had proved unavailable for duty: some, because of the short notice, could not be reached; others had gone out of town, or to nearby beaches for the weekend; some, because of lack of nerve or dedication, had changed their minds at the very last moment. In all only about a third of those expected showed up, and some groups were harder hit than others.

A young Captain Pilafort, who had painstakingly recruited as many as 150 men over a period of months, now saw that he could count on only 50; but with these and the help of three reserve officers he successfully seized the XIX Corps headquarters.

Meanwhile, at the heart of the military communications of all Algeria, the Centrale Protegée at Mogador, the Abbé Cordier, with four young rebels, had successfully seized the prize: the main telephone switchboard.

One by one, the post office, Radio Alger, and the Centre d'Écoutes at the Bois de Boulogne, the censors' listening post, all fell.

General Staff Headquarters was soon occupied, its troops confined by the rebels to their barracks.

H hour for the arrival of the Americans was supposed to be 2 A.M. The last moments, as the rebels tied up the city, were not without touches of humor.

A group of rebels burst into the bedroom of the Prefect of Algiers.

"I'm a faithful partisan of Marshal Pétain and Premier Laval," he kept mumbling as he pulled on his pants.

"It took him," reported one of the rebels, "a whole half hour to catch on."

The Governor General of Algeria, Yves Chatel, was absent from his official residence and had left the Palais d'Été in the hands of his wife. At pistol point Mme. Chatel was politely ordered to her *salon* but, the moment the rebels turned their backs, tried to escape. At the gate, asked by a young guard for a whiskey, she stuttered everything but "soda" and was thereafter not left out of sight.

The Governor General's secretary Ettori, at home and unable to reach his chief, presented himself at the Commissariat on boulevard Gallieni, where the rebels put him in touch, via their private phone, with the Central Commissariat.

"What's going on?" asked Ettori.

At the other end of the line Guy Cohen turned to his noisy companions: *"Fermez vos gueules bandes de cons,"* he shouted. *"Vous allez tout faire rater!"* Then, as deferentially as possible, he spoke into the mouthpiece: "We're not quite sure, *Monsieur le Sécrétaire Général;* but your presence here would seem indispensable."

"J'arrive," announced Ettori; and he did, just in time to save the rebels from having to go arrest him.

Meanwhile Achiary, with a special squad, had gone through a whole list of authorities capable of making trouble, and had put them under lock and key.

While all this silent and effective activity was taking place, Guy Cohen, at the Central Commissariat, kept a notation of each operation.

Shortly after 2 A.M., and right on schedule, he closed this dossier and handed it to Henri d'Astier, who returned to 26 rue Michelet. There he found Rigault and Saint-Hardouin.

"We're masters of the city," said d'Astier.

It was 2:35.

Everywhere the *coup* appeared to have succeeded as planned, and, most extraordinary, not a drop of blood had been shed. At each key spot, civilian rebels stood guard before the darkened buildings, their white armbands visible in the light of the risen moon.

All that remained was to deliver the city to General Mast.

Solemnly Rigault and d'Astier set off to find the general at the Caserne Pelissier. But Mast was nowhere to be found. He had left, with his most immediate collaborators.

Back on the sidewalk Rigault turned to d'Astier. *"Mon cher,* here we are with a city on our hands. *Ça devient drôle."*

It was time for the Americans.

6

IN THE DIRECTIVE he had received from Eisenhower's headquarters Murphy was led to expect Allied landings in the vicinity of Algiers any time after 2 A.M. of November 8; he had therefore requested Algerian patriots to start seizing the city as of midnight, by which hour he had sent guides to the beaches.

Three hours later, with the city at his disposal, Murphy still had seen no sign of the Americans.

"We were told," says Kenneth Pendar, "that the transports had missed the landing spots near Algiers and hit some 25 to 30 kilometers away."

But this explanation did not satisfy Pendar. "I have always suspected," he says, "though I have absolutely no proof of this, that the 'mistake' was deliberate. The British and American navies do not generally drift that far off course. I suspected that both the British and American authorities at home were far from confident about our collaborators, and that they simply did not trust them not to betray the exact point of the landings."

What Pendar suspected was perfectly true.

The fleet, having taken the sensible precaution of sending submarines to act as beacons, along with pilots to indicate to the troops the precisely designated landing spots, had arrived where it intended, and well before midnight.

What happened is bluntly revealed by the official military historian of the United States Army: "The Eastern Assault Force plan for capturing Algiers did not rely on possible assistance by friendly French elements ashore but was based on an analysis of the terrain and the defenses."

While the United States "vice-consuls" and their French friends waited on the nearby beaches, the Allies calmly landed on more distant shores, there to be further delayed by a slight wind, trouble with their landing craft, and general inexperience.

Having gone to the trouble of recruiting members of the top local intelligence organization to help them ashore, the Allies acted without them.

To add to the confusion, Murphy, like a neophyte bridge player who refuses to establish a suit, decided to play *all* his top cards at once.

At the very moment the rebels were seizing the city at his request, Mr. Murphy was requesting "the quiet-mannered, cautious head of Juin's Deuxième Bureau intelligence service," Colonel Chrétien, to accompany him up to the residence of General Juin, Commander of all French forces in North Africa.

Pendar, armed with an automatic and a large rebel bodyguard, was to follow in Murphy's own car up to Juin's Villa des Oliviers above Algiers in the suburb of El Biar.

As the consular vehicles drove through the city, it was still too early for any sign of untoward activity. At the gates of the ancient yellow palace where Juin had his residence, huge black Senegalese troops saluted Murphy and his escort.

Remaining in the car, Pendar watched his chief disappear with Chrétien into the villa, gazed for a moment at the outlines of the nearby Fort l'Empereur, Algiers military headquarters, with its single monolithic obelisk visible in the pale moonlight above the flowered gardens of the villa, then closed his eyes for a badly needed nap.

In the villa, Juin came to the Arab-style living room in a pair of pink striped pajamas to be informed by Murphy that the landing of a large American expeditionary force could be expected any moment.

"What!" exclaimed Juin. "You mean that convoy we have seen in the Mediterranean is aimed at us?"

Murphy nodded.

"But you told me yourself," said Juin, "not more than a week ago, that the United States would never attack *us.*"

Murphy replied that the American force was not coming to

attack, but at the invitation of the French, to collaborate in the liberation of France.

"Whose invitation?" asked Juin.

"General Giraud's," said Murphy. "He is expected momentarily."

For several minutes Juin paced the floor expostulating that this went far beyond their agreement of October 13th, that Murphy had placed him in a terrible dilemma by not taking him into his confidence.

To this Murphy pointed out that as Juin had taken a personal oath of allegiance to Marshal Pétain and given his parole to the Germans, the Allies had not wished to put him in "a situation embarrassing to an army officer," but that, knowing his sentiments, they expected him to rally to the Allies at the proper time.

Juin shook his head. Were the matter solely in his hands there would be no resistance to the American landings. But Darlan was in Algiers. No matter what Juin said, his orders could be immediately overruled by Darlan, who commanded *all* French forces.

"Very well," said Murphy. "Let us talk to Darlan."

Juin agreed to phone his superior, who was sleeping at Fenard's villa about a mile away, and inform him that Murphy had an urgent message for him.

Such are the quirks of history, had Murphy waited only a few minutes, this *démarche* would no longer have been possible, for at that moment the Abbé Cordier was busy cutting the power to the telephone lines.

As it was, the phone rang in Fenard's own bedroom, where Darlan was sleeping, and was answered by Mme. Darlan, who woke her husband.

The admiral agreed to come right away, and Chrétien in turn woke Pendar to ask him to fetch Darlan at Fenard's villa.

It was 1:30 A.M. when Pendar arrived at the villa Sidi Aloui. Darlan, short, heavyset, pasty-faced, with deep-set shifty blue eyes, dressed in a civilian double-breasted suit, was standing on the steps of the villa, nervous and strained, accompanied by his chief of staff Admiral Battet.

On their way to Juin's they exchanged not a word with Pendar, who, from their behavior, realized that they had not yet been advised of the landings.

In Juin's *salon,* Darlan's reaction to the news was to turn purple and exclaim, "I have known for some time that the British were stupid. I always believed the Americans to be more intelligent. Apparently you have the same genius as the British for making massive blunders."

For the next fifteen minutes Darlan paced the floor while Murphy tried with "every argument he could advance" to persuade Darlan it was to the interest of both France and the United States for him to "seize this golden opportunity."

Both Juin and Darlan were aghast at the prospect of another commando-style raid such as the recent disaster at Dieppe, in which the Allies had been butchered and from which the French had suffered severe reprisals.

Were the present Allied landings to fail, it would be the Germans who successfully invaded North Africa, said Darlan, and this would render France's position even more desperate.

In vain Murphy tried to convince Darlan that the Allied landings were by no means a raid. Darlan remained convinced that Murphy was bluffing, and asked Juin to send his chief of staff, General François Sevez, to get in touch with Vice-Admiral d'Escadre Moreau, to find out what was happening along the coast.

But just as General Sevez tried to leave the villa, he was blocked by a young man with a leveled rifle.

Unnoticed by the dark Senegalese sentries, the entire grounds of the villa had been surrounded by a group of d'Astier's men under the command of an Artillery cadet, Bernard Peauphilet.

Pendar woke up to realize that the shrubbery round the villa was filled with armed civilians, some of whom surged forward in the half-light thrown from the villa windows, pointing their guns from the waist.

By now General Juin, Mme. Juin, Colonel Chrétien and Murphy had appeared in the villa doorway, followed closely by Admiral Battet. All, says Pendar, looked surprised and disturbed. Chrétien commanded the officer in charge of the insurgents to step forward, but Peauphilet cautiously refused, advising them from the darkness that no one was to leave the house with the exception of Mr. Pendar, who could take the car he was driving.

Murphy and the French retired within the villa; and when Darlan realized what was happening he was furious, accusing Murphy of having drawn him into a trap.

Murphy denied that he had anything to do with the armed civilians, and offered to send Pendar downtown "to find out who had placed the watchdogs and have them called off."

The effect on the French commanders of being surrounded by a handful of youths was indicated by Chrétien's pompous remark to Murphy: "If *these* are your friends, their behavior is revolting."

As for the young insurgents, the sight of Darlan, archcollaborator with the Germans, vacillating on the edge of further betrayal, was even more revolting. As one of them was to remark, "Had we not believed that on the morning of liberation Darlan was to be judged by a court-martial and shot, we would have disposed of him then and there."

Back at 26 rue Michelet, Pendar tried to find Mast or Jousse to ask if they were responsible for surrounding Juin's villa. But he could find neither of them.

As a precaution, now that events were taking on a more complex aspect, he abandoned his pistol and bodyguard, both of which appeared to be more of a hazard than a help.

The secret headquarters was in great excitement as reports poured in from young men who had taken the post office, the radio station, the telegraph office, the Préfecture, the whole city, in fact. But the guides sent to the beaches to greet the landings had not yet returned; General Mast was still unfindable; and the radio gave no news of what might be happening at Bône, Oran or Rabat.

Everyone, says Pendar, asked him if Chrétien—who had played such an elusive game with both sides—was now with the rebels.

Pendar found Rigault "paler and tighter-mouthed than ever"; he wanted to be driven to Juin's to find out what was happening.

When they arrived there Darlan asked if he could return to Fenard's to sleep; Rigault refused to let him go.

Meanwhile Murphy drew Pendar aside and asked him to go back to town, only not to hurry. He was stalling, he said, until the landings had actually taken place, so that his bargaining power would be greater. Darlan, according to Murphy, was beginning to talk politics, and it looked as if both Darlan and the officers who recognized his authority, and possibly even the French fleet, might fall into Allied hands. Juin, said Murphy, wanted to help, but felt obliged to defer to Darlan as his superior.

Once more Pendar chauffeured Rigault back to 30 rue Michelet, where they found Saint-Hardouin worried that the rebels would be overwhelmed if something were not done right away. The only solution, said Saint-Hardouin, was to reach Admiral Fenard, whom the rebels had purposely left undisturbed in order to use him as an intermediary with the Navy in case of necessity.

This decision had been made before it was known that Darlan would turn up in Fenard's villa that night. During the afternoon d'Astier had learned from Saint-Hardouin of Darlan's presence and had wanted to surround the villa and immobilize its occupants, but by evening he had not been able to do so, partly because the Allies had not furnished the necessary weapons with which to confront the well-armed naval personnel which guarded the villa, and partly for lack of sufficient conspirators.

So Pendar and Saint-Hardouin drove back to Fenard's villa to impress upon him the fact that the underground was in complete control of Algiers, and that the Navy should rally to them.

As they approached the luxurious Victorian villa, they saw the windows still brightly lit. The admiral, fully dressed, was puffing at his pipe.

When he was told by Saint-Hardouin of what was happening in town, "Fenard's pear-shaped face turned yellow." Then he brightened: *"C'est rudement bien joué,"* he said, clasping both of Saint-Hardouin's hands.

As they talked, Mme. Fenard's anxious face peered from above a black kimono through the portiere to the hall.

Fenard agreed that Darlan must be prevailed upon to prevent the Navy from shooting. But how?

Raising his hands and shrugging, he complained that since Darlan had been summoned to Juin's villa he had given no sign of life.

On the way up to Juin's, Fenard asked Saint-Hardouin for details of the plot and, hearing them, said he was much impressed. At the villa Murphy came out looking depressed. He had worn out his arguments on Darlan and whispered to Saint-Hardouin, "Pity that Admiral was here. Without him, I believe General Juin would have come along."

For the past hour they had been upbraiding Murphy on several counts: that he had lied to them about the date; that the Americans had arrived not as allies but as conquerors; that they had called in Giraud, a man with no legal authority. "He is not your man," said Darlan. "Politically he is a child. He's a good divisional commander, nothing more."

To top it all, Murphy had now organized a local *coup* which was causing chaos in the regular command, threatened to crumble the unity of the armed forces and to start a civil war between rival French factions.

Murphy's position was not to be envied. There was no sign of the Allies. He had no way of knowing if the landings had gone wrong, been postponed, or even if someone had made a mistake with the date. Overworked, overtired, at a disadvantage as a civilian arguing with high-ranking military, playing a game that few of his compatriots had mastered and on which the lives of thousands of them depended, it is understandable that at this point Murphy could have been ready to make almost any concession to Darlan in order to prevent Vichy forces from opening fire on the Americans.

In the presence of Fenard, Murphy argued desperately that the Allies could put 500,000 men in the field, with an assault wave of at least 100,000, and reminded Darlan of his promise to Leahy that he would lead the French if the Americans came in sufficient strength.

The admiral continued to shake his head, insisting that his orders were to defend North Africa against *any* aggressor, that the marshal was bound by an armistice he had honorably sought from the Germans, that it was not up to Darlan to tear up so solemn an engagement on the simple demand of Murphy. Without the authority of Pétain, to whom he had given his personal oath, there was nothing, said Darlan, he could do: "For the last two years I have preached to my men in the Navy and to the nation, unity behind the marshal. I cannot now deny my oath."

Would Darlan, asked Murphy with a glimmer of hope, cooperate if the marshal authorized him?

"Yes indeed," answered Darlan.

"Then why not send a message," suggested Murphy, "asking the marshal for his authorization?"

Darlan agreed and—in the presence of Murphy, Juin, Fenard, and Battet—sat down to draft a message in which, according to Langer, he stated that "an American landing operation involving half a million men was happening in French North Africa" and requesting the marshal to give him liberty of action.

On the envelope Darlan scribbled: "To be sent urgently. F. Darlan."

Pendar was asked by Fenard to deliver the message to Admiral Leclerc at the Admiralty.

Everyone, says an eyewitness, was radiant. But Saint-Hardouin pulled Murphy aside and whispered to him, "Do you know what is in that message?"

"Heavens, no," answered Murphy.

On the way downtown, Pendar, less (or perhaps more) diplomatic than Murphy, asked Saint-Hardouin to open the envelope and read him the contents; but Saint-Hardouin thought it better to wait till they reached their headquarters, where an expert could steam the envelope open.

All around them Algiers was still quiet. Somewhere in the night a church bell struck three.

From Admiralty Point a single searchlight snapped on, then slowly probed the night. Stopping on a cloud, it focused, moved on, threw a sudden beam of light on the tall white façades of Algiers' silent buildings.

Then the light was extinguished and only the stars illuminated the dampish night.

To Algerians who had got up to look from their windows, a faint rumble was audible out at sea; there followed the sound of a solitary air-raid siren from Admiralty Point, echoed in turn by nothing more than the howling of dogs; the other sirens in the city had all been silenced by the rebels.

Then three warning shots were fired from the Admiralty, followed by a barrage.

As Pendar maneuvered downtown, an air-raid patrolman stopped his car. Saint-Hardouin, uncertain of the patrolman's sympathies, and unsure whether the rebels were still in control of the city, cautiously produced both his passes: A V.P. armband and the urgent letter from Admiral Darlan—all of which was too much for the air-raid warden, who quickly acquiesced with a *"Bon, bon, ça va."*

At 26 rue Michelet, Pendar and Saint-Hardouin found d'Astier and Rigault, avid for news, and when the Abbé Cordier had opened the letter and Rigault had read it, Rigault folded it and put it in his pocket with the words "Tell Bob we cannot possibly forward this cable. It is not a matter of courtesy. It is giving the enemy a weapon."

Saint-Hardouin thus reported the scene: "It was a telegram to be sent to Vichy not even asking for instructions, but saying that he, Darlan, had answered the Americans that he had to carry out the orders of his government to resist them.

"In view of the fact that we had not foreseen these conversations with Darlan, I declared to Cole, the senior American present, that I would not, despite the accord in principle of Murphy, assume the responsibility of letting Darlan get in touch with the Admiralty, where just then fighting was in progress, and through the Admiralty with Vichy, without instructions from General Mast.

"Admiral Darlan is now a prisoner of the French who have taken it upon themselves to neutralize the defenses of Algiers. We cannot allow him to give to his ships and to the Vichy government the impression that he is in a position to implement and direct defenses."

"Needless to say," Pendar comments, "the telegram was not sent. I can't believe Darlan ever thought it would be."

The text of the message, as later reconstructed, ran as follows: "Admiral Darlan to Marshal Pétain: I was summoned at 0115 this morning by General Juin and found with him Mr. Murphy who declared to me that on the demand of a Frenchman, General Giraud, President Roosevelt had decided to occupy French North Africa with important forces this very morning, to save France which they wished to maintain in its integrity.

"I answered that France had signed an armistice convention and that I could but comply with the orders of the Marshal to defend its territories."

In Darlan's defense it is worth pointing out that there was not much else he could say in a message bound to be intercepted by the Germans.

Be that as it may, as Pendar headed back for the Villa des Oliviers, the situation was to be further complicated by another Allied blunder which was to cause a lot of bloodshed and unnecessarily threaten the position painfully established by the rebels.

What the searchlights on Admiralty Point had picked up was the silhouettes of two British destroyers, H.M.S. *Broke* and H.M.S. *Malcolm,* attempting to pierce the barrier to the port in order to land troops on the Quai de Dieppe.

As Darlan's shore batteries opened up on the invaders, the turmoil of their cannonading roused the whole city—and not only the city, but officers and officials of Vichy who had been peacefully sleeping.

A great number of them, presenting themselves singly or in small groups at the key places occupied by the rebels, such as the police stations and the barracks, were promptly apprehended. But the more that came in, the worse the situation became for the rebels. With fewer than 400 men they could hardly take care of a garrison of 12,000 soldiers reinforced by an estimated 30,000 SOLs.

Some of those arrested were, it is true, quite pleased to be held: "It saved them any painful search of their conscience." Others were even annoyed at the rebels for not having let them in on the secret and enabled them to participate in the rebellion. But the majority posed a dangerous threat.

Worse still, this direct naval attack by the Allies had roused to action the Vichy forces in the harbor. The conspirators had known all along that Darlan's navy was almost certain to resist. *Their* plan had been to have the Allies land at nearby safe beaches such as Pointe Pescade, from which they could move into the city and cut off the navy from behind, not only physically but psychologically.

Once isolated, the shore batteries could much more easily have been taken through negotiation or stormed from the rear with a minimum loss of life.

As Pendar—once again—drove back to the Villa des Oliviers, there was considerable confusion in Algiers, especially in the high part of the city where the people, roused from their sleep, milled around in the dark, looking for shelters.

Along the narrow staircase streets of the Casbah—where 10,000 Moslems lived together in a space of less than 100 acres—a flow of humanity descended to gush forth from the exits, half awake, half dressed, almost everyone carrying a bundle in one arm and a child in the other.

Desperately the conspirators tried to hold their ground, speaking to the crowds which jammed into the place du Commissariat: "You have nothing to fear. Our friends are coming. The Americans have landed near the city. Giraud '*l'Africain*' has rallied to the Allies."

At 26 rue Michelet the conspirators realized the situation to be precarious. "Vice-Consul" Woodruff, back from a long walk on the beaches, had seen no sign of the Americans. A third radio message to Béthouart in Morocco was still without answer. The only word which had come to those listening to the secret radio, had been a brief message that the landings *would* take place. The only rumor was that the Allies had landed at Cap Matifou, some 30 kilometers east of the city.

At the Villa des Oliviers Pendar found Murphy walking up and down in the garden and told him of the content of Darlan's telegram.

"I don't give a damn," muttered Murphy, "what Darlan said to Pétain. What's happening to the landings?"

When Pendar told him the rumor about Cap Matifou, Murphy exploded: "What the devil are they doing out there, 30 kilometers from the city!"

Just then Rigault entered the villa and told Fenard he could take Darlan home on the condition that Darlan agreed to consider himself a prisoner on his word and would not try to communicate with anyone outside.

Fenard raised his hands to heaven. "The Admiral is furious. This is hardly the time for me to take him such a message."

Through the open door Rigault could see Darlan in the next room, puffing on his pipe.

Turning to Peauphilet, Rigault gave strict orders that no one was to enter or leave the villa. Catching sight of Murphy "walking up and down, rubbing the short grass of the lawn with his toe in the mechanical gesture of someone troubled with a problem he cannot resolve," Rigault asked what progress he had made.

Briefly, Murphy reiterated that he could get nothing out of Darlan.

"At least," asked Rigault, "are you sure your boys will turn up?" He looked at his watch. It was after 4 A.M. "I only guaranteed our operation for this one night. Your friends were supposed to be here at 2 A.M. Now they are three hours late." Looking up at the sky, he saw that the dawn was already tinting the moon. "At 7 o'clock it will be daylight. I cannot answer for what will happen after that."

Something was already happening: A short French Air Force major dressed in a brown business suit, returning to the Palais d'Hiver, seat of Juin's official headquarters, found the entrance barred by some thirty young civilians with white armbands. One of these explained to him courteously that he could not pass, that they were acting in the name of General Giraud and that General Juin was being held under house arrest.

Outraged, the major, who was Juin's adjutant Dorange, immediately decided to free his commanding general. Foreseeing that all the other centers, both civil and military, would have been occupied, Dorange decided to approach the Admiralty, not along the blocked mole but by crossing the port in a small fishing boat.

From the beginning of their plotting the conspirators had decided against trying to storm the Admiralty, which stood at the very end of the western jetty, cut off from the city by the water of the port and steep banks, and was heavily defended.

Just as Dorange, accompanied by a Medical Corps captain by the name of Dupuy, boarded a small skiff, the two British destroyers made their appearance in the entrance to the port and began to skirmish with the coastal batteries, lighting up the night sky all around them.

Clambering up the rough jetty walls to the Admiralty, Dorange and Dupuy found Admiral Leclerc cut off from the mainland by a force of insurgents at the end of the mole. Under the circumstances, Leclerc considered it his duty to apply the existing orders to oppose any landings whatsoever.

This he was doing when, from along the mole, a vehicle slowly approached under a sign of truce. It was a rebel car; from it descended a young army officer with an order signed by General Mast—and some startling news.

The Germans, said the young officer, had landed in Tunisia; American forces, called on by Marshal Pétain, were therefore landing in North Africa to bring aid to the French. French troops were to help the Americans land.

"Who," asked Leclerc, "gave the original order?"

At the young rebel's silence, Leclerc decided he had better check directly with his commander in chief, General Juin.

Only how? Telephone service had been cut off, and there was not a single car at the Admiralty.

Major Dorange stepped forward. "Leave it to me, *mon amiral.* I will reach the commander in chief, if you will provide me with a weapon."

Puzzled, Leclerc turned to his assistant chief of staff on whom he spotted a huge 1874 revolver, which he turned over to Dorange. Dorange, in turn, used the weapon to requisition the young rebel officer's car. Climbing in, he ordered the driver to speed him to the Caserne des Tagarins—headquarters of the Vichy Garde Mobile, heavily armed riot police provided with tanks.

Because of its distance from the center of the city, and its heavy armament, the conspirators had purposely decided to forgo trying to take this barracks by force or by threat, just as they had forgone trying to seize the Admiralty.

At the barracks Dorange immediately called upon the commander of the Garde Mobile, Colonel Zwilling, and devised a cunning stratagem.

Having asked the colonel to form up his men in a square, Dorange harangued them: "Guards: This is the greatest day of your lives. The Germans have invaded Tunisia and the marshal has enjoined us to throw them into the sea. The Americans are landing in North Africa to aid us in our task. We shall now go to meet them and help them ashore."

He paused, while the guard, so he later reported, "*frémissait,*" and the soldiers cried out, "*Vive la France! Vive le maréchal!*"

On a signal from Dorange, the colonel now addressed them: "Men. It appears that General Juin is a prisoner in his villa. Our first job is to set free our commander in chief."

While the troops raised a shout of approval and were being mustered for the task, Dorange took the extra precaution of sending a messenger to the commander of the 1st Regiment of Zouaves, to put him on guard "against the disorder which appears to be spreading."

To Dorange—who was almost psychically reacting to Darlan's own plan—the worst threat was that the African Army might crumble into separated and divided pieces, and cease to serve as a controllable force.

At the head of the first platoon of the Garde Mobile, Dorange set off for the Villa des Oliviers, a good four kilometers away.

Just then, a dozen kilometers farther to the west, at a spot on the coast where 122 years earlier Marshal Bourmont had landed to avenge a slap in the face given by the local bey to the local French consul (and thus, incidentally, to occupy Algeria for France), a flotilla of small landing craft was heading for the beach near Cap Sidi Ferruch.

The night was balmy. Along this particular stretch of coast, normally used as a summer resort for Algerians, the sea was calm.

In the villa of a onetime senator from Algiers, an old gardener was awakened by a sound which seemed to him to be a motor launch at sea.

Jumping out of bed, he went down to the beach just in time to greet a group of silhouettes helmeted in a remarkably German fashion.

It was a delicate moment, especially as the American commanders of the expedition had neglected to send with each landing party someone who spoke either French or Arabic. But when the old gardener saw the Stars and Stripes sewn onto the soldiers' tunics, he was reassured and led the Americans past a small French garrison toward the local fort.

In the U.S. Army's official report: ". . . no resistance was offered by shore batteries or other French elements at Sidi Ferruch." The assault wave of Company A, 168th Infantry, met General Mast near Fort Sidi Ferruch and received his assurance that they would meet no opposition; and they did not.

Even more interesting is the American company commander's own report: "We received no opposition whatsoever from the beach and if we had, in that condition of landing, it would have been a complete failure in my opinion, as the troops in the wallowing boats and those in the water would have been helpless against enemy fire."

Thanks to the conspirators, the first of the Allies had landed safely in Algeria.

At Juin's villa Murphy and Pendar, unaware of this momentous event, were still walking up and down in the gravel driveway.

Admiral Fenard came out of the villa with an envelope for Pendar. It was a second message from Darlan to the marshal, and Fenard asked if the first had gone off as scheduled.

Answering evasively, Pendar said he had given it to be sent, then climbed into Murphy's car.

Backing it away, he was hailed by Murphy, who ran up to ask him to send an urgent message to the fleet by radio. Pendar carefully recorded it in his little black notebook: "Western Task Force Commander from Murphy. It is urgently necessary that some Allied troops arrive in the city of Algiers as quickly as possible. Situation well in hand but unwise to let this endure too long."

"Allied?" asked Pendar in surprise. "You mean American?" Murphy firmly repeated "Allied."

This, Pendar later admitted, was the very first knowledge he had "that the British were actually landing with us."

And such was the tenseness of the two diplomats, neither realized that Pendar had written Western for *Eastern* Task Force.

But the message failed to get far.

Just as Pendar swung the car to take off, a group of Vichy Garde Mobile police burst through the gates of the villa, seized Murphy, dragged Pendar from his car and forced them both at gunpoint to the porter's lodge, where they were ordered to stand with their hands above their heads and were searched and stripped of all their papers.

The two Americans were addressed by one soldier in German, which led Pendar to suspect they were Germans disguised as Frenchmen. Murphy even overheard one of the soldiers give the order to have them taken out and shot.

"Luckily this item escaped me," said Pendar, "or I couldn't have answered for my dignity."

At which point Dorange burst upon the scene, still in his tweed suit, wildly waving his huge revolver and crying, "What have you done? What have you done?"

Some of the Garde Mobile police tried to arrest Dorange, who, in a fury, turned on them shouting, "I am Major Dorange. You are under *my* orders."

He then addressed Murphy. "You knew how I felt. What made you do such a stupid thing?"

Neither Murphy nor Pendar could answer. Pendar complained later that even if he had had an answer, Dorange was so excited he would not have listened.

In the midst of what Pendar calls "this Gallic scene," Juin, Fenard and Chrétien appeared in the doorway and asked that Murphy be brought to the villa.

Staunchly, Murphy insisted that Pendar be included. "I regret," said Juin rather formally, "having to do this. But your action in making me a prisoner leaves me no alternative."

Murphy and Pendar, who had been holding Darlan and Juin as *their* prisoners, now traded roles.

At the sight of Dorange waving his revolver and supported by his Garde Mobile men, the insurgents who had been lurking in the bushes, in the word of one eyewitness, "volatilized."

Similar tragicomic scenes occurred at other key points. At the headquarters of the XIX Corps, General Koeltz, who had been arrested in his pajamas, choking with rage at his enforced impotence, managed to throw a message from the window calling on the 3rd Chasseurs d'Afrique to come rescue him with tanks. At the instant of his liberation, he canceled Mast's orders, relieved him of his command and replaced him with General La Roubertie (also recently freed) with strict orders to contest Allied landings.

Entering the salon at Villa des Oliviers, Dorange found Juin gritting his teeth, pacing the floor with great strides, while Admiral Darlan, impassive, leaned against the mantelpiece.

Darlan had just received a message from Admiral Moreau, to inform him that the Hotel Saint-Georges, where he had his command post, was now free and that the maritime defenses were in action.

Darlan was thinking of transferring himself there, but Dorange persuaded him and General Juin to go to the nearby Fort l'Empereur where elements of the Garde Mobile and of the 1st Regiment of Zouaves could better insure their security.

So Darlan drove off, leaving the official representative of the President of the United States under house arrest in the villa.

Meanwhile Admiral Fenard, who had remembered Darlan's second message to Pétain, went out to find Pendar to make sure this message was dispatched at once.

Pendar, complaining that all his belongings had been removed, made a second search through his pockets only to find that the Garde had taken everything *but* the message.

Surrounded by his captors, their submachine guns leveled, Pendar climbed once more into Murphy's car and headed again for the Admiralty.

"*Enfin!*" sighed one of the Garde policemen, addressing his fellow, whose machine gun was pointed at the back of Pendar's head. "*Enfin,* we're getting out of that silly situation of the last two years. *Now* we shall fight against the Boches."

Pendar pricked up his ears, remarking that he hoped they would do just that.

Surprised, the policeman answered in German.

Pendar retorted that he spoke better English or French than German.

"Why?" asked the policeman. "What are you?"

At Pendar's explanation that he was an American vice-consul there was stupefaction among his captors. Thanks to Dorange, they had taken him for a German agent.

His identity restored, Pendar insisted on delivering Darlan's message directly to Admiral Leclerc at the Admiralty.

"What proof," asked Leclerc, "do I have that this is Admiral Darlan's signature?"

"Only my word," said Pendar. "But I will be delighted to take anyone you suggest up to Darlan to confirm it."

"I will go," said Leclerc. "And you will stay here."

Once more Pendar was a prisoner. Disconsolately, seated beneath a huge portrait of Pétain, whose face Drew Middleton aptly described as "lugubrious and with watery eyes, the very negation of all that France had stood for in the past," poor Pendar was obliged to witness the slaughter of his compatriots by fire from the Admiralty guns a few hundred yards down the quay, as they approached from H.M.S. *Broke.*

Having failed three times to enter the port, on the fourth attempt H.M.S. *Broke* had sliced through the barrier "like a knife through butter" and, though it missed its planned point of mooring, debarked its men at 5:20 A.M. on the Mole Louis Billiard.

"I want you to hit that dock hard," the colonel had ordered this Minnesota regiment, "then light out like stripy-arsed baboons up the wharf until you can get some cover. Then fight like hell." This the Minnesotans were doing, while being heavily fired on by Vichy forces in the harbor.

At 6 A.M. Admiral Leclerc came back to the Admiralty to free Pendar (having authenticated the second message, in which Darlan informed the marshal that American troops appeared to have landed from Morocco to Algeria and that British troops might be heading for Tunisia).

Halfway up the rue Michelet on his way to the American Consulate, Pendar was once more arrested by the Garde Mobile and taken to the barracks of the 5th Regiment of Chasseurs d'Afrique, which was humming with activity, tanks rumbling by, ambulances coming and going, as the Vichy forces set about recapturing from the rebels each carefully neutralized point in the city.

By dawn, safely installed in Fort l'Empereur, Darlan was ordering resistance to the Allies wherever they landed.

When Pendar was finally released from the barracks of the 5th Chasseurs, on orders from General Juin, it was already broad daylight. The streets of Algiers were crowded with "excited and mystified passersby, all streaming towards the harbor." Overhead planes were performing acrobatics, and Pendar could see the puffs of ack-ack in the clear blue sky, their crackle mixed with the sound of Sunday church bells.

At Blida airfield, where General Giraud was expected to land anytime after 6:30, Lemaigre-Dubreuil and Pierre Alexandre were impatiently scanning the skies for a sign of Giraud's plane, becoming more nervous every minute.

Blida, a town of a few thousand inhabitants, 45 kilometers southwest of Algiers, boasted a sizable military garrison, under the command of Brigadier General Monsabert, known to his troops as "Strawberries and Cream" because of his red face and snowy hair, who was pledged to the conspirators.

But the actual airfield, as an autonomous air force base, was under the command of Colonel Monstrelet, whose superior officer, General Jean A. Mendigal, chief of the local air force, had just been released from his villa. From him Monstrelet had orders to fight the Allies.

So Monstrelet's *tirailleurs* of the air base faced Monsabert's *fantassins* in trenches a few hundred yards apart "weapon to cheek, elbow to ground."

Monstrelet, not knowing whom to obey, was toying with the idea of arresting Lemaigre as a scapegoat. The latter, sensing that the atmosphere might render his position untenable, discreetly slipped a raincoat over his uniform, pocketed his *képi,* put on a pair of dark glasses and headed back for the city.

In Algiers, the other leaders of the conspiracy, after a dismal breakfast at 30 rue Michelet (where the Alexandres' cook had served over a hundred meals), realized that even if Giraud did arrive, it would take him over an hour to get into town, and decided that something drastic was needed to save the situation.

"Though we have no Giraud," said Saint-Hardouin, "we can still use his name. The city is awake. Let us broadcast Giraud's appeal over Radio Alger. It may rally the people and save the day before we are overwhelmed by the military."

Immediately two rebel sympathizers were dispatched to rue Berthezène, where the conspirators were still in control of the radio station. For lack of Giraud, Raphaël Aboulker impersonated the general's voice, with a broadcast appeal written by Saint-Hardouin in which there was an echo of de Gaulle's "We have but one passion—France": the phrase Giraud was happily to adopt as his motto and as the title of his book *Un Seul but: la victoire!*

This was followed by the rousing strains of the Marseillaise.

Hoping the appeal might even help the insurgents in Morocco, Rigault sent off a message to Béthouart: "Listen to Radio Alger at 7 A.M. for important announcement."

But from Béthouart there was no more sign of life than from Giraud.

On their way back from Blida Lemaigre-Dubreuil and Alexandre ran into a British patrol, which had not been given the password and nearly disposed of the conspirators as spies, putting them up against a wall despite their repeated cries of "Whiskey."

Released, they ran into Colonel Jousse at the corner of the avenue de la Bouzaréa, also back from Blida, extremely depressed. There was no sign of Giraud. A serious *bagarre* had only just been avoided at the airfield when, after a night's march from their landing beaches at "Apple Green" and "Beer White" and with the aid of some transport provided by General Mast, the Allies reached Blida to find Monstrelet willing to allow Allied aircraft only to land but not take off.

Now a volley of fire from some ambushed Indochinese troops interrupted Jousee's roadside parley and he was able to control the fire only after several civilians had been wounded.

Turning the incident to account, Alexandre placed two of the wounded in his car, shouted to the Orientals that he was a doctor, and proceeded at full speed to the center of Algiers, where he found d'Astier and José Aboulker.

After another brief council they decided the only hope was for Alexandre to head for Sidi Ferruch and plead with the Allies to rush troops immediately to the center of town.

Rigault had the same idea and asked Woodruff to head for the nearest Allied landings near Saint-Eugène.

Alexandre rushed off; some Vichy troops tried to stop him but he accelerated and escaped in a rain of bullets. Woodruff, more lucky, after taking several small roads through the *faubourgs,* managed to bypass the Vichy forces, make his way to the coast and reach Pointe Pescade.

Five or six kilometers from Algiers he ran into a column of Allied troops advancing cautiously in groups of four or five, looking from side to side. According to plan, they were encircling

Algiers along the high ground, and had no intention of entering the city until this textbook operation had been properly completed. And there was no one among them with authority to change the orders.

Luckily, on the road to Sidi Ferruch, Alexandre ran into his old friend, Consul John Knox, who had returned with the Americans, impressively uniformed as a colonel.

They proceeded to a conference with the American officer in command of the entire assault force, the United States 34th Infantry's Major General Charles W. Ryder.

"Why aren't you already in the city?" pleaded Alexandre. "By noon it will be too late."

"Impossible," said Ryder. "At least till tomorrow. I have only 2,400 men with which to insure all of the Algerian Department, and no heavy equipment."

"If you act immediately," said Alexandre, "the city is still in our hands. If you delay till tomorrow you will be opposed by 12,000 Frenchmen who are now in their barracks, plus 30,000 armed SOLs who haven't yet been mobilized. In forty-eight hours the Germans can land parachute forces in support of Vichy."

Convinced by Alexandre's pleading, which was strongly supported by Knox, Ryder decided to advance right away.

At 10 A.M. of the morning of the 8th, eight hours behind schedule, the Allied columns abandoned the encircling movement and headed for the center of Algiers.

It was none too soon; inside the city the position of the rebels was desperate.

7

AT A DOZEN SPOTS in Greater Algiers, half a thousand insurgents with an arsenal of superannuated weapons were defending themselves as best they could against a large well-armed force of regulars.

The position of the insurgents had been further weakened by the escape from the Central Commissariat of an officer of the 5th Chasseurs, who managed to rejoin his barracks and inform his superiors of all he had overheard during the night of the weakness of the rebels, and of their actual numbers in the various key places.

At the Central Commissariat, José Aboulker was flooded with phone calls from rebel outposts wanting to know what to do. Should they, if attacked by superior forces, give themselves up, or try to fight it out?

Against his inner feelings, Aboulker ordered surrender, then went to see for himself what was happening, slipping the one submachine gun delivered by the Allies (on the night of Cherchel) into the hands of Guy Cohen, who groaned, "But I don't know how to use it!"

"Makes no difference," said Aboulker. "You will have to surrender, just like the others."

At 11 A.M., the insurgents who were holding the Central Post Office under a young officer named Dreyfus were forced to barricade themselves against Vichy troops who started to lay siege to the building.

Across Laferrière Square came a figure with a white flag of truce. Spotting the Vichy parliamentarian, Dreyfus went out to meet him and was asked to surrender. Politely, but firmly, Dreyfus refused. The two men parted; as each moved toward his own lines a shot rang out. The bullet struck Dreyfus in the back, wounding him mortally. (For this act of ignominy the marksman was awarded the *Croix de guerre* by his Vichy superiors.)

At almost the very same moment at the Central Commissariat a Vichy colonel, Jacouin, sped past the entrance and let loose a burst of machine-gun fire which cut down a young rebel, Captain Pilafort. With his dying breath Pilafort fired his old revolver at the colonel, and the other rebels fired their rifles. Dragged from his car, the Vichy colonel was found to have fourteen bullet holes in his body.

By noon the insurgents were everywhere overwhelmed. Many, locked into dungeons, awaited execution by firing squads.

Shortly after noon virtually all the arrested Vichy functionaries had been freed. The whole situation, so beautifully organized by the rebels, had collapsed—for lack of American support.

From the terrace of the Villa des Oliviers, Murphy and Dorange could plainly see the Allied warships moving back and forth at sea, while American planes attacked the coastal batteries of Musoir.

Vehemently Dorange reproached Murphy for the incredible situation in which he had managed to put the French, reminding him of the terms of their October 13 conversations.

Murphy, says Dorange, seemed depressed by the struggle which was taking place before them, and by the bad news from Morocco where the Allies had run into serious opposition.

According to Dorange, Murphy affirmed that he had never wanted any of this, that he had honestly believed Giraud's appeal represented the thoughts of the majority of Frenchmen. With a touch of bitterness he added that he could not see why Admiral Darlan would not consider his proposal to join the Allies.

Dorange replied that Giraud, no matter what his renown in the Army, had no formal authority and that without such authority no Frenchman could act.

Murphy expressed his regrets, and Dorange suggested that the solution to the drama might lie not in Algiers but with General Noguès in Rabat, who might still be able to take the necessary steps to stop the fighting.

Murphy nodded thoughtfully and agreed with Dorange that the Resident General of Morocco, "the best man of government in North Africa," might get a quick decision from Vichy or, in case of failure, take the necessary steps to stop the fighting.

Dorange offered to leave immediately by plane for Rabat and take with him Darlan's chief of staff, Admiral Battet.

Murphy accepted. But Darlan had just quit Fort l'Empereur to install himself in the Hotel Saint-Georges and could not be reached.

In the port, where the duel had resumed between French coastal batteries and H.M.S. *Broke* (whose troops were ashore attacking the seaplane base and the electric plant), one of the shore batteries got the range of the destroyer and began to inflict heavy damage on her. Putting up a smoke screen, the *Broke's* captain sounded a siren to recall the troops and began to pull out of the harbor, firing back at the coastal batteries.

Six British Albacore dive bombers arrived and soon silenced the coastal batteries, but not before the *Broke* had been so badly hit that she soon sank. (For this anti-Allied action Darlan requested from Vichy, and obtained the same day, Leclerc's promotion to the rank of vice-admiral).

To console Murphy, Pendar arrived at the Villa des Oliviers with some shaving material, a clean shirt, and a bottle of Scotch.

Properly shaved, and having had a drink "under the disapproving eye of Mme. Juin, an Algerian heiress with a reputation for adhering to the strictest neutrality," they went downstairs to see Chrétien and Fenard.

"It was only too evident," Pendar said later, "that Giraud, though he was admired by all the secret pro-Allied forces in North Africa, which included most of the Army, was not going to be able to take the heads of that Army into our camp with him. We would have to have Juin and the others; and to get them, we would have to have Darlan. With true French logic, everything had to follow legitimate succession."

To which Pendar added pithily, "Darlan was holding off to see how strong our forces were going to prove to be."

Seated at a small table in a dusty office, dressed in a brown business suit and brown fedora, Darlan was playing a triple game: If the landings failed, he would have strengthened his position with the Germans for having opposed the Allies (much as Boisson had done against de Gaulle and the British at Dakar). Were the Americans to succeed, Darlan's stand would still help Vichy with the Germans by allowing the marshal to show that the French had actually resisted.

Paradoxically, the *more* Darlan resisted the Americans, and the more he could command the obedience of the French, the greater would be his bargaining power with the Americans. In the night-long argument with Murphy, Darlan had realized that he could out-last his opponent, that Murphy was ready to give in to almost any conditions that would salvage his position and stop the fighting.

Sometime between 8 and 9 in the morning Darlan received a secret message by private wire directly from Pétain: "I have received your messages via the Admiralty. I am happy that you are there. You may act and inform me. You know you have my full confidence." The message was in a code known only to Admiral Paul Auphan, Pétain's Navy chief, and to Darlan's aide, Admiral Battet. It had been specially set up so that Darlan could communicate top-secretly with Pétain, presumably in case of an Allied landing in North Africa.

With this message in his pocket, Darlan felt he could afford to temporize with the Americans.

In Algiers he had the situation in hand!

By lunchtime, helmeted Garde Mobile police, aided by SOLs with muskets, were patrolling the streets.

Radio Alger, which had been broadcasting Giraud's proclamation all morning, between recordings of martial music, reverted to a program of light music, then went off the air.

No newspaper had appeared on the streets, and the BBC, the only other source of information, was being successfully jammed by the local Vichy censors.

Lunching at the Villa des Oliviers, Murphy and his "vice-consuls" could see a great fire burning near the port, and hear the sound of firing. As they ate, three American dive bombers, says Pendar, swept down on the port.

Fenard stepped outside onto the terrace to discover the damage they were doing and came back muttering, "This must be stopped. This is ridiculous."

He was voicing, says Pendar, what everyone thought.

Even Darlan, by this time, had come to the same conclusion. Shortly before noon he sent another message to Pétain warning that the city might be taken by nightfall, that the Allied forces advancing from east and west would eventually encircle the city.

Not that he remained idle. His subtle reaction to this new situation was neatly to sidestep the issue by dividing the North African command into two: the eastern half he placed under General Louis Jacques Barré in Tunisia, the western half under General Noguès in Morocco, thus virtually dispossessing Juin of all authority outside the city of Algiers, and at the same time placing the two halves of North Africa directly under Vichy control.

Darlan then let it be known that as soon as his trusted Battet could be found, he was ready to talk business with the Americans.

Pendar was asked to find Battet. Weary from his night's experience, Pendar asked Dorange to issue him a safe-conduct. Dorange, who had "recovered from his hysteria of the night before," and was now "calm and suave in an immaculate new uniform, and also convinced that the Americans were here to stay," agreed to drive Pendar to Fort l'Empereur. There Pendar witnessed the coming and going of generals and colonels, receiving news of French resistance all along the coast.

"I remember," says Pendar, "hearing Sevez answer a call from Oran with the news that things were going well for the Vichyites in the town proper. A bulletin from Morocco said the Americans had tried to land at Safi but had been repulsed, and that there was very severe fighting going on at Port Lyautey and near Casablanca."

As for Algiers, the only Allied group to have reached the heart of the city was a detachment of some twenty-five men commanded by Colonel Doyle of the 1st Battalion of the 168th Infantry.

Arriving at the Palais d'Été about 3 P.M., they succeeded in capturing it, but concealed snipers opened fire, killing Colonel Doyle. The rest of the battalion was pinned down near El Biar, while flanking parties, having overcome some French armor, were approaching the vicinity of Fort l'Empereur.

Dorange reappeared with a pass for Pendar and urged him to find the American commanding general in order to start talking terms.

From this Pendar knew that Juin wanted an armistice, "as Dorange never took responsibility except under Juin's orders."

Not knowing where to locate Battet, Pendar tried the Central Commissariat; there he found d'Astier and Cordier and a lot of people milling around the bloodstained body of Colonel Jacouin.

Pendar then tried Villa Sinéty (where the OSS had a secret radio) and was told by Cole and Boyd that the Allies were at Sidi Ferruch.

Heading in that direction, Pendar rounded a corner to see the harbor of Chergas filled with hundreds of gray ships, the road crammed with companies of American soldiers marching toward Algiers through a throng of curious French and Arab onlookers.

At about 4:30 General Sevez warned Juin that it was time he made up his mind either to move out of Algiers at the head of his troops and leave Darlan to handle the political situation in the city, or stay where he was and be surrounded.

By this time the Americans were already moving down the boulevard Gallieni. Darlan phoned to say he wanted Juin to stay and negotiate as quickly as possible a cease-fire valid only for the Algiers garrison. "There is no point," said Darlan, "having people killed uselessly. Let us not prolong a resistance which is hopeless."

Immediately Juin ordered Dorange's doctor friend Dupuy to get in touch with the American officer in charge of the landings, or with anyone who could discuss a cease-fire. At the same time he ordered French forces to withdraw on Fort l'Empereur so as to avoid tangling with the Americans.

From the periphery the Americans were dropping mortar shells onto the casements of the old fortress, whose crumbling brick was none too resistant, and had already killed a dozen Frenchmen including another full colonel.

By 5:30, with no word from Dupuy, and as contact was about to be made with the Americans in the more brutal form of a counter-attack from the Caserne des Tagarins, Juin ordered the attack suspended and sent out Dorange to back up Dupuy.

By this time Pendar had found General Ryder, the tall, thin, stooped commander of the Eastern Task Force, at his temporary headquarters behind a roadside hedge on the outskirts of El Biar. With him were General Mast and Captain Randolph Churchill, son of the Prime Minister.

It was there that Dupuy managed to join them. To show that he was well disposed to a cease-fire, Ryder seized—so reports an eyewitness—both hands of the Frenchman, with an effusion of friendly words.

"What," asked Ryder, "are your intentions, and above all, *who* is in command here?"

Ryder then outlined his terms: easy if the French surrendered at once, harsh if they refused, with the stipulation that Pendar find Murphy and have him present at all negotiations.

On his way back to Algiers Pendar ran into his chief near Juin's villa. By this time Darlan had sent a French car and chauffeur for Murphy; but the first group of Americans Murphy ran into would not believe his story—at least not until he had the wit to convince their commanding officer, a Lieutenant Geiser, by the wisecrack: "You're the best looking Geiser I've seen in a long time."

Accompanied by Pendar, Murphy was then allowed to drive off to meet Ryder. On their arrival, they found Dorange ready for the formal surrender of Fort l'Empereur.

What followed, says Pendar, was wonderfully French. "Dorange stood before six French soldiers, lined up in an arrow shape, and handed the sword of surrender by the blade, hilt extended, to General Ryder, announcing that with this sword he surrendered Fort l'Empereur, and the City of Algiers to the American Consul General."

The protagonists then entered Darlan's limousine.

With Knox at the wheel they headed for the fort, accompanied by a volley of tracer bullets from Colonel O'Daniel's troops, which whizzed above them as they sped toward Voirol hill.

It was, says Pendar, a grotesque situation, what with the British Navy offshore still bombarding the Admiralty, and the batteries of Fort l'Empereur still sending back salvoes against the ships at sea.

As they crossed the lines in El Biar, which the Americans insisted on calling by its old name Lambiridi, and were approaching the fort, they suddenly heard, through the windows of the limousine, the French signal for a cease-fire: "trumpet blasts, blown with great bravura."

Passing the gates, Murphy solemnly acknowledged the salute of the French, then went to closet himself with Ryder and Juin, who stood waiting behind a green baize table. Overhead the bomb from an American plane whistled past and exploded a hundred yards down the road.

An ecstatic smile, says Murphy, spread over Ryder's face as he exclaimed, "How wonderful! This is the first time since World War I that I have been under fire."

His pleasure, added Murphy, was not shared by the French.

All that was now necessary to stop the hostilities in Algiers and its suburbs was a few words of agreement between Juin and Ryder. After a slight hesitation, Ryder, on his own responsibility, agreed to let the French keep their arms, "in view of the nature of the operation which had just taken place."

As dusk settled on the city, the shooting ceased, and with nightfall came the first full blackout accompanied by the sound of sirens.

Those who should have had most reason for celebration and fraternization, the original conspirators, those who had worked so hard to bring the Allies ashore, were, of course, the most discomforted of all. Many of their leaders were now in jail or in hiding, and their titular head, Giraud, had not even dared to make an appearance.

Yet news of the armistice, which was brought to the Five late in the afternoon, had been a relief, and they had gone to visit Murphy at his villa so as to celebrate with champagne (provided by Lemaigre-Dubreuil) and discuss their next moves, which meant largely how to handle or be handled by Darlan.

That evening at 8 P.M. a conference was to be held at the Hotel Saint-Georges, Darlan's headquarters, where Ryder was formally to meet the French Commander in Chief.

Murphy, delayed by his talks with the Five, did not arrive till close to 10 P.M., accompanied by Ryder and Holmes, to find Darlan surrounded by his senior officers, Juin, Moreau, Fenard, Battet, Koeltz, Mendigal and Sevez, and the inevitable Dorange.

Murphy apologized for being two hours late. Fenard answered, "Not two hours; three years."

They then got down to business.

Ryder mentioned that a suspension of arms might be extended to the whole theater of operations.

Darlan answered that outside Algiers he could do nothing without first consulting Marshal Pétain.

Darlan asked Ryder if he had any suggestions to offer.

Ryder retorted that he too could not speak without the authority of General Clark, who was due the next day, but wished that Algiers be cleared so that his men and equipment could move toward the east, leaving the French administration intact.

"Under what government?" asked Darlan.

Ryder said he had expected to find an insurrectionary government, and was not competent to speak without Clark.

As neither could, or would, speak without the authority of his superior, the conference was postponed till the morrow, and, in the manner of the Orient, and no doubt to show that his interlocutors were as much his guests as his conquerors, Darlan turned to Murphy and asked, "Would the general accept a cup of coffee?"

"Certainly," answered Murphy, "with pleasure."

At this socially relaxed moment Lemaigre-Dubreuil, Saint-Hardouin, d'Astier and Rigault were seen to enter the room, Lemaigre asking what had become of Giraud, and expressing himself in bitter terms.

No one seemed to know, and it was suggested to Lemaigre that it would be better for all concerned if Giraud did not arrive to increase the confusion.

Saint-Hardouin argued quietly but firmly with Fenard that the Murphy-Giraud agreements should serve as the basis for any further discussions.

But the only request to which Darlan agreed was that the Allies should have immediate access to Algiers harbor, where their transports could shelter from a wolf pack of Axis submarines steaming toward an easy kill.

Turning to Juin, Murphy said, "It is calm tonight in the city of Algiers."

"Yes," retorted Juin. "There is no one on the streets but the air-raid wardens."

With this diplomatic badinage the protagonists drew the curtain on the first day of the landings.

But while Murphy and Knox drove home through the quiet city their problems were far from over.

In Oran and in Morocco French and Allied troops were busy massacring each other, and in Tunisia no steps had been taken to prevent a German invasion. If Darlan would not act, could Giraud?

8

TRANSFERRED from the *Seraph* to a Catalina flying boat, Giraud had been landed at Gibraltar late in the afternoon of the 7th, still dressed in his wrinkled business suit, his face unshaven and pale from lack of sleep, his mustache drooping, but his cold gray eyes grim and determined.

Eisenhower again demurred at the prospect of seeing so formidable a Frenchman before the landing operations had even started, sensing that Giraud might "ask for the moon."

Then he relented. At 5 P.M. Giraud was led down a 2,000-foot-long gallery to the 10-foot-high blockhouse which served as operations room, its walls lined with maps on which the various forces had been pinpointed. For privacy, Eisenhower took Giraud into the tiny office reserved for General Clark.

Using Holmes as interpreter, Eisenhower discovered that Giraud —whose five stars outranked his own three—still believed himself to be in supreme command of the entire Allied operation, and would accept nothing less.

Eisenhower offered Giraud the governorship, or, in the words of Clark, "virtually the kingship" of North Africa, as well as sufficient funds to build up an army of his own; but "the old General declined in seven languages, each meaning 'Prestige.' "

Butcher reports that Eisenhower would argue with Giraud for an hour, then rest while Clark took over.

What would people think, Giraud kept asking, if he didn't become Allied Commander in Chief within forty-eight hours?

By nightfall, after a prolonged and heated discussion, during which no agreement whatsoever was reached, Eisenhower stiffly accompanied Giraud to the door. Coming out, Giraud brusquely told Beaufre that the Allies were not acting in good faith, that he intended to return to France via Spain, and that in the meantime he was going to catch up on his sleep.

Sunday morning, invasion or no invasion, Giraud and his son disappeared to an early Mass, leaving Beaufre to sit between Clark and General Alfred Gruenther at a breakfast of fresh eggs and orange juice. Beaufre, whose English was excellent, astutely used the opportunity to discuss some means of ironing out the Giraud impasse.

Clark agreed to call another meeting at General MacFarlane's for 10:30—at which Eisenhower once more said that he was prepared to recognize Giraud as head of the civil government of North Africa and as head of all French forces.

Somewhat mollified by a good night's sleep, and the news that the landings had gone off more or less as scheduled, Giraud agreed to a face-saving compromise.

The supreme command would go to the French as soon as they had the largest number of units, newly equipped, in the field. This satisfied Eisenhower's orders from the Combined Chiefs, but kept the command firmly in his hands. Cheerfully the meeting broke up for lunch.

Unaware of what was happening in Algeria, Eisenhower sent off a signal to the War Department in Washington to the effect that Giraud would proceed to Algiers on the morrow "to do all in his power to stop all French resistance to the Allied forces and to begin the organization of French forces for use against the Axis."

While Eisenhower retired for a nap, Giraud spent the afternoon shopping in the narrow bazaar streets for underwear and shoes.

Little did either general suspect that just then Admiral Darlan had retaken control of Algiers, and that in Morocco Noguès and Michelier had settled down to fight Lieutenant General George S. Patton and Rear Admiral Henry K. Hewitt.

Roused late in the afternoon with the news that Admiral Darlan was in Algiers and that Ryder had "grabbed him," Eisenhower wondered how this would affect Giraud and was faced with the problem of what to tell him.

Afraid that Giraud might start another marathon argument, Eisenhower decided to send him directly to Algiers in the morning, without benefit of the intelligence about Darlan, and let him work it out for himself on the spot.

So, on the morning of the 9th (and only four days late), Giraud was placed in a Hudson bomber and dispatched to Algiers along with his son and Beaufre, having been told to keep General Clark constantly informed of any steps he might take to stop French resistance.

At the same time, General Clark, accompanied by his aide Darryl F. Zanuck and by the British General Sir Kenneth A. N. Anderson, who was to take over Ryder's forces for the push toward Tunisia, took off in a B-17 to set up an advance echelon of Allied Force Headquarters in Algiers, stopping on the way to see how the fighting was progressing in Oran.

In Algiers, where the sun kept peeping out from behind light clouds, crowds gathered on the terraced streets to watch Allied ships debarking British troops in the busy harbor.

Poor Ryder, anxiously waiting for Clark, kept postponing from hour to hour his scheduled meeting with Darlan, becoming more and more nervous about obtaining a cease-fire so as to clear the way for the British to move eastward toward Tunisia, where the Germans were already landing on the airfields.

When Ryder could no longer postpone a conference with Darlan, he went along to see the admiral at the Hotel Saint-Georges. It was just after 5:30 P.M. and an air raid of some 30 Junkers began to pound the shipping in the harbor and the airfield at Maison Blanche.

Surrounded, as usual, by Fenard, Moreau, Juin, Koeltz and Mendigal, Darlan greeted Ryder.

From his briefcase Ryder produced two armistice conventions prepared in Washington. One was lenient, in case Darlan showed himself willing to cooperate. The other was harsh, in which the

French were to be disarmed and confined to barracks, in case Darlan refused to be helpful; Ryder insisted he must take such measures so as to insure the security of his own forces.

Juin interjected that it would be an affront to the French to remove their arms just as they were about to be required to use them against the Germans.

To smooth things out General Koeltz, Commander of the XIX Corps, suggested that his troops be allowed to keep their weapons so long as they stayed in their barracks.

Darlan added that all their munitions, except what they might need "for the maintenance of order," could be placed under American guard.

But the crucial question of a cease-fire elsewhere in North Africa remained unsolved.

In return for a cessation of hostilities everywhere, Ryder offered to allow French ships to fly their own flag, and to retain the regular French administration.

Darlan asked if this meant that the negotiations were to be carried out in the name of the marshal. In other words, did Ryder recognize the authority of Vichy in North Africa?

Ryder answered that he was not qualified to do so without General Clark's approval.

At that moment Clark's B-17 was landing at Maison Blanche in the midst of the German raid. From the airfield Clark drove directly to the Saint-Georges, where he walked in on the conference about an hour after it had started.

Clark's first move was to bluff Darlan with the news that a great number of Allied troops had already landed, letting drop the figure of 150,000 men, and requesting that all French resistance cease immediately. Actually, at that time, according to Colonel Holmes, there were some 3,400 troops ashore in the Algiers area. Darlan and Juin were, in any case, unconvinced.

Clark then said he wanted to discuss the situation with Murphy; so the conference was postponed till morning.

As soon as they were alone, Murphy said to Clark, "Where are all your tanks? Run your tanks through the main streets. Show them some force."

"O.K.," answered Clark. "If you insist, I'll have all three of our available tanks put on a show."

Subdued, Murphy accompanied Clark to send a signal to Eisenhower that the presence of Darlan had rendered obsolete their agreement with Giraud.

Left to themselves, Darlan and his cohorts noticed that the Americans had either forgotten or intentionally planted on the table a large manila envelope which contained the terms of the harsher of the two armistices.

Having studied it carefully, Darlan asked all those present, starting with the lowest rank, what they thought should be done. The prevailing opinion was that the French could no longer resist, and that it might be better to accept the lenient terms than risk the imposition of harsher ones.

Without expressing his own opinion, Darlan said he would refer the decision to the marshal, and see them in the morning.

At 8:30 P.M. Darlan cabled Pétain a résumé of the mild armistice, saying that he had told Ryder he was not qualified to discuss, and could only refer, but that Ryder had insisted on an answer by the following evening at 10 P.M.

Darlan knew the Germans would intercept his message; but it contained a key word which, according to Darlan's son Alain, was a code between Pétain and Darlan to verify messages in case of a resumption of the fight against the Germans. The word was one of Darlan's Christian names: Xavier.

At the same time, by his secret channel, unknown to the Germans, Darlan added that his general officers judged the terms acceptable and that he agreed with their opinion.

In answer, and to help Darlan make up his mind, came a secret cable from Auphan saying that the marshal was "in intimate agreement with Darlan," but that the official position of the government could not be given until after the return to Vichy of Premier Laval from his discussion with the Germans.

With Pétain's tacit approval, Darlan considered himself in a position to deal with the Americans as he saw fit.

His only problem was Giraud, who—still believing himself to be officially invested as Commander in Chief of all French forces in

Africa—had arrived at Blida airport early in the afternoon of the 9th to a reception he had not expected.

"Giraud?" asked Colonel Monstrelet, who by then had recovered control of the airfield for Darlan. *"Connais pas."*

It was an insolent blow, and to add to Giraud's discomfort, he discovered that his luggage, which contained his uniform, had been mislaid.

It was a nasty scene, and it might have been worse had not Murphy chanced to arrive on the field in search of General Clark, and promptly placed one of his cars at Giraud's disposal to dispatch him to the Five.

Instead of being driven in a motorcade through an applauding crowd, Giraud's limousine slipped noiselessly through the twisted alleys of the Ruisseau quarter and drew up among the garbage cans that lined the imposing gateway to Dar Mamieddine, the center of the rebel conspiracy.

There was no one at the villa to greet Giraud, with the exception of Lemaigre's private secretary. As Giraud passed under a wisteria-covered pergola, the sky was still palely tinted, but a dismal dusk was about to fall.

At the Saint-Georges, furious at the turn of events, Achiary, Jousse and Jacques Brunel had gone to see Murphy.

Spotting them in the lobby, Dorange informed them that if they so much as stepped back into the hotel, Darlan would have them arrested by the American.

In Murphy's office the trio heatedly confronted the American with what they considered a perfectly valid complaint: that he had no right to deal with a traitor such as Darlan, especially after having worked with the real Resistance for almost two years.

Murphy answered that he was sorry, but could do nothing about it, adding laconically, "I have my orders."

Still furious, the trio went out, slamming the door.

At Dar Mahieddine the conspirators turned up one by one for dinner, and each attacked the "chief" for not having arrived at the time of the landings.

They urged him to make up for lost time; but Giraud shook his head. He had come to fight. If Darlan, his superior, was in charge, there was nothing he, Giraud, could do about it.

In vain the Five tried to argue that France would never stand so good a chance among the Allies with Darlan as it could with Giraud, who had the support of the Americans. As commander, he must act to assert his authority.

"I'll think about it," said Giraud.

Van Ecke, who had been blocked for two days in Constantine, arrived from downtown Algiers to report that everywhere the opposition was winning, that Darlan was becoming entrenched. Worse, the heads of the Resistance were to be subjected to disciplinary measures for having failed to fulfill their personal oath to Pétain and would have to go into hiding.

Throughout the city many young rebels who had been acting in secret for the benefit of France, not even knowing the identity of their real leaders, were now in jail, unaware that the Allies had landed, convinced that their *coup* had failed.

It remained for Lemaigre, archplotter and *éminence grise,* to find some way of redressing their disastrous position.

Did they not still have the Giraud-Murphy accords? Were they not personally initialed by Roosevelt? Were they not more generous to France, by far, than any terms Darlan was likely to obtain?

On these he intended to capitalize.

By now the city of Algiers was once more white with moonlight.

Clark, with his intimate staff, had gone to bed in Darlan's Hotel Saint-Georges, under the joint guard of Allied sentries and the admiral's naval personnel who patrolled the gardens in their blue-black uniforms and white puttees.

Along the gravel path Major Dorange was seen to walk with General Juin to his superior's car, then head through the night toward his own quarters in the Palais d'Hiver—for what seemed like a well-earned night of rest.

He was not to get it.

At 11 P.M. the telephone rang. It was Colonel Chrétien. "Would General Juin receive M. Lemaigre-Dubreuil?"

"En principe, oui, je pense," said Dorange. "But I must be able to inform the general with what the meeting is to deal." Dorange was stalling, trying to guess what the "spy" colonel could mean. Then it dawned on him that one of the main protagonists of the drama had yet to make his entrance upon the stage. Almost casually Dorange posed the question: "By the way, Colonel, what ever happened to General Giraud?"

At his end of the wire, the perpetually solemn Chrétien must have smiled. "Why," said he, "General Giraud arrived here this evening."

"Then I suppose," said Dorange, "the most urgent step would be to get in touch with him. You know that he is tied to General Juin by an old friendship."

"Let us make a date," said Chrétien.

Thus was knit the first stitch of a new conspiracy.

Shortly before midnight Dorange and Colonel Chrétien entered the patio of Dar Mahieddine, where young men of the Chantiers de la Jeunesse, in green berets, still guarded the entrance.

Introduced to Dorange, Giraud found himself squarely before the dilemma of whether to impose his authority—as urged by his co-conspirators—or submit to the supposed "legality" of Darlan. Dorange exposed the kernel of the problem with one short phrase: "General Giraud legal, yes. Rebel, no."

Worn out with fatigue, almost as much at the end of his rope as Murphy had been with Darlan on the night of the landings, Giraud said softly that any solution would suit him, so long as it led to a resumption of hostilities against the Germans, that he would be happy to hand over the charges of government and devote himself to his military duties, adding that he was confident that Juin, his junior, would accept a command at his orders.

Dorange, quick to seize an opening which would subordinate Giraud to Darlan, as official heir to the marshal, replied, "In that case, *mon général,* let us work to install an organ of government. It will make no difficulties in assigning to you the mission you have so well conceived."

Despite the late hour, Juin agreed to meet his old comrade in arms. By the time they reached the Villa des Oliviers, it was 3 A.M.

and they found the villa well protected by tanks, Juin in his bath-robe, Mme. Juin pale from the excitement.

Juin summed up his reasons for this marriage of convenience. Giraud had the support of the Allies, Darlan that of the senior French Army and Navy commanders in North Africa. Someone had to unite the two, so that Darlan could bring the French to the side of the Allies without breaking their oath to the marshal.*

The interview ended (in Dorange's romantic language) with Giraud walking down the broad steps of Juin's villa "wrapped in the mantle of Commander in Chief of the French forces, which, of his own initiative, Juin had conferred on him."

But poor Dorange still had a chore to perform: to persuade Darlan to accept Giraud.

Knocking at Darlan's door at 4 A.M., Dorange found the little admiral "fatigued and dejected."

"Yes, yes," mumbled Darlan, "I certainly had a feeling of friend-ship for Giraud. I suppose I still do. But it is too early yet."

Clearly Darlan dared not give up even a vestige of his power till he had coped with Clark in the morning.

November 10th was a bright hot day. The meeting between Clark and Darlan took place at 10 A.M. in a small ground-floor room of the Saint-Georges—a typically Mediterranean tourist hotel of rambling white buildings shaded by palm trees. Through the windows the military could enjoy the autumn flowers against a backdrop of the azure Mediterranean.

In an obvious move to gain time, even minutes, Darlan slowly went through the motions of studying the armistice terms, of which he knew the content in detail.

Though he had accepted a cease-fire for the city of Algiers, Darlan was still hedging for the rest of North Africa. In Morocco Noguès was resisting; in Oran General Robert Boisseau was hold-ing out against the Americans who had encircled the city. In Tunisia the Germans were pouring in troops.

Becoming impatient, Clark nudged Murphy, and Murphy ad-

---

* An oath of allegiance personally to the marshal had been imposed first on ministers and civil servants, then on the army, the magistrature, and every-body holding public office.

dressed the admiral: "Time is pressing. General Clark intends to settle the political question. Are you ready, Admiral, to have hostilities cease in North Africa?"

Darlan shifted in his chair; his hands fumbled with the papers on the table in front of him. Ill at ease, he explained that he had sent Ryder's armistice proposal to Pétain during the night, with his own opinion, supported by that of his generals, that it would be foolish to pursue the fighting. He was convinced, said Darlan, that the marshal shared his views, and that an answer would be forthcoming that evening, or, at the very latest, the following morning. In the meantime he could do nothing, as only the marshal was empowered to act. Pulling a handkerchief from his pocket, Darlan mopped his bald head, then gave his reason for stalling: Laval was at that very moment on his way to Munich to see Hitler, and the marshal had ordered Darlan to do nothing to spoil Laval's chance of strengthening Vichy's position with the Germans.

"In that case," said Murphy, "the general sees no reason for continuing the conversation. He must take immediate steps which he deems essential to his security."

Darlan then offered to send another message to Vichy.

"No," said Murphy. "That is not possible. The matter is urgent, and must be settled in thirty minutes."

As Darlan continued to stall, pleading that he only happened to be in North Africa by chance, Clark lost his temper and threatened to bring in Giraud to sign for the French.

"Do you want Giraud without the Army?" answered Darlan. "Or the Army without Giraud?"

Juin interjected, "Giraud has no power. General Noguès commands in Morocco, and General Barré in Tunisia. No one will follow Giraud."

"In that case," said Murphy to Darlan, "though the situation is as painful for him as it must be for you, General Clark is going to find it necessary to take you under his protection."

"That's my last word," said Clark.

As he spoke, American soldiers ranged themselves before the door, and according to one witness, there was the clicking of rifle bolts.

Unmoved, Darlan retorted, "*Je m'en fous.*"

Clark rose to end the meeting; but General Juin, who had been sitting at Clark's left, reached up and "laid his war-maimed hand on the American's arm." He was so desperate he spoke in English: "Five minutes, please," he begged. "Give me five minutes."

"O.K.," said Clark. "Five minutes." Whereupon he withdrew from the room, followed by his staff.

After eight minutes of impassioned argument, which, says Holmes, could be plainly heard by the Americans beyond the closed doors, "roly-poly Admiral Raymond Fenard burst out with the news that Darlan had been won over."

The Americans trooped back. In the silence that followed, Darlan asked Murphy to please translate for the general: "*J'accepte.*"

Without further ado, "though pale and shaking," Darlan began to draft a directive to the various chiefs of the French armed forces requiring them to break off hostilities with the Americans and observe the strictest neutrality.

"In the name of the marshal," said Darlan, "I assume authority in North Africa. The present military chiefs retain their commands, and the political structure and administration remain intact. No changes may be effected until further orders from me."

He then turned to Murphy. "All French troops retain their weapons?"

Murphy looked at Clark, then nodded. "The high military authorities subordinate will make contact with the local commanders of the American forces in order to apply the armistice."

So Clark obtained his cease-fire.

Darlan, however, insisted that the French officers who had aided the Allies be branded as traitors.

"There are some officers," said the collaborationist admiral, "who have failed in their military duty." He then mentioned Generals Mast and Monsabert by name, as well as several others. "They have failed," said Darlan, "to keep their oath. I do not wish to collaborate with these people. I will not accept an officer who disobeys his chief!"

Clark replied, "I understand your position. They will never hold command so long as Admiral Darlan remains Commander in Chief."

Darlan raised the question of General Giraud, who, as the Allied choice for Commander in Chief, had not even been allowed to attend the morning conference. But on this point Clark stood firm, answering that the problem could be settled only after the cease-fire had been put into effect.

And so the conference ended. On the way out Darlan, who spoke much more English than Clark had realized, paused to say to Murphy, "Would you mind suggesting to Major General Clark that I am a five-star admiral. He should stop talking to me as if I were a lieutenant, junior grade."

As for Clark, he immediately signaled Eisenhower in Gibraltar, summing up the complex French situation: "I now have two granddaddies on my hands"—meaning Giraud and Darlan.

Meanwhile Darlan signaled Marshal Pétain, outlining the results of the conference and urging him to approve what had been done.

Supported by Weygand and Auphan, the marshal agreed to act at once; he even considered ordering the fleet to sea, and the French garrisons in unoccupied France to take to the hills.

But Darlan's message about the armistice with Clark reached the Germans almost as fast, and they immediately confronted Laval (as he was about to face Hitler) with this unpleasant bit of news.

Furious, Laval threatened to resign on the spot, and forecast such dire reprisals against France by the Germans that Pétain reversed himself and reinstated his order to North Africa to continue resisting the Americans; on the theory that Darlan would by now be a prisoner of the Allies, he named General Noguès as Commander in Chief for North Africa.

Meanwhile Murphy and Clark, bent on finding a way to honor Eisenhower's engagement to Giraud, and despite the cease-fire they had obtained from Darlan, now tried to double-cross Darlan and install Giraud as both civil and military leader in North Africa, with their full support.

Giraud, his mustache bristling, pompously refused. "I am no statesman. I merely wish to command the armed forces of France."

In vain Clark and Murphy tried to shake him from this position.

After half an hour's struggle Clark and Murphy went away with no visible alternative but to continue to deal with Darlan.

Then, to climax this Molière piece, just as Giraud decided to go make his own obeisance to Darlan, the latter received the message from Pétain disavowing him and appointing Noguès. As Giraud entered Fenard's villa he was thunderstruck to hear Darlan exclaim, "I am lost. I can only give myself up."

When Clark and Murphy turned up a few minutes later, they could hardly believe their ears when the admiral announced that he must annul the orders he had given in the morning.

"Damned if you do," said Clark.

"Then you'll have to make me a prisoner," said Darlan.

"That's O.K. by me," answered Clark.

So Darlan remained a prisoner in Fenard's villa, on his word, and a few sentries were posted in the garden.

Luckily the cease-fire orders had already gone out, and could hardly be countered.

But Clark was now at a complete loss for what to do next.

To Saint-Hardouin he complained that Darlan was worthless, that he could not even bring over the fleet or apply the armistice he had signed that morning.

Overhearing the remark, Giraud brightened and suggested that perhaps after all *he* should be allowed to take over. This was too much for Clark, who by now wanted to do nothing but let matters ride, hoping that if nobody rocked the boat, the cease-fire might go into effect before the news got around of Darlan's collapse.

To complicate the imbroglio further, yet another secret message arrived for Darlan from Admiral Auphan, in effect disavowing the disavowal, which Auphan explained had been made under duress from the Germans.

Once more Darlan revived. With the news that two armored and eight other German divisions had begun to cross into Vichy France, his mind was made up.

Bolstered by Pétain's secret cables, Darlan now felt himself capable of assuming control of North Africa.

For public consumption he sent a message to Vichy saying that since the Germans had broken the armistice and the marshal was no longer free, he, Darlan, "faithful to the marshal's inner thoughts," would do what was best for France—a remark which led Churchill to comment that if called upon to shoot the old marshal, Darlan would happily do so in the name of Pétain.

Yet Darlan was still in a quandary: Secretly encouraged by the marshal, he was without *official* power and had no means of commanding the various North African authorities, such as Admiral Edmond Louis Derrien and General Barré in Tunisia, who had been told by Vichy to listen only to Noguès. Nor could Darlan reveal the marshal's secret encouragement by either radio or wire, as the Germans had all French codes with the exception of the one secret link to Pétain. There was nothing Darlan could do but wait for Noguès.

To try to get some action in Tunisia and forestall the Germans, Juin cleverly dusted off the old rule that no French soldier could take orders from a chief who had fallen into enemy hands—as had Pétain, with the German occupation of southern France—adding that the rupture of the armistice by the Germans freed Frenchmen from being bound by its conditions, and from their oath to the marshal.

"On va taper sur le boche," he said heartily to Barré on the phone; then gave orders for Koeltz to start moving his XIX Corps to the east and for Lorber in Bône to march to Barré's support.

But this was too much for Koeltz and company, who still counted on saving their positions by acting in a strictly "legal" manner, and who maintained, not illogically, that Juin's orders were no more legal than Darlan's, and that they would have to wait for the arrival of Noguès.

So Juin annulled the order, and the Germans consolidated a Tunisian bridgehead at the very moment when it could have been wiped out by the French, saving the Allies six months of bitter fighting.

Outraged, Clark, who, after all, had been partly responsible for the entire situation since Cherchel, threatened to arrest every

Pétainist general and admiral in Africa—which was just what the Five had been waiting for.

Now that his uniform had arrived and had been freshly pressed, Giraud was acting much more like a chief. All that he needed, said the Five, was a suitable setting.

What better place, suggested Lemaigre, than the seat of the Algerian government, the Palais d'Été?

Forthwith Giraud's aide was dispatched to the palace to induce the unhappy Mme. Chatel to remove the slipcovers in some of her salons.

"Luckily," said Lemaigre, "today is November 11. All we have to do is get Giraud in full uniform to place a wreath on the tomb of the unknown soldier. This will evoke the glory and enthusiasm of 1918."

And so it did.

Puffed up by the applause he received, and happy in his new surroundings, Giraud revived to the point of issuing a new proclamation in which he took over North Africa in the name of the marshal, so as to lead it in war against the Axis. So confident did he become that when Clark summoned him to the Saint-Georges, Giraud retorted that it was up to the American general, his junior, to visit Giraud.

In this he overplayed his hand. Clark wrinkled his mouth, agreed, but cunningly planned to have the last word. Having noted that Darlan's orders were obeyed despite the weakness of his position, Clark decided to support Darlan.

Accompanied by Murphy, Clark went down to the Palais d'Été to see Giraud. There they ran into Beaufre, radiant at the French general's latest proclamation, but abashed when he saw Clark "assume his movie actor expression" and heard from him in surprisingly diplomatic language that though Giraud was a great soldier and all that, he had best "understand the necessities of the present hour" and lie low.

As was to be expected, Giraud instantly deflated, declaring himself happy to accept any military command under Darlan.

So another night was lost.

In Gibraltar, sitting in his underpants while his orderly tried to remove an inkspot from his trousers, Eisenhower, "irritated at French garrisons for failure to step in and fight Huns in Tunisia," turned to Butcher and remarked that the French, "don't seem to know which side of the bread is buttered."

9

NOGUÈS ARRIVED from Morocco during the afternoon of November 12th accompanied by his aide, Commandant Bataille, a financial and economics expert, who had just flown back from Vichy (which he had left one step ahead of the Germans) with orders for Noguès direct from Pétain. With them came the ubiquitous Dorange.

From Fenard's villa, where he had been shut up, Darlan came out, remarking, *"Enfin on me débloque."*

Seeing that Darlan was no longer a prisoner and that he appeared to be in effectual control, Noguès returned to him his full command. Together they convoked the senior French generals and admirals, as well as the Governor General of Algeria, Yves Chatel, who had also just arrived from Vichy via Constantine where Bergeret had induced him to forget his protestations of loyalty to Vichy and trim his sails to the new breeze.

In an exotic lounge at the Saint-Georges, with Moorish arches and blue majolica tilework, these top Vichyite Frenchmen were to hold a conference with General Clark at 6 P.M.

Giraud, who had been summoned, was at first excluded by the "legitimists" and then kept waiting in an anteroom.

At the meeting Noguès expressed his relief that the fighting was over, but said he did not believe it possible to reverse steam so precipitately and join the Allies, an attitude which he maintained despite the contrary advice of Juin.

Pendar, who was present as an interpreter, says that Noguès had no intention of bringing Morocco into the war on our side:

"He proposed merely to give us 'the right of passage'; exactly the amount of cooperation, in other words, that Vichy gave the Germans on the Syrian airports. Noguès seemed really afraid for French, and for his own, sovereignty in Morocco. His tenseness and unhappiness went far beyond that of the other Vichy leaders in North Africa at the time."

Noguès, says Pendar, kept wanting to send Bataille back to Vichy to discover "the old man's intimate thoughts."

But Clark at last put an end to this with a stern statement: "Please impress it upon General Noguès, once and for all, that there can be no question of communicating with Vichy. We have broken relations with that government. In our eyes it no longer exists."

Albert Kammerer, author of *Du débarquement allié en Afrique du Nord,* says that Noguès showed that his main preoccupation was not with resuming the war against Germany, but in "maintaining the marshal's national revolution in Africa, perpetuating the Vichy spirit, and eliminating his 'bête noire' Giraud."

At Clark's words, Noguès made a move to leave, muttering, "Then we have nothing more to say." But Darlan held him by the sleeve, and requested a private conversation with Clark, in the course of which Noguès insisted they would have nothing to do with Giraud. "There was a General Giraud," said Noguès pontifically. "There is no more."

Clark, at the end of his patience, read them an ultimatum he had just received from Eisenhower.

If they did not come quickly to terms, he would put Giraud in charge, or rule by military dictate.

He then insisted on rereading the ultimatum to them in the presence of Giraud.

When the Allies' favorite advanced with hand outstretched, Noguès put his own hand behind his back and said, "I will not speak to a rebel general."

He was then heard to mutter between his teeth an unwilling *"Bon jour,"* to which he added an almost inaudible *"traître."*

Again General Juin saved the day by turning on Noguès with a sharp *"Assez de votre sale politique.* We are going to fight the Germans."

The remark cleared the air; Noguès buckled, and though still maintaining it would be impossible for the Army to change sides without a transitory period of neutrality, he suggested that Giraud might go ahead and form a corp of volunteers to fight beside the Allies.

Again the argument flared. As—in Clark's words—"no peace pipe was smoked," he decided to break the impasse by agreeing to leave Noguès in political charge in Morocco while Darlan assumed the role of chief political executive in North Africa in the name of Pétain.

It was a comedown, especially for Giraud, who was limited to recruiting some volunteers while Juin retained command of the "legitimist" Army.

All of this, of course, went on behind closed doors, and was being kept as secret as possible from Algiers and the world at large.

But Clark had to face the Allied correspondents with some sort of story about what was going on. With what Drew Middleton described as "the pleased smile of a comedian telling his very best jokes," Clark assembled the reporters at the Saint-Georges and informed them he had wired Eisenhower that the "YBSOBS" had come to terms. YBSOBS, Clark explained with a grin, was an old West Point abbreviation for yellow-bellied sons-of-bitches.

"This," said Middleton, "was a delightful introduction to diplomacy as practiced by some generals. Clark seemed to think he had scored a diplomatic triumph."

To hear the results of what had developed at the Saint-Georges, the Five congregated in the big hall of the Palais d'Été and waited for Giraud. But it was from Beaufre they were to get the details.

Outraged at the news that Darlan had been accepted as political chief, that Noguès was to remain in power in Morocco, and that Juin had recovered his command of the armed forces to the detriment of their protégé, who was to be relegated to the insignificant role of commanding a group of volunteers, the Five decided to insist that Giraud reverse the situation.

But Giraud had retired to bed.

Once more Lemaigre got on the phone to Murphy and made a date for as early as possible the following morning.

In the meantime another day had been lost in the race with the Germans for Tunisia. To get things moving in the right direction, Juin made a desperate effort that night to induce the French to work together, by the only effective means he could think of.

Inviting to the Villa des Oliviers the senior French officers from each branch of the armed forces for a private dinner, he suggested that the best way to resolve their differences was to fight the Germans.

When all present had agreed, Juin delightedly ordered his aide to phone General Barré in Tunis and tell him "*qu'il me foute des coups de fusil, vite, dès ce soir.*"

All present, recounts an eyewitness, understood, and felt relieved that "this was it!"

But the real reason that the dinner went on so smoothly and that no one contested Juin's idea, was the presence of a man who was soon to play an increasingly important role in the future proceedings, and who seemed bent on seizing the reins of power: General Jean Marie Bergeret.

Early on Friday the 13th, Dubreuil, Saint-Hardouin and Rigault went to see Murphy. They insisted that the Americans honor the conventions signed *before* the landings. Giraud, they said, must be given full command of the armed forces, as the only means of balancing the political power of Darlan.

Nodding noncommittally, Murphy proposed that they talk to Clark.

Clark listened in silence, then said he had no objection, but that it was a matter for the French to work out among themselves. His only stipulation was that they reach an agreement *that* morning, because his Commander in Chief was arriving at noon and wanted everything settled so he could fly back to Gibraltar by dusk.

At the Saint-Georges the trio ran into Giraud.

At that same moment Noguès appeared. Sensing this to be the best opportunity for getting them together, Dubreuil whispered to Juin.

Juin rose to the occasion and approached Noguès:

"Come, come, *mon général,* we can't abandon a five-star comrade with such a tiny command. It's a question of France. Let us all march together. I am ready to place myself at Giraud's orders."

Noguès, to whom Darlan had shown the secret cables from Pétain during the night and who was by now much more chastened, held out his hand and agreed that Giraud should command the army, but on three conditions: that de Gaulle not set foot in North Africa, that Giraud place himself under Darlan's orders, that he hold his command in the name of the marshal.

Giraud accepted. The gang was united.

Even Vichy's Chatel was to remain in power as Governor General of Algiers.

Beaufre ran to tell Clark: "Everything is set. They all agree. Giraud has given up his corps of volunteers and assumes command of the Army. France is no longer neutral. She is with the Allies."

Clark, equally happy to have fulfilled his own orders, drove out to Maison Blanche to meet Eisenhower, whom he took to lunch at Cole's Moorish-style villa.

At 2 P.M. Darlan, Giraud, Noguès and Juin met with Eisenhower at the Saint-Georges. Using Murphy and Holmes as interpreters, Eisenhower said he had heard that an agreement had been reached among the French; he then confirmed that Darlan was acceptable to him as "Head of State" and that he would submit the agreement to Great Britain and the United States.

To Clark, as his deputy, he delegated the implementation of the deal, saying that Clark spoke for him.

Eisenhower's only condition was that the French attack the Germans in Tunisia. Darlan replied that the French would respect the agreement scrupulously.

"To his surprise," says Butcher, "Eisenhower discovered that they still felt a loyalty for Marshal Pétain, and that the group insisted on sending word to Pétain of their action."

At 3 P.M. Eisenhower and his small party set off again for Gibraltar—taking Murphy to help Eisenhower draft a cabled explanation of his deal with Darlan for the benefit of Washington and London.

Left to themselves the French surveyed their position, and Darlan decided to send off yet another secret message to the marshal, asking for his approval of this latest arrangement.

From Auphan came the reply: "You have the intimate accord of the marshal and Laval, but official decision has been submitted to occupying authorities."

Though a bit enigmatic, the substance of the message was clear enough to Darlan, who happily explained to his French colleagues: "*On a l'accord du vieux monsieur.*"

As a final adieu, Darlan sent off one more secret message to Vichy: "*Affections à tous.*"

The secret line was then destroyed by a naval technician.

French North Africa was officially severed from the mother country. Darlan was on his own. Assuming the role of Chief of State—in lieu of the marshal, who was considered "impeded"—and the title of High Commissioner, Darlan proclaimed the news to the people of North Africa in a masterpiece of sophistication. Pétain, said Darlan, no longer being free, the Germans could force from him declarations which in his heart the old marshal repudiated. Warning that Pétain would "publicly disavow me and condemn me for my action," Darlan insisted the marshal would be doing so only out of patriotism, to lighten the burden of the German occupation. "It is a game," said Darlan, "which must be repulsive to our chief, whose conscience is all clarity."

In Gibraltar, Eisenhower received from General Bedell Smith a signal to the effect that while there was no objection to the deal with Darlan from the United States, it was being coldly received in the British capital.

Eisenhower, explaining his acceptance of Darlan, cabled Washington: "Existing French sentiment in North Africa does not remotely resemble prior calculations and it is of utmost importance that no precipitate action be taken which will upset such equilibrium as we have been able to establish. . . . The name of Marshal Pétain is something to conjure with in North Africa. From the highest to the lowest everyone attempts to create the impression that the shadow of the marshal's figure dominates all his actions and, in fact, his very life."

But despite his full powers, and his agreement with Giraud, Darlan moved very cautiously.

All that was given out to the public was his proclamation, which the papers were obliged to run as received, to the effect that Noguès had passed to Darlan the powers he had received from Pétain, and that this invested Darlan with full responsibility for French interests in Africa. As might be expected, it ended: *"Vive le maréchal."*

On the 14th Darlan's police seized the entire issue of the local magazine *TAM* merely because it carried a picture of Giraud, whose appointment as chief of the armed forces Darlan wished to keep secret at least until the 16th, so as to give Bergeret time to see Boisson in West Africa.

This was another trump up Darlan's sleeve.

For years President Roosevelt and the Chiefs of Staff had been worried about the possibility of Dakar's falling into enemy hands, with its potential submarine base on the Atlantic.

Were Darlan to obtain for the Americans this important naval and air base (which could shorten the bomber ferry route by a third), not only would Darlan deal a severe blow to de Gaulle, who had failed to deliver the territory, but it might well counterbalance Darlan's unsavory political past in American eyes.

As a clue to what was going on in Darlan's mind, his notes for the 14th are revealing. "Order," noted Darlan, "and discipline must be maintained in the interior of the empire. The struggle of parties must be suspended. When the Axis is beaten the population of France and its empire will provide the political regime and chiefs of its choice."

To secure his immediate position, Darlan quickly saw to it that as many key positions as possible were given to reliable Vichy personnel, and that the SOL and PPF were allowed openly to reorganize. In Morocco they were organized into shock troops like

Nazi SA. Instead of tearing down the portraits of Pétain with which Algeria was plastered, similar (but smaller) portraits of Darlan appeared alongside those of the marshal.

As for the Gaullists, the simplest and most expeditious way of disposing of such rivals in Algeria was to put them in jail, at the same time imposing an absolute censorship on the very name de Gaulle.

With some 400 censors, and a completely controlled press, and with the police-state laws of Vichy (which allowed for the tapping of phones, both French and Allied), Darlan could block *all* political news.

But to insure his control, Darlan needed one more thing: an inside track to the Americans. As he did not yet dare to count on himself for this role, he resolved on the next-best move—to incorporate in his government those who were clearly closest to the Americans: the Five.

But the Five appeared undecided. Lemaigre thought it best to abstain from the whole affair. The others felt it would be better, so long as they could not manipulate their puppet Giraud, to control what they could.

So Darlan sent around Fenard with the message: "Please don't sulk. Come along with us." His counsel prevailed. At 10 A.M. Sunday, November 15th, the Five—with the exception of Van Ecke—were lined up before the admiral, who, hands behind his back, appeared to pass them in review, looking at them curiously.

For the details of this scene there are the notes of Saint-Hardouin.

Darlan, says the diplomat, congratulated the Five on their good work, then intimated that it had merely paralleled his own efforts.

Kammerer, who also reported on the scene, says that though Darlan displayed a great deal of bonhomie, he did not bear up well, was vacillating, as if at bay, constantly puffing on his empty pipe and giving the impression of a weak personality, which caused "a general letdown among the Five."

Darlan's first attack was directed at de Gaulle and de Gaullism, for which, says Saint-Hardouin, "he is full of hatred." But Darlan then went on to say that he was happy with the turn of events which had brought about what he had always dreamed of and even foreseen.

For a long time, so the admiral confided to Saint-Hardouin, he had been informed of their activities and it was thanks to his efforts that their clandestine conspiracy, on which he was informed in detail, had gone unmolested.

But now they must move with caution. Before naming collaborators in his new government Darlan said he wished to await the return of General Bergeret from West Africa, expected the following day.

Once this was done, he counted on having the aid of the Five.

Once the conference was ended, Admiral Fenard worked out with the Five the composition of Darlan's Cabinet, in which Fenard was to reserve for himself the key spot of Economic Affairs.

For the moment the announced members of Darlan's Cabinet were to be Saint-Hardouin at Foreign Affairs and Rigault as Minister of the Interior, also in charge of information, with, as his chief of all the police for North Africa, Henri d'Astier de la Vigerie. Bergeret was to act as deputy to Darlan.

The deal concluded, a dinner was arranged to seal the accord.

That night at Dar Mahieddine, which was all lit up for the occasion, Darlan, flanked by Fenard and Battet, came to dine with Giraud and the Five in the presence of Murphy.

Lemaigre, says an eyewitness, was an indulgent host. Champagne flowed, and Darlan, says Saint-Hardouin, "was very gay, very cordial, and *très commun*."

But the conspirators could hardly have been expected to stomach giving up all they had gained with their champion Giraud.

As Admiral Docteur was to put it, "Having put d'Astier and Rigault at the heads of the police forces of North Africa, Darlan established around himself the very net which was one day to strangle him."

As for Lemaigre—who still seemed to prefer anonymity—now that his "man Friday" was strategically placed in the key position of Minister of the Interior, and that Saint-Hardouin was in Foreign Affairs, he felt safe enough to proceed with the next and more advanced step in the conspiracy. He prepared to attack the citadels of actual power—in New York and Washington. To accomplish this maneuver he had himself put in charge of a diplomatic mission to America: he would thus be able to deal not only with key figures in the business and financial world, but directly with Murphy's superiors, Secretary Hull and President Roosevelt.

A clue to what Lemaigre intended to do in America can be obtained by a careful scrutiny of the members appointed to the economic section of Darlan's government, which was one of the best-kept secrets in North Africa.

The mere fact that Darlan placed his "Economic and General Secretariat" above the other two bureaus of Foreign and Political Affairs, was indicative of its prime importance.

So little known was the man who was to become Director General for Economics that few had ever heard of M. Alfred Pose. In the events that followed he was to play a significant role.

10

ON NOVEMBER 17th President Roosevelt made an announcement calling Darlan a "temporary expedient" who would soon have to go. It was a broadside which badly hurt the admiral's position.

According to Robert Sherwood, in Washington, the storm of criticism over the Darlan deal "had reached such proportions that Hopkins, Rosenman and I strongly urged the President to issue a statement to the press."

This the President did, making "even stronger and tougher" the language of a draft prepared by Elmer Davis and Archibald Mac-Leish.

In his statement the President made it clear that he had accepted Eisenhower's political arrangement "only for the time being" but that "in view of the history of the past two years, no permanent arrangement should be made with Darlan."

The President then qualified the arrangement as "justified solely by the stress of battle."

In both Algeria and Morocco the President's declaration was strictly censored by Rigault. No newspaper was allowed to carry it, and the BBC was jammed; as a result, the main distribution Roosevelt's words received in Africa was from the Free French Station at Brazzaville—such a thorn in the flesh of Boisson that in return for his subservience to Eisenhower he specifically insisted it be cut off the air!

Darlan expressed his resentment at being labeled a "temporary expedient" by coining an equally catchy phrase with which to rebut the Allies: he said they planned to use him and discard him "like a squeezed lemon."

Pretending to do whatever the Allies requested, Darlan set about consolidating his position, instituted an even severer censorship, and began concentrating on building up a strong personal army at Allied expense.

When stories in the conservative London dailies revealed that "in French Morocco, a new army is being formed by Admiral Darlan that will have as its basis men who until now have been training in Pétainist youth camps and are well inculcated with Fascist tendencies and doctrines, plus Axis sympathies," Darlan insisted that his censorship be extended to cover Allied correspondents.

His technique for imposing such a censorship on AFHQ was described by John MacVane of NBC who quoted the admiral as saying to an American official, "I have four hundred censors who control press, radio, telegraphs, telephones and the mail. I can manage them for you. But if we disagreed and I resigned I would take my four hundred censors with me, and what could you do? You couldn't replace them. Your military secrets would be secrets no longer. All security censorship would become chaos. But you need have no fear. I have no intention of resigning."

In his basic accord with the Allies—which was to be formalized in Algiers November 22 between Darlan and Clark—a co-censorship clause was written into the agreement, giving Darlan what he wanted. But though the Allies recognized that Darlan, as the High

Commissioner in French Africa, would be responsible for "maintaining order," the admiral was obliged to give way to Clark on several of the other twenty articles of the accord—at least on paper.

To an alarmed Lemaigre it looked as if Darlan had abrogated a great deal of what the Five had painfully achieved with the Murphy-Giraud agreements. There was no longer any question of the French holding the supreme command; they were not even considered as full-fledged Allies.

To the Five it looked as if Darlan had abandoned a great deal of the French sovereignty they had so carefully protected with Murphy.

In France the astonishing agreement between the Allies and Darlan inspired the cynical comment: "A fine thing when you can't trust even your own traitors!"

Quietly, Lemaigre set about putting things straight. According to Saint-Hardouin, Lemaigre went to see Giraud and issued him an ultimatum: either he prepared a secret civilian cabinet ready to succeed the admiral, or the Five would no longer support him. Reluctantly Giraud agreed.

Noting this undercurrent of activity, an observant Gaullist, René Capitant, editor of the clandestine newspaper *Combat,* warned that Darlan was sailing into troubled waters. In a prophetic article dated November 23, Capitant was to speculate on who could replace the admiral at the helm: "Apart from Giraud, who claims he does not want the job, could it be Peyrouton . . . or the Count of Paris?" Capitant then wrapped up the subject to his own satisfaction: "It is a question of finding another Clemenceau. Luckily he exists. His name is Charles de Gaulle."

That same day, November 23rd, Eisenhower flew in to Algiers, with the rear of AFHQ, less preoccupied with the political situation than with the military one in Tunisia, on which, after all, his career depended.

With him came his worst enemy: winter. Shivering—for there were only a few small fireplaces to heat the Saint-Georges—he set up his headquarters in three bedrooms and a parlor.

There now came an even worse blow to Darlan's position: On November 27th the Toulon fleet scuttled itself.

At midnight the Germans reached the port and attacked. While French sailors resisted with small arms and machine guns, special crews set about destroying every vessel in the harbor. By dawn 73 ships had gone to the bottom, including several modern battleships, many with their captains and part of their crews, and the harbor was covered with a pall of smoke visible thirty miles.

"Ike," says Butcher, "took it calmly, trying to foresee just what it would mean, immediately appraised it as beneficial so far as keeping the scuttled units from the Germans, but wondered why in the world the French naval officers haven't responded to the call to join the Allies immediately after D-day."

It did not seem to strike Eisenhower that his and Patton's attitude at the time of the landings, when they had sunk 13 French ships and killed more than 1,000 sailors, might have its influence on a French navy already embittered against the Allies by the British slaughter at Mers-el-Kébir.

Darlan, less squeamish about the past, quickly attempted to take credit for the scuttling by writing to President Roosevelt: "I have always declared since June 1940 that the fleet was to remain French or perish." And to Churchill: "The willing destruction of the fleet in Toulon now proves I was right; though I am no longer its chief, the fleet executed the orders I gave it, despite the wishes of the government of M. Laval."

But the loss to the Allies of the fourth most powerful fleet in the world looked more like a defeat than a victory for Darlan. At least it did to the Germans.*

All along, the American objective had been to get the fleet to come over to our side. There was evidence that its sailors would not have fought with the Germans, and evidence that the Germans did not have the requisite personnel to man the ships themselves. Had the ships joined the Allies, they would have constituted a real threat to the Axis in the Mediterranean.

---

* Italy's Army Chief of Staff, General Mario Roatta, who was present at the Brenner Pass meeting between Hitler and Mussolini at the moment of France's collapse, quotes Hitler as saying of the French fleet: "The very best possible solution would be for the French to sink it. The worst: that it join the British."

In any case, Darlan was now Admiral of the Fleet in name only. Admiral Jean de Laborde, who commanded the Toulon squadron, and was known as an Anglophobe, had even wanted to bring out the fleet not with but against the Allies, and had answered Darlan's plea to join the Allies with the one word *"Merde."*

Vichy took away Darlan's French citizenship and exposed him as a profiteer, revealing that 500 pounds of strictly rationed coffee and 800 pounds of even harder-to-get sugar had been found in his house along with a large number of hams and seventeen admiral's uniforms.*

On November 30th, in a desperate attempt to consolidate what was left of his position, and without breathing a word of it to the Allies, Darlan summoned Noguès, Boisson, Chatel, Bergeret and Giraud to form an Imperial Council with which to rule all of French Africa by decree.

On December 2nd Darlan allowed an announcement of the formation of the Council to be printed in the local papers, but veiled the real significance of the measure.

In the House of Commons when members demanded an explanation from Eden, he described Darlan's action as "the unilateral inspiration of himself," and as "binding the British government in no way."

From the United States Chief of Staff in Washington Eisenhower received a long message conveying Secretary Hull's wish that civil matters in North Africa be turned over to the State Department as soon as military operations permitted.

But before he could even start to comply, Eisenhower received a blow to his own plans as severe as the one sustained by Darlan. The attack mounted by General Anderson with the objective of throwing the Germans out of Tunisia by Christmas was unexpectedly smashed by the enemy: it was a rebuff which rendered the political situation in North Africa all the more difficult.

* Hubert Cole has reported that Darlan was so avid for luxury and display that his personal train, equipped with two bathrooms, was the most well-appointed in Vichy and that a twenty-four-piece naval orchestra accompanied him everywhere on his journeys.

PART THREE

TUNISIA

AND MOROCCO

11

IN TUNISIA at 2 A.M. of November 8th, United States Consul General Hooker A. Doolittle had called on the French Governor General, Admiral Jean Pierre Esteva, at his shiny white residence in the moonlit city of Tunis.

Despite the late hour, this white-bearded old man in his seventies —a highly decorated appointee of Darlan's who had been chief of French naval forces in the Mediterranean at the opening of World War II—received the United States emissary dressed in full uniform, but still wearing his Arab bedroom slippers.

Doolittle presented the admiral with a message from President Roosevelt, much like the others of that night, asking for free passage of American forces through Tunisia.

Having carefully read it, Esteva answered officially that he would refer it to his government, but that in the meantime he must execute his standing orders from Vichy to resist any attack.

With a change of tone he asked, "Out of curiosity, where have the landings taken place?"

"Er . . ." said Doolittle, "everywhere: in Morocco, Algeria, and Tunisia."

"Not in Tunisia," said Esteva. "I would have been informed. The nearest port is Bône. How long will it take your forces to reach here?"

Unable to answer (indeed Eisenhower would have been hard put to do so), Doolittle temporized by saying, "They may well be on their way, right now."

"In that case," replied Esteva, "they had better hurry up; because the others will be here within forty-eight hours."

Everyone in Tunisia, says Kammerer, was in a mood to resist the Germans: not only General Barré in command of the armed forces, even old Esteva himself. But what they needed was some sort of order from above.

All through Sunday the 8th nothing happened. In Tunisia they received no further orders other than to defend themselves against attack. But no one was attacking.

On the morning of the 9th at 7 A.M. Admiral Esteva summoned Barré to the Residence and without a word of comment showed him a message phoned to him via Admiral Derrien who held the naval base at Bizerte. It was from Darlan in Algiers.

"The Americans," said Darlan, "having attacked us first, are the aggressors, and we must fight them, alone or assisted."

The existence of this message, unknown to the Allies, might have changed their attitude toward Darlan.

All that morning, while in Algiers Ryder was impatiently waiting for Clark, in Tunisia the French were equally anxiously looking for the arrival off Bizerte of an Allied force which could have seized the port without a shot, or for land forces to appear, equally uncontested, across the Tunisian border.

Instead, at 12:30 P.M. German planes began to circle the Tunis airfield of El Aouina, coming in for a landing.

Barré, who had the airfield dominated by French troops and light artillery, could have destroyed the Germans with ease.

Instead, he asked their commanding officer, Colonel Fiedler, "Was it not agreed that no German plane would present itself without higher authorization?"

Calmly the German produced a copy of the order which Esteva had received from Darlan that morning. The original had been issued by Laval.

Blocked by both Laval and Darlan, Barré felt himself obliged to take no offensive action while the German planes continued to arrive.

By 3 P.M. they were 25; an hour later they were 60; by evening 100. Bivouacked beside the airfield, the troops "sang their sad songs, then fell asleep along the seashore" an arrow's shot from the ancient walls of Carthage.

When Darlan finally capitulated to Clark, it was almost noon of the 10th, and Darlan's orders to Barré did not go out for several hours.

By the evening of the 10th 150 heavy German troop carriers had landed with reinforcements of artillery. Using giant Bloehm and Voss three-motored hydroplanes, the Germans were able to land as many as 80 fully equipped infantrymen at a time.

Hitler had decided on a full-scale effort to hold a beachhead in North Africa. Laval had given the necessary orders; Darlan would not oppose them.

By the morning of the 11th, his forces too weak to cope with the Germans, Barré decided to move away toward a defensive position in the hills in the direction of Algeria.

Meanwhile Admiral Derrien, with his naval units in Bizerte harbor, and his coastal guns trained out to sea, was still hoping that an Allied fleet would turn up.

All through the 10th he saw neither Allies nor Germans.

Then came the cease-fire orders from Darlan. Derrien was to oppose any Axis attempt at a naval landing, but be neutral toward Axis aircraft unless they acted in a hostile manner.

So far not a shot had been fired by either Frenchman or German. Their respective forces merely skirted each other "like a couple of mastiffs."

Then came the dreadful turnabout when Pétain disavowed Darlan. The news was soon known in Tunisia, where orders arrived from Vichy to support the Axis and resist the Allies.

Yet Darlan could not inform them in Tunisia by radio or phone that he had secret orders from Pétain.

Juin made a desperate personal attempt to break the impasse on the afternoon of the 11th by phoning to Derrien. This was enough for Derrien to launch a proclamation to his forces that the moment had come to fight the Germans. But when Juin's order was overruled by Koeltz and Mendigal pending the arrival in Algiers of Noguès, due the afternoon of the 12th, Derrien was obliged quickly to rescind his proclamation in favor of a strict neutrality.

At noon on the 12th two Axis freighters, protected by five destroyers, appeared off Bizerte harbor.

Forbidden by all his superiors to open fire on the Germans, and not wanting to be considered a rebel, Derrien, who may have wanted nothing more than to attack the Germans, stood by and watched a whole German battalion, followed by an Italian battalion, land on his moles with all sorts of heavy equipment including tanks—thus earning for himself the sobriquet "*l'amiral de rien-du-tout.*"

Vainly Auphan wired from Vichy to convey him a hint. "Follow Noguès. He has the marshal's confidence."

When Derrien urgently phoned Algiers, he was told that Noguès had arrived but "was in conference and could give no orders."

Noguès was just then arguing with Clark about a period of neutrality before the French could join the Allies.

When, later that night, Juin finally put through an order to shoot at the Germans, it was to arrive too late. "Fight now?" answered Derrien. "How can I? My coastal batteries will not fire inland. The Germans and Italians are entrenched behind me!"

He was not only outflanked but outnumbered, and the Germans controlled his port. What had been isolated Axis units on the 9th and 10th were now a well-established and coordinated bridgehead, constantly being reinforced by sea and air.

As for Barré, he kept edging away from the Germans as their

numbers increased. When the order from Juin finally arrived on the night of the 12th, Barré was in the very worst possible conditions, his poorly armed troops spread out and on the move from one position to the next, an easy prey for the heavily armed and strongly concentrated Germans.

Barré therefore continued to retreat toward the high ground west of Tunis.

For Derrien in Bizerte it was the end.

Once the Germans had encircled his naval forces, they issued him one of the most brutal ultimatums of the war. He was given precisely thirty minutes in which to deliver to the Germans his forces, including all the French warships in Bizerte naval base. Failing to do so, or in any way sabotaging them, Derrien and all his forces were to be treated as outlaws and shot to the last man.

Trapped, Derrien gave in; for this surrender he was later to suffer a humiliating court-martial.

Barré was luckier.

Falling back toward the Algerian border, he did not feel himself strong enough to implement Juin's order to attack the Germans first. With some 9,000 troops he had approximately 125 kilometers of front to hold. But while he reorganized his forces he was able to sneak out from under the noses of the Germans' 147 train locomotives and 2,500 freight cars, leaving the Germans nothing but some dilapidated rolling stock. He also managed to save about 300 trucks.

His weapons were nothing but the antiquated ones "almost of Napoleonic vintage" he had been able to hide from the German armistice commission, now dug up from their caches: altogether about 250 machine guns, 400 automatic rifles and half a dozen 47-mm artillery pieces.

General Pequin, head of the Tunisian air force, got out of a hospital bed to join Barré and managed to salvage 75 ancient French planes, useful mostly as trainers.

On November 17, after sending Barré a telegram—"All united in our love for France and the marshal. We have only one mission: Victory"—Giraud set off with Juin for a quick tour of this Tunisian front. "Hold on three or four days," Giraud exhorted the troops. "Then you will be taken back, armed and instructed. You will then be better equipped than the enemy."

"On this fable," says Chamine, "with which Giraud himself was duped," the French were to protect a slow Allied concentration not for four days but for a good four months "with not much more than their bare bodies—of which they were to sacrifice all of 8,000."

Allied forces, "which had been immobilized by the political situation," now began to trickle forward.

On November 19th, the German commander in Tunisia, General Walter Nehring, worried at Barré's withdrawal, sent an ultimatum. Barré rejected it.

Just before noon on the 19th, in the fields of asphodel along a eucalyptus-lined road beside a small silvery stream not far from an olive-covered ridge which was to become famous as Long Stop, Barré at last fought the Germans.

A few Britishers joined in but had to retire on the 20th for lack of ammunition. The first really serious fighting did not come till the 22nd, the day before Eisenhower arrived in Algiers.

By November 25th the British 78th Division managed to launch one of its brigades toward Bizerte and the other toward Tunis. After four days the Allies were at Mateur and Djeideïda, a mere 20 kilometers from their objective. But two days later weak infantry, feeble artillery, and inferiority in the air (our bases were 300 miles from the front) allowed the Germans to counterattack and throw the Allies all the way back to their starting line. The weather turned atrocious. Rain reduced the dirty roads to mud ponds; cannons could barely be dragged by mules. More Germans poured into Tunisia.

On December 6th, while shaving, Eisenhower reported to Butcher that we might have to retreat.

General Anderson reported that because of reverses, the major attack planned for December 9th was now out of the question.

As Butcher described him, Eisenhower was "like a caged tiger, snarling and clawing to get things done."

But if Tunisia was a disaster, Morocco was even more depressing. There the conspirators' plans had all been based on the premise of action *late* in November; and it was not until after the Cherchel meeting, and Giraud's agreement in principle, that Rigault decided at the beginning of November to deliver Giraud's message to the Moroccan army personnel siding with the plotters. The military posts he had to visit were several hundred miles apart. To cover them, Rigault needed a car; but he was afraid of using an official one provided by the Americans lest it attract too much attention.

Kenneth Pendar, who had originally been posted in Morocco and had left his private car there, offered to chauffeur Rigault on this dangerous tour.

Murphy agreed; Pendar was to fly to Morocco to meet Rigault on November 2nd. This was the very day Murphy had been allowed by higher authority to inform Giraud that D day was for the morning of the 8th.

That morning, when Murphy joined Pendar for an early Monday breakfast at Cole's house where they were both staying, Murphy seemed "under such tension beneath his calm and pleasant exterior" that Pendar blurted out, "Bob, am I wrong when I believe our landings will take place toward the end of November?"

Murphy nodded.

After several more queries—which Murphy answered by nods or shakes of the head—Pendar established that "the landing would come the following Saturday night: at 1 A.M. in Algiers and Oran, and at 4 A.M. in Morocco: at Safi, Fedala and Port Lyautey."

In Casablanca Pendar found everyone in a state of intense activity trying to perfect a secret radio link with Tangier and Gibraltar, to be used for communicating with the Allied fleet; but no one yet knew the actual date of the landings.

Rigault had worked out a plan with General Béthouart, who commanded the Casablanca Division, to help the Allies ashore, much like the plan devised by General Mast in Algiers. The plotters were to neutralize the commander of the army, General Georges Lascroux, the commander of the air force, General Lahoulle, and the theater commander, General Noguès, so that only Béthouart's orders to the French to aid the Allies would then be followed. To avoid a conflict with Vichy naval units based in Morocco, resistance forces were to neutralize the Casablanca naval base by cutting it off from the rear. As in Algiers, they would occupy the radio and the phone central, and paralyze Vichy reaction.

Two hours before H hour of D day, Béthouart would encircle the high command at Rabat and neutralize the Resident General, Noguès.

To Pendar, sitting in the white building which housed the American Consulate, it was excruciating to listen to these plans and know they would be aborted by a change in the Allied schedule.

The next day, as he and Rigault set off on the first leg of their journey to Marrakech, where Rigault was to attempt to bring over —by means of a letter from Giraud—the local commander, General Henri Martin, Pendar was in such mental anguish, wondering whether it was more dangerous to break security or risk having the Americans land without assistance, that he finally decided it would be safer for Rigault to know the exact date, and turned to him: "I'm afraid you will have to change your plans with Béthouart and the other generals. The landing in Morocco is scheduled for the early morning of November 8."

"*Et vous pensez qu'il valait mieux me le dire?*" answered Rigault.

As in every crisis they had been through, says Pendar, Rigault revealed no emotion. This time he simply asked Pendar to stop the car, got out and stretched, "as if he had to let his emotions come out somehow," then climbed back in muttering, "*Ce chameau, Bob.*" Then he smiled. "Why didn't he tell me? This changes everything."

Suddenly he looked grave. "*Mon dieu!* My wife will be caught in France."

Pendar suggested he arrange for a third person to telegraph her to take an earlier boat, but Rigault replied, "No, I'll never do that—the risk is too great. I am certainly suspect, and she, as my wife, may be too. She knows the risks involved and will certainly understand."

Rigault, says Pendar, was not being melodramatic. Just before they left Casablanca, a member of the intelligence bureau of the French Army had warned Rigault that the Germans knew of his presence in Morocco, and members of the Vichy police had been sent out to arrest him.

Yet Rigault was the only person who could accomplish the job at hand; he was the only one who knew the various top members of the conspiracy. "All the sections," he explained to Pendar, "act independently. The civilians do not know the military, and vice versa. I am the only one who can put all the pieces together. To do so I would need at least ten days. We have three. It will be a nice mess. Don't be surprised if you Americans get yourselves shot at."

At Marrakech Rigault handed Giraud's letter to General Henri Martin, and hinted that the Americans might one day be arriving. Would he open his airfields to them and take care of the German armistice commission?

Presuming the other generals were already in on the plot, but as anxious as any of his colleagues to act only within the framework of legality, Henri Martin asked if the orders would come from the Residence.

"*En principe,* yes," answered Rigault. "Though circumstances may necessitate some other channel of communication."

"Then how will I be warned?"

"You will be signaled either by the Residence or by the headquarters of General Béthouart."

By now it was midnight between the 3rd and 4th of November.

Coming out of the interview, Rigault climbed into Pendar's car and they headed back for Casablanca.

There, at 10 P.M. on the 4th, Rigault had a long conference with Béthouart at his divisional headquarters in the presence of his chief of staff, Colonel Eugène Molle, and several other officers.

Back at the American Consulate Rigault outlined Béthouart's new project to Vice-Consul David W. King. Béthouart strongly recommended that the Americans avoid any frontal attack on the heavily fortified towns of Casablanca, Fedala and Port Lyautey, where naval guns on ship and shore were bound to fire back at the Americans. Béthouart suggested instead that they land at such safe spots as Rabat, Salé, Mazagan and Safi where the Americans could be helped ashore by Béthouart's forces.

Most important, said Rigault, was to avoid an immediate conflict with the Navy. If, while American forces were landing north and south of Casablanca, American escort vessels were to stay well out to sea in front of Casablanca and Fedala and make no hostile move, the conspirators would make a direct approach to Admiral Michelier, in charge of the Vichy Navy, inform him of the Murphy-Giraud agreements, and try to persuade him not to fire on the Americans.

By encircling Casablanca and the other strong points the conspirators and the Americans could not only take the Navy from the rear but prevent them from being reinforced by troops from winter garrisons in the interior.

Meanwhile Béthouart would go personally to Rabat to talk to Noguès, then proceed to the coast near Rabat to wait for the American commander to take over.

It was an excellent program, providing they could get the Americans to coordinate with it.

At the Consulate Rigault drafted a long cable for Gibraltar, which Pendar translated into English, to be forwarded to the commander of the fleet at sea, requesting the Americans to acknowledge the French plan and urging them to radio any suggestions for modification.

"Unfortunately," says Pendar, "this vital information was never acted upon by the Americans," adding that perhaps it was never received.

True, there was some unfortunate difficulty with the Casablanca secret radio which operated from a roof near the port, due to what the U.S. Army historian calls "unwillingness of the operator in Gibraltar to adopt procedures which the operator at Casablanca deemed necessary in the light of experience"; all of which rendered the contact imperfect, especially at night.

But searching through the official files after the war, the historian was able to find the actual message slugged "King to Eddy in Gibraltar," dated November 5, 1942. It was also received by the fleet.

Once the radiogram had been sent, there was nothing more for Rigault and Pendar to do in Casablanca; still without sleep, they set off at 4 A.M. on November 5th, for a 1,300-kilometer drive back to Algiers via Rabat, Fez, Taza, Oujda and Oran where they had other conspirators to alert.

Early in the morning of November 6th Pendar finally arrived back in Algiers. That same day in Casablanca, Béthouart was informed that H hour was set for 2 A.M. of the 8th. He begged King for more details. King knew of none, other than that the invasion "was to take place simultaneously on the beaches and all the major ports."

"*Invraisemblable,*" commented Béthouart.

With still no precise information as to where the Allies would land, or how, he decided to go ahead with the plan he had radioed to the Americans, hoping they would comply.

His most difficult problem was to decide whether to warn individual local commanders *in advance* (and risk having them request confirmation from the higher command in Rabat) or wait till the very last minute.

With clear orders from Giraud and Rigault, Béthouart decided on a compromise. He would wait till the very last minute to try to convince Noguès, Lascroux and Lahoulle, having first done everything in his power to reduce them to impotence, in case they declined to go along.

Colonel Pierre Magnan, in command of Béthouart's Moroccan Regiment of Colonial Infantry, agreed to deploy his battalions along the coast at Rabat and Mazagan to help the Allies ashore. The Rabat battalion was given orders to encircle the Residence and headquarters of the Moroccan high command. General Raymond Desré, commanding the local subdivision, agreed to hold Casablanca while Béthouart went to neutralize Noguès.

To deal with the French Navy, Béthouart assigned his chief of staff, Colonel Molle, who was to call on Admiral Michelier and explain the situation.

Béthouart had already prepared letters for both Noguès and Michelier. To be sure that the letter for Noguès would be delivered to him in person, Béthouart assigned the job to his adjutant, a nephew of Noguès, who, as a member of the family, could obtain entry to the Residence even at that late hour.

At 11 P.M. on the night of the 7th, in a sudden downpour of rain, Béthouart got into his car at Casablanca and drove the 80 miles to Rabat. There he found that Magnan's forces had surrounded the Residence.

Noguès's nephew had succeeded admirably in his mission; Noguès, his trim figure neatly corseted, studied the letter and the documents which were intended to substantiate Béthouart's claim that the Americans were landing in Morocco. For a moment the result hung by a thread.

Everyone agrees that had Noguès been *convinced* the Americans were actually out at sea, and in great strength, he would have rallied. But because the Allies had left Béthouart too little time, the documents did not have the proper seals or the signature of Giraud, and this puzzled Noguès.

At the very same moment, in Casablanca harbor, Colonel Molle had presented himself at the Admiralty and managed without much difficulty to obtain entrance to Michelier's headquarters.

Michelier also glanced at the letter and the documents, which explained that the Americans were coming to support Giraud because the Germans had invaded Tunisia.

Michelier, described as "cold and level-headed and approachable only with incontestable facts and precise figures," was also dubious. He decided to check with Noguès.

Noguès said that he too doubted the authenticity of the documents. "Do you think," he asked "that a large American landing is imminent?"

"According to what I hear from Vichy," replied Michelier, "and from my coastguardsmen, there is absolutely nothing to report."

Ironically, a signal had been sent to Michelier from the Admiralty in Vichy at 9:15 that night, warning him of possible Allied landings in North Africa; but it had been received at Casablanca only at 12:15 A.M. of the 8th and its decoding was delayed by later events, so that it served no purpose.

Furthermore, it was a pitch-black night, pouring with rain. For lack of fuel Michelier had been unable for some time to send night patrols out at sea. Nor could he send out a plane before dawn.

To Michelier, the whole idea of a large Allied landing in Morocco in November, when the sea was only likely to be calm one day out of seven, appeared out of the question. The most the Allies might attempt would be a commando raid in conjunction with a Gaullist uprising: exactly what he and Noguès most dreaded, since it would give the Germans an excuse to occupy Morocco.

So Michelier agreed to act to relieve Noguès at the Residence; and fearing a *coup* might also be aimed at his own command, he ordered the Admiralty secured against attack from land. Still not believing there was anything to worry about at sea, he failed to order his ships to raise steam. Turning to Molle, he chided him for being *naïf*. "You are nothing but children. There are no ships at sea. You've been duped, most probably by the Gestapo, who want an excuse to occupy Morocco."

Meanwhile in Rabat, Béthouart, who was in control of the situation to the extent that he had Nougès surrounded, sent out orders to all the coastal defenses other than naval, telling them not to fire on the Americans, but to welcome them ashore.

Béthouart could now only hope that the Americans would land where he had suggested.

But the Americans, without even informing their own representatives in Morocco, let alone Béthouart and his conspirators, had changed H hour from 2 to 4 A.M., a delay which was to be extended by bungling.

From behind the blinds in their Consulate in Casablanca the American staff, reduced to helplessness, could observe truckloads of Vichy soldiers, "a stream of little Citroëns, and motorcycles and bicycles, hastening through the city toward the port and coastal batteries."

As time passed to 5 A.M. and there was no news of American landings, even Béthouart began to have doubts. Both Noguès and Michelier assured Béthouart that there was no sign whatsoever of any Americans at sea.

Unwilling to unleash a fratricidal civil war, Béthouart ordered his battalion to return to its quarters and gave himself up to Noguès.

Noguès issued orders to repel any possible landings and began to move troops toward the coast from their winter positions in the interior.

In Casablanca, Colonel Desré, who had stood in for Béthouart in command of his division, now got cold feet. When ordered by General Lascroux—once more in command of Morocco's 60,000 land forces—to prepare to defend himself against possible landings, he abandoned Béthouart and protested his allegiance to Vichy. Summoning his officers, Desré addressed them: "Gentlemen. We had a lovely dream. Now we must forget it."

Thus, during the very hour before the Allies were to land (and an hour after they could have been safely ashore), the entire situation was reversed, in many cases to the tragic despair of local subordinate commanders, who were now obliged by their superiors to prepare to fire on their Allies.

In the absolute darkness of November 7 a huge convoy of troopships and cargos, flanked by 40 destroyers, guarded by the battleships *Texas* and *New York* and the aircraft carrier *Ranger,* split into three separate forces and took up their positions before Safi at 11:45, before Fedala at 11:53 and before the mouth of the Sebou River by Port Lyautey at precisely midnight.

During the 4,500-mile crossing of the submarine-infested Atlantic, no one had spotted them.

Aboard the armada's flagship, the cruiser *Augusta,* a West Point classmate of Eisenhower's, Lieutenant General George C. Patton, Jr., in command of all the landing forces, announced in an odd falsetto, "Never in history has the Navy landed an army at the planned time and place. If you land us anywhere within 50 miles of Fedala and within one week of D day, I'll go ahead and win. We shall attack for sixty days, and then, if we have to, for sixty more. If we go forward with desperation, if we go forward with utmost speed and fight, these people cannot stand against us."

More dangerous even than Patton's Army/Navy rivalry was his intention to disregard the orders of the United States Chief of Staff, General George C. Marshall, whose directive, approved by the President (as well as by Churchill and his staff), was that: "No offensive action is to be taken against French forces unless they first take definite hostile action against us."*

To Patton this was nonsense. He had even intended, if the circumstances were advantageous, to go ahead and attack Casablanca on D minus 1, giving an ultimatum to the "governor of Casablanca" saying "I will accept his surrender and give him all honors of war and parole his troops; or . . . I will bombard him from the sea, bomb him from the air, and attack him on the ground."

"It is my belief," added Patton, "this bluff will work."

The folly of such a move is curtly disposed of by Samuel Eliot Morison in his *History of United States Naval Operations in World War II:* "Casablanca was so well defended that any attempt to seize the harbor by a surprise attack would have been suicidal."

As it was, Patton's inefficiency caused his three-pronged attack to be fatally delayed.

The objective of the southernmost attack group was to seize the small port of Safi, 140 miles south of Casablanca, where General Ernest N. Harmon could place his tanks directly onto the docks, along with 6,500 United States troops.

The objective of the most northerly attack group, 250 miles up

---

* To make sure that even Patton could understand this order it was followed by the comment: "Action contrary to this spirit may have repercussions far-reaching in their effect. Every precaution is to be taken to avoid unnecessary damage to ships and harbor installations." This was further spelled out in unequivocal language. "1. The French must be permitted to take the first hostile action. 2. A hostile act by an isolated unit should not necessarily be interpreted as indication that all units in that area have hostile intent. 3. Once resistance in any particular area ceases, Allied forces should abandon hostilities unless the French resume the operation."

the coast, was to land 9,000 soldiers at the mouth of Sebou River in order to take possession of Port Lyautey and its airport.

Meanwhile the center attack group, which was the main one, was to place about 19,000 United States soldiers on the beaches of Fedala, a small fishing town and beach resort 15 miles north of Casablanca, the principal objective.

As of 3:20 A.M., the French garrison in Safi at the southernmost point of attack received a warning to be prepared to resist enemy landings, but could see no immediate threat.

The last of the old moon—"a pale ghost gondola skimming the southern horizon," as Morison describes it—had long since set.

To the Americans, who were lowering their landing craft, the lights of Safi were clearly visible on the horizon. But out at sea everything was black, and the embarking operations were so fouled up and slowed down that H hour had to be postponed till 4:30.

Finally, at 4:38 Admiral Davison gave the signal "Play Ball" and the landing craft headed for shore. At 4:45 the first American troops landed in French Morocco and hastened along the mole of Safi's port.

An Offenbach touch was added to the scene by native Moroccans who gathered in awed crowds to observe the naval shelling, "disdainful of small arms fire."

"A soldier," reports the Army's historian, "would snake his way painfully through rock and rubble to set up a light machine gun, raise his head cautiously to aim, and find a dozen natives clustered solemnly around him. Street intersections were crowded with natives turning their heads like a tennis gallery in trying to watch the exchange of fire. The wounded were poked and jabbered at."

The French garrison resisted as best it could, but the Americans were quickly in possession of the harbor, the railroad station, the post office and the highways which entered the city from the south, just as Béthouart had suggested.

By 9 A.M. of the 10th Harmon had enough gasoline ashore to head his tanks northward for Casablanca, still 140 miles away.

Meanwhile the most northerly prong of the attack, which had for its objective the airfield at Port Lyautey, had run into considerably more trouble.

Arriving off the coast just before midnight, the transports could clearly see the lights ashore less than three miles away. But during the last stage of the approach the transports lost their formation, so H hour here also had to be postponed till 4:30.

The delay caused Béthouart's arrangements for silencing the coastal batteries on shore to fall through just as the Americans were ready to arrive.

Half an hour earlier they had authorization to help the Allies.

Instead, the battle was to become prolonged and complicated as the Americans were obliged to fight inland from the coast against some 3,000 French troops already in position, on easily defensible ground, protected by a swamp and a large curve in the shallow Sebou River, reinforced by mechanized cavalry with 45 tanks from Rabat.

To avoid a long-drawn-out and unnecessary slaughter, a gallant attempt was made by one of the few really able American military attachés of the prewar era, Colonel Delmas F. Craw, known as "Nick" to his friends.

In a jeep, flying a white flag of truce, and accompanied by Major Pierpont M. Hamilton, Colonel Craw headed toward the town of Port Lyautey to take a letter to the French commander from the American commander, Lieutenant General Lucien K. Truscott, similar in import to President Roosevelt's broadcast.

French troops directed them toward their headquarters; but at a fork in the road as they neared the town a Moroccan machine gunner opened up point-blank and killed Colonel Craw.

Major Hamilton was taken prisoner, and his mission was doomed, with the result that the Americans had to struggle four days to attain their objective. They had, of course, been warned in advance by Béthouart that any direct attack on Port Lyautey was likely to be easily contested.

Meanwhile the main American attack against Casablanca was being carried out by landings in and around the small fishing port of Fedala.

Just before midnight, through intermittent rain squalls, the center attack group arrived off its target. As they anchored 4 to 8 miles offshore they could watch the lights of Casablanca being extinguished. From Fedala, notes Morison, no light showed, but "a pungent smell of charcoal smoke floated out with the offshore breeze to suggest that land lay within striking distance."

Unfortunately an unexpected current carried the ships a few miles from their proper stations, causing the transport formation to become so badly deranged that H hour again had to be postponed.

In the pitch-darkness "many troops showed a natural repugnance to letting themselves down the nets," and "many fell and were drowned."

The guide boats, sent ahead, got tired of waiting and started back toward the transports just as their signals were most needed.

Finally, at 4:45, the landing craft started their first fifteen-minute run toward the beaches.

Some of the transports and landing craft had never even exercised at putting men ashore. Landing craft were generally assigned to fishermen or merchant seamen, but were seconded by young recruits some of whom "had now seen the sea for the very first time in their lives."

Faulty navigation brought the troops to widely scattered points. Some of the craft were swamped, others went on the rocks. By dawn 162 landing craft could be seen being battered against the beaches. According to Morison, "despite the perfect weather half were lost for lack of know-how," and "several soldiers were drowned in the landings simply because they were unable to regain their feet after being rolled over by a wave."

Luckily they ran into very light French opposition along the coast, which had been denuded with the arrival of winter.

But the effect of this disaster on the overall operation was serious. According to Admiral Hewitt, in command of the naval forces, "the damaging effect of such heavy losses on the build-up of troops and supplies ashore was felt throughout the operation. This misfortune was one of the factors which made swift investment of Casablanca impossible."

From nearby airfields the French could throw some 50 fighters and 30 bombers at the landing forces.

Also, the naval base at Casablanca, with its 2nd French Naval Squadron of submarines, destroyers, one heavy cruiser and the uncompleted battleship *Jean Bart,* was only 12 miles from the United States transports.

With the first glimmer of daylight, French coastal batteries opened up a few minutes after 6. By 6:10 United States destroyers at sea were firing back at them, followed by salvos from the cruiser *Brooklyn,* which appeared on the scene, "handsome," as Morison describes her, "as a bridal bouquet with her guns spouting orange bursts of flame."

In a bombardment lasting 85 minutes the *Brooklyn* fired 757 rounds of 6-inch shells, culminating at 7:42 in "two furious minutes of continuous rapid fire." Only subsequently was it discovered that this bombardment was unnecessary, as the French petty officer in command of the shore batteries was negotiating with an American officer of the 30th Infantry to give up the position, but was unable to communicate this to the American command.

At 7 A.M. the aircraft carrier *Ranger* took up a position which would enable it to have its squadrons airborne over assigned targets just before the actual sunrise.

The American planes had orders to destroy French planes on the ground *before* they could take off, and help destroy French naval forces in Casablanca harbor *before* they could move out to sea.

At ten minutes after sunrise, and without any ultimatum whatsoever, and no hostile action from the French in Casablanca, 18 bombers from the *Ranger* let loose against the French submarine base in the harbor, while a rain of heavy-caliber bombs fell on the Delure jetty and on the *Jean Bart,* immobilized at its mooring. Moments later three French submarines were sinking. Three steamers were listing in flames; the dead and wounded were being carried ashore.

What choice, asks the French historian Mordal, was left to Admiral Michelier? "Even if he had wanted to open his arms to the

Americans, they gave him no chance to express his thoughts. . . . What could he do, in the circumstances, but answer their fire?"

Yet there was nothing, says Mordal, to prevent Admiral Hewitt from keeping a respectable distance and starting *pourparlers*. So long as they did not approach, American ships ran no risk from French guns. "Never," says Mordal, "would Lyautey's admonition have been more applicable: Show your strength so as not to have to use it."

Had Admiral Hewitt arrived at high noon, says Mordal, with his armada in full view, Noguès would have buckled like a scarecrow.

But the real question in French minds was why, if the Americans really wanted to avoid a bloody battle, Patton had sidestepped the areas of Mazagan and Rabat, devoid of coastal batteries and safely out of reach of the French 2nd Navy Squadron, in order to attack Port Lyautey, one of the strongest garrisons on the coast, well defended by coastal batteries, and Fedala, whose landing areas were directly under the massive guns of the *Jean Bart* and within minutes of the French naval units in Casablanca.

Had the Americans landed at Rabat as suggested, and on schedule, they would have been met by Béthouart who was in control of the entire Moroccan high command, which the Americans could have taken without firing a shot.

An example of the complete lack of understanding of what the American military were heading into at the time was the escapade of another daring American colonel, William H. Wilbur.

A classmate of Béthouart's at Saint-Cyr, who had lived a long time in France and spoke fluent French, but who, despite his position on Patton's staff, knew nothing of Béthouart's recent activities, the colonel made a rush in a jeep through the French lines in the hope of reaching the French commander of the Casablanca Division and persuading him, for old times' sake, not to oppose the Americans.

Successfully reaching Béthouart's office, Wilbur was amazed to find the general absent and to hear he had been jailed.

His replacement, Colonel Desré, took Wilbur to see Admiral Michelier. But at the Admiralty they arrived just as Michelier was being informed of the damage caused to his ships by the American air raid. Hardly the propitious moment.

To make things worse, at that very instant Noguès phoned Michelier to inform him that he had received orders from Algiers to oppose the Americans with all his forces.

In an attempt to find a way out of his predicament, Noguès had wired urgently to find out what General Juin, technically his superior, was doing in the circumstances.

The answer he received (via the Admiralty at 5:20 A.M.) was that "Algeria is defending herself." This was followed an hour later at 6:28 by a message to the effect that Admiral Darlan was in Algiers, and that as Commander in Chief of all French forces he was in complete accord with General Juin, "who is acting in defense of North Africa."

So Noguès passed on to Michelier these orders to resist.

All through the night Michelier had anticipated nothing more than a Gaullist uprising, or, at most, a commado raid, and so had prepared against attack from land.

His naval units were alerted, but not stoked up.

At 1:30 A.M Admiral Gervais de Lafond, commander of the 2nd Squadron, arrived at the naval base on a bicycle and was told to expect a Gaullist uprising at 5 A.M.

At 5:45 the Casablanca air-raid sirens sounded as thousands of leaflets fell on the sleeping city written in French and Arabic, with pictures of F.D.R. and Eisenhower and the news that the Americans were coming "only to destroy your enemies."

Michelier now ordered four submarines to sea to fan out round the entrance of the port. A few moments later the horizon lit up like fireworks as Americans opened fire on the coastal batteries of Fedala.

At last Michelier ordered his ships to stop the Allied landings. There was, however, no question of having the *Jean Bart* leave port, as it was chained to the jetty. Still this 35,000-ton battleship constituted a formidable threat with its 15-inch main gun turrets, its many antiaircraft guns, and its modern direction-finding equipment.

Aware of the threat of these guns, the American naval squadron headed for the French coastal batteries at El Hank, then northeast, paralleling the coast to put it in the best position to fire on the *Jean Bart*. It was getting light. The swell had completely abated. The sea was like a mirror. At 8:04 A.M. bombers from the *Ranger* circling over the Casablanca port began dropping their bombs on the submarines in the harbor.

The guns of the American warships *Wichita, Tuscaloosa* and *Massachusetts* opened fire on the *Jean Bart,* while Douglas Dauntless dive bombers attacked in waves.

At 8:07 the *Jean Bart* opened fire with two shells from its 15-inch guns. But she had to fire sparingly since she had only 100 rounds in her magazines. Besides, the visibility was poor. A slight haze made it difficult for the French to discern what was facing them out at sea, and the smoke raised by the ships which were heating up in the harbor was drifting out to sea.

It took the *Massachusetts* twenty-one minutes to land a hit on the *Jean Bart,* which, though struck by three shells, still maintained its full firepower.

All around, the port was a shambles as French ships small and large were hit, then foundered and sank. By a great piece of fortune two loaded oil tankers were missed or the whole port might have been set on fire.

With their steam up, the ships of the 2nd Squadron which had not been sunk now passed out of the port while the chaplain of the cruiser *Primaguet,* Father Lenner, stood on the mole in a rain of bombs, "a solitary black figure, blessing the French units as they passed on their way to certain death."

In three parallel lines the French squadron steamed toward its fate. Admiral Michelier's orders were to sneak along the coast and break up the landing operations at Fedala, his only desperate chance of defeating the "invasion."

The 8th of November had developed into a "blue and gold" autumn day with bright sunlight on a smooth sea, almost unruffled by the light offshore breeze, over which skimmed sea gulls with black-tipped wings.

De Lafond's plan was to advance between the coast and the opposing naval units so as to keep the sun in his enemies' eyes (as it rose steadily behind the city of Casablanca) and use the breeze to spread a smoke screen toward the Americans.

What he did not know was that since he had last used such a tactic against an overwhelming British force off the Syrian coast in 1941, the Americans had installed radar on their ships, and could see him clearly through the smoke.

Nevertheless the situation was quite dangerous for the Americans. There were barely ten nautical miles separating the French naval units from the United States transports off Fedala, and the only American force in a position to intervene consisted of the two destroyers *Wilkes* and *Ludlow,* which "were dancing ahead like fox terriers," their main batteries "yap-yapping" while behind them at some distance followed the "queenly *Augusta,* with a high white wave-curl against her clipper bow, her 8-inch guns booming a deep 'woof-woof,' and finally the stolid, scrappy *Brooklyn,* giving tongue with her six-inchers like ten couple of stag hounds."

But because of the smoke and the confusion, the French admiral mistook the bunched silhouettes of the United States transports as a prolongation of Cap Fedala, and did not immediately attack them.

United States air force reaction to the sortie of the French units was immediate. Wildcat fighters supported by bombers from the *Ranger* attacked the French destroyers, which had few antiaircraft guns with which to defend themselves. Slaughter to French personnel was dreadful, especially from strafing, though damage to the ships was minor.

On the French destroyer *Albatros* 80 per cent of the personnel on the bridge was hit, and 20 per cent of the machinists.

The same occurred on the *Milan.* Even Admiral de Lafond was wounded.

Though the French gunners could not see much in the mist, the *Albatros* nevertheless fired 450 rounds, mostly at the two United States destroyers.

Deciding on the most gallant type of action, Admiral de Lafond prepared to use himself as bait with which to lure the big American ships into range of the *Jean Bart* and the coastal batteries at El Hank.

But being out of radio communication, he did not know that a freak hit by an American dud had just put the *Jean Bart's* guns out of commission by jamming the turrets.

What were the French ships to do? Turn tail and disperse, hoping that by a passive attitude the Americans would hold their fire? Admiral Hewitt, as Mordal points out, could hardly have allowed the French ships the opportunity of coming out after dark to attack him.

"The ships," says Mordal, "were condemned to death."

With all hope gone, the French turned to a desperate attack. On board one of the French destroyers, the *Boulonnais,* a young navy lieutenant in command decided on a suicidal approach with torpedoes against one of the large American units, so as to inflict the greatest damage before going down.

Raising his pennant, he headed straight for the line of American cruisers. He was promptly followed by a comrade, the *Brestois.* So rapid was their rate of acceleration that the stern funnel of *Brestois* became incandescent.

The Americans had a hard time stopping them. In the words of one historian, "throwing 8 and 16 inch shells at these small ships was like trying to hit a grasshopper with a rock."

Finally, as the French destroyers came in close enough for their suicide attacks, the Americans got their range. The *Boulonnais* was hit by two shells, one of which decapitated a French sailor, while the other hit the boiler and lowered the steam pressure. Covering herself with smoke, the *Boulonnais* went right on firing, her captain withholding his torpedoes till he could be within 12,000 meters of his target.

Loudly the telemetrist sang out the range till the destroyer was 11,800 meters from the American ship, but the order to fire was never given.

Five American shells landed all at once, engulfing the destroyer with flames and green smoke.

At 10:35 a full salvo also hit the *Fouguex* and set the bridge on fire; it sank by the bow almost immediately.

The Americans now concentrated their fire on the *Primaguet,* which was hit again and again.

An aerial bomb hit the bridge, killing half of those on it. Soon only 106 of the ship's complement of 300 hands remained alive, and of these the majority were suffering wounds or burns, or both.

According to one French account, as the captain and most of the officers lay wounded, a horrible scene developed: "The ship's pigsty had been shot to pieces, and the animals wandered over the ship, attacking those who lay suffering and helpless. The roar of the guns prevented the cries and the moans of the men from being heard, and before their plight was noticed most of the wounded sailors had been mauled to death by the beasts, who seemed to be possessed of a sanguinary rage against the helpless men. . . . The surviving sailors of the crew had just finished killing off the pigs when fire broke out between decks."

Just as gruesome was the plight of the wives and children of these French sailors, who, from the top stories of Casablanca buildings, could see, especially with binoculars, not only the familiar silhouettes of their ships but details of their death throes.

By nightfall Admiral Michelier informed Vichy that all the ships of the 2nd Squadron were either sunk or out of commission.

Some 1,000 French sailors were casualties in the defense of Morocco. Michelier then rounded up the survivors, armed them with rifles and five rounds each of ammunition and formed them into battalions with which to defend Casablanca from land.

Leaning on a cane, Admiral de Lafond passed them in review before loading them aboard trucks to move up to the front.

Under their surviving officers the sailors were ordered to oppose the Americans on the road from Fedala.

Patton, furious at the "goddamn Navy" because they had "demolished the kitchen of the house he had selected for his headquarters at Fedala," was steaming at everyone's general incompetence. His orders to "grab the enemy by the nose and kick him in the pants" were not working out to his satisfaction.

Up before daylight of the 9th of November, Patton went to check the situation on the beach.

He considered it "a mess." To Patton the shore parties seemed neither energetic nor resourceful in moving the matériel already on the beach. "In a state of exasperated frustration," reports the U.S. Army historian, "over the slackness which he observed and over some cases of fright during a French air attack about 0800, he remained on the beach until after noon, then set up headquarters in the Hotel Miramar."

Tuesday the 10th, while in Algiers Clark and Darlan were arguing about terms for a cease-fire throughout North Africa, Patton was back aboard the *Augusta*. Toward noon word came to him that two small French coastal gunboats, the *Gracieuse* and the *Delage*, had slipped along the coast and were shelling the advanced American positions on land.

As two nearby American destroyers had not yet managed to put a shot on either of these gunboats, Admiral Hewitt, who was standing beside Patton on the bridge of the *Augusta*, decided to deal personally with these diminutive pests.

What neither Patton nor Hewitt knew was that during the course of the 8th a French industrialist, having abandoned a boar-hunting jaunt, had volunteered to work all day on the jammed turret of the *Jean Bart*. By evening he had repaired it; to fool the Americans, the captain ordered the turret to remain in its jammed position so as to be reported out of action by Allied reconnaissance.

At 12:20 P.M. on the 10th, as the *Augusta* was steaming into range at some 30 knots, the captain of the *Jean Bart* ordered action stations. His gunnery officer requested to be allowed to fire only when absolutely sure of getting the *Augusta*, which could not know it was heading for a trap.

"Nineteen . . . eighteen . . . seventeen . . . ," sang out the telemetrist. The captain was waiting for 15,000 meters to be absolutely sure of his shot. But the sight of the two small French gunboats being pounded by the *Augusta* was too much for him. At 12:30, while still at 17,000 meters, he ordered fire.

For some inexplicable reason the first salvo fell short. The gunnery officer ordered higher range, and at 16,000 meters the second salvo went way beyond.

What the gunnery officer did not know was that in the trajectory of the *Bart's* guns stood a giant giraffe crane, invisible to the personnel aboard, which had been volatilized by the first salvo, whose impact had nevertheless been insufficient to explode the armor-piercing shells.

Aboard the *Augusta,* apart from Patton and Hewitt, were two rear admirals, a major general, and several war correspondents. To save this important personnel, Admiral Hewitt decided to break off the engagement.

The *Augusta* made a violent turn and belched smoke as it picked up speed. Not till the fifth salvo did the *Jean Bart* finally get the *Augusta's* range and place two shells right beside her.

On the two tiny gunboats the French sailors threw their hats in the air and resumed shelling the Americans.

By 12:50 the *Bart's* sixth salvo grazed the stem of the *Augusta* and drenched the American officers on the bridge with a shower of yellow water.

Furious at having to change his clothes, Admiral Hewitt signaled in clear to Rear Admiral Ernest D. MacWhorter aboard the nearest flattop to send his planes and "get rid of that yellow painted ship." (The *Jean Bart* had been painted yellow as port camouflage.)

From the *Ranger,* Douglas Dauntlesses set off to pound the *Jean Bart* with 1,000-pound bombs. This they did, causing her to sink from the stern with 19 dead and 42 wounded.

And what irony. Clark had by then obtained his cease-fire from Darlan. Already on *our* side, the *Jean Bart* could have been of considerable help against the Axis.

As a further bit of irony, it was then realized that all that day the *Jean Bart* could have trained its long-range rifles on the large troop-ships standing before Fedala at a distance of from 25,000 to 28,000 meters—well within its range, and sitting targets.

"But this," says Mordal, "never crossed the mind of the French commander. This was a fight between gallant sailors. In his heart he wanted those troops to help liberate his country."

Nor was this all of the tragedy. As late as November 13th, forty-eight hours after the cease-fire, the French submarine *Conquérant* was sunk by a United States Catalina flyingboat off the Moroccan coast. And the *Sidi Ferruch,* having put its wounded aboard a Spanish freighter, was sunk by three American planes while it was heading for Casablanca after receiving by radio news of the cease-fire order. To the bottom went its three officers and 65 men.

Michelier himself did not hear that Algiers had signed a cease-fire till 3:30 P.M. local time of the 10th. At almost the same moment he received a message from Vichy ordering him to continue to fight. Shortly thereafter he received the news that Darlan had canceled his order of that morning, and had surrendered himself a prisoner. When Michelier tried to get in touch with Noguès in Fez, he found the phones were out and could not be re-established before evening.

Luckily at 8:20 P.M. Admiral Auphan in Vichy saved the day with a message so carefully worded as to give Michelier the chance for an honorable peace. "Marshal orders are to continue fighting so long as it is possible."

Without a plane or ship left, and with Patton's land forces at last in a position to overwhelm him, Michelier could safely contemplate honorable surrender.

It was because he had feared just such a mix-up that Juin had ordered Dorange to Morocco armed with a copy of the order to cease fire, signed by Darlan.

Despite the urgency of Dorange's mission, the Allies delayed him at Maison Blanche and did not allow him to fly off till 5 P.M. This forced him to stop at Oujda at nightfall. Realizing he might not get through at all, Dorange tried to reach Noguès on the telephone. But Noguès was not at his command post. A Major Moraillon who picked up the phone said he could hardly stop the war on just anyone's say-so. He did, however, recognize Dorange's voice (they had had a girl friend in common) and Moraillon promised to transmit the message to Noguès and assure him it had come from Juin's adjutant.

Michelier was not reached till 9:10.

Disaster still threatened.

All this time no one had managed to get through to the Americans!

At 7 A.M. on the 11th, Admiral Hewitt, aboard the *Augusta,* still had not heard the news of the armistice. At Patton's request he had ordered the battleship *New York* to take up position to bombard and destroy the city of Casablanca; planes from the *Ranger* were already airborne, minutes from their target.

Had the French not managed to get an envoy through to General Truscott, Casablanca would have been largely destroyed.

In Gibraltar Eisenhower, "demoralized to realize the radio functioned badly or not at all," tried to get messages to Patton by plane, but the aircraft were shot down.

On the 12th Butcher complained that "for some reason our set of codebooks and Patton's don't jibe." He discovered later that Patton's codebooks had been stowed at the bottom of an as-yet-unloaded ship.

During the course of the 11th, American and French commanders in Morocco did manage to meet before the Casbah at Mehedia and arrange for a truce.

At Fedala—where, for the occasion, he had summoned out an honor guard and a band of musicians—Patton waited on the steps of the Hotel Miramar surrounded by a group of his officers.

Michelier arrived about 1 P.M., and after an exchange of courtesies Patton asked Michelier if he would care to join him for lunch.

"*Avec grand plaisir,*" said the admiral.

"In that case," said Patton, "I will get in touch with Admiral Hewitt who is still on the *Augusta* and ask him to join us."

When Hewitt arrived, the erstwhile combatants sat down to lunch in the Hotel Miramar. After this friendly meal, at about 3 P.M., Noguès arrived with Lascroux and Lahoulle.

A short and polite ceremony took place between Noguès and

Patton who exchanged compliments on the fighting qualities of their respective troops.

An armistice was discussed, but the terms offered by Patton were so severe that Michelier scribbled to Noguès on a scrap of paper, "*Inacceptable.*"

Very ably, Noguès refused to face the armistice terms directly by saying it was inadvisable to talk about a Moroccan convention while Eisenhower was dealing with Darlan for all of North Africa.

No accord was signed. But according to the French, "from its beginning Franco-American cooperation was total, sincere, confident and friendly."

The meaning of this is perhaps best exemplified by the opening remarks of Noguès to Patton: "As for Béthouart, he has betrayed and must be punished. We all did our duty as ordered, though many officers would have preferred to do as he did. It is inadmissible that an officer act thus."

Confined to prison cells as common malefactors, Béthouart and his chief of staff, Colonel Molle, along with five subordinate officers, were stripped of arms and rank; charged with rebellion, they were to be brought before a court-martial in the morning.

When Béthouart asked his court-appointed defense what the punishment for such a "crime" might be, the answer was "death."

The official United States Army historian—who can hardly be accused of bias—recorded the situation:

"In French military hands they were actually in danger of paying with their lives for anticipating the orders which their superiors were to issue four days later, after Darlan had taken the responsibility on his shoulders."

Luckily, on November 15th, Eisenhower intervened and requested their immediate release. On November 17th General Béthouart and Colonel Magnan (who had surrounded Noguès's residence) were flown to Algiers by American plane.

As for the situation which they left behind them in Morocco, the United States Army historian summed it up dispassionately:

"For an undue length of time pro-American French remained in custody, while those hostile to the Allies before the landings, followers of Pierre Laval, remained in positions of trust and power. The Frenchmen of authoritarian sympathies, some of them members of fascistic societies like the Service d'Ordre Légionnaire des Anciens Combattants and the Parti Populaire Français and others in less formal associations seemed prepared even to assist an Axis counterinvasion. They propagandized against the Allies. Frenchmen of pro-Allied views, whether Giraudist or Gaullist, were the object of their surveillance and open hostility. Specific denunciations of these anti-American individuals to American civilian officials were of little or no avail, for their hands were tied by military control. The position which General Patton took was that 'the anti-Darlan-Noguès group does not have the personnel nor is it in a position to control Morocco if given that mission.' "

To this the historian adds that Noguès "was suspected of maintaining ties with Vichy and perhaps thus with the Germans even after 15 November. In general, he was the victim of the lack of forthrightness which characterized his political, as distinguished from his military role. . . . General Patton became in effect a defender of General Noguès as an indispensable agent who could keep the native population in hand while the French in Morocco were in general kept friendly and neutral."

PART FOUR

THE END

OF DARLAN

12

IN MID-DECEMBER Patton flew to Algiers to report to Eisenhower, whom he found not only mired in the military problems of the Tunisian front but about to face a fresh storm on the political one.

Eisenhower's British political advisers, fresh from a trip to London, reported to him that the animosity toward Darlan in Britain was such that it would be wise, as soon as Tunis could be captured, if Darlan were dismissed.

But if Darlan were to go, who could replace him? Giraud did not want the job. Noguès, Boisson or Chatel would mean no change whatever. Of the Five, who still needed some manageable figure at the top, Lemaigre-Dubreuil was bold enough to suggest neutralizing and controlling de Gaulle by making him minister of war in a provisional government to be set up in Algiers with Lemaigre-Dubreuil as premier. But this would not work, for Lemaigre was even less well known than Bergeret and would be a more unpopular choice.

Oddly enough, Darlan too seemed for a while in favor of resolving the situation by offering de Gaulle the vice-presidency of the Imperial Council, and had gone so far as to dispatch two officers to London to sound him out. But the officers were waylaid at Gibraltar; and in any case de Gaulle would never have agreed.

It remained for Henri d'Astier to produce the dramatic solution. "What figure," he asked, "can be found, sufficiently well known to need no buildup, yet with a political mantle broad enough to cover the various litigant factions?"

He answered his own question: Prince Henri d'Orleans, Count of Paris, pretender to the throne of France.

It seemed to d'Astier that the count could come not as a restorer of the monarchy but as mediator.

In this bold venture d'Astier was supposedly supported by M. Alfred Pose, and by another former Inspector of Finances, M. Davernas, co-director with Pose at the Banque Nationale pour le Commerce et l'Industrie and former *Chef de Cabinet* of Pierre Pucheu at the Vichy Ministry of the Interior. The stage was set for a new and extraordinary drama.

The plotters' next problem was how to get rid of Darlan peacefully.

This they decided to accomplish by means of a French law of 1872, passed shortly after France's defeat at the hands of Prussia, which granted to the regional legislative bodies of the various departments of France, known as the General Councils, the legal powers of the government of France if ever she were incapable of exercising such powers herself.

Algeria (considered an integral part of France) had three departments, with three duly elected heads, or councilors general: A. Froger for Algiers, P. Saurin for Oran, and L. Deryron for Constantine—the last two also deputies to the national parliament.

So d'Astier, the monarchist, met with these three republican representatives—mostly at Algiers' most elegant restaurant, the Paris, described as "eloquent of the *ancien régime* with its mustached and monocled clientele, its bar crowded with American businessmen and war correspondents." There d'Astier suggested that in order to re-establish constitutional law, they call in the heir to the throne.

The three democratically elected councilors agreed with d'Astier to draft a letter to Darlan, pointing out that since the marshal was a prisoner of the Germans, and Algeria was now liberated, Pétain's delegation of authority to Darlan in Africa was *ipso facto* void. They therefore suggested to Darlan that he step down from his post.

"Having reflected on the matter," wrote the councilors, "it behooves us to see if other men and other methods should not guide France."

Darlan ignored their letter.

The councilors sent a similar letter to President Roosevelt. It also received no answer.

This approach having failed, the plotters decided on a further step. Supported by "certain military figures," the councilors general would call on Darlan at his office and request that he step down. If necessary they would eject him bodily, then summon the Count of Paris to fill his empty seat.

The date for this *coup* was set for December 18. To obtain the count's adherence to the plot, M. Alfred Pose, as an ostensible emissary of the three councilors, set off (early in December) to call on the count at his villa in Morocco (near enough to Rabat for him to cycle into town on business), where he lived "surrounded by his numerous children, his blonde, royal Brazilian wife, and the remnants of a small court."

Ever since his father, the Duc de Guise, had retired from the embattled arena in 1940, the count, now in his thirty-fourth year, had been in the thick of plots aimed at the restoration of the monarchy with himself as King Henry VIII of France.

Banned (as were all pretenders) from setting foot in Metropolitan France, and having unsuccessfully tried to enlist at the beginning of the war in both the French and the British armies, the count had joined the French Foreign Legion, from which he had been demobilized at the time of the armistice.

For a moment, at the beginning of the Vichy regime, it looked as if even the Germans were considering the possibility of restoring the monarchy, but their *ballon d'essai* was punctured when the count's entourage let it be known that Henri VIII "would never impose the return of the King of France with enemy bayonets."

He had also kept up a correspondence with Pétain, and just three months before the landings in North Africa had a secret meeting with the marshal, at the Château de Charmeilles, in a suburb of Vichy.

"In case of probable Allied landings in North Africa," the count asked Pétain, "would you come there to head up a resistance movement?"

Pétain's answer was to repeat that one could not defend France by quitting it, and that he was afraid the Germans would install a *Gauleiter* in France and "Polonize it," were he to do so.

To see how his chances stood of regaining the throne the count also saw Laval, who, according to one historian, Hubert Cole, offered the count a trial position in the government where he might show his mettle.

"If you are successful in the post I offer you," said Laval, "I can assure you that within six months you will have all France at your feet. Would you care, *monseigneur,* to take over the Ministry of Food?"

As a last resort, just a few weeks before the landings, the count flew to Rome to see Pope Pius XII, who expressed his worry at the prospect of a Soviet victory all over Europe.

When the representative of the councilors from Algiers arrived in Morocco to put forth their proposition, the count listened carefully, then declared himself prepared to agree on two conditions: that there be no bloodshed; that the Allies approve the move.

It was, he stipulated, not as a pretender to the throne that he would take the lead, but as a conciliator.

According to Soustelle, a provisional government to replace Darlan's was already discussed. One list had the Count of Paris as

Premier with de Gaulle as Minister of War; another had de Gaulle as Premier, with the count as Chief of State. In the lineup Giraud was to be Commander in Chief of the Armed Forces, Lemaigre-Dubreuil Minister of War, Henri d'Astier at the Interior, the Gaullist General Georges Catroux at Foreign Affairs, Pose at Economic Affairs and, curiously, Darlan as Ambassador to the United States.

This at least showed that the *coup* was supposed to be bloodless. But the key to success, of course, was the approval of the Allies.

To see if the moment was indeed propitious for him to step forward, the Count of Paris agreed to send a delegate to Algiers.

In answer to the count's key question as to what the Allies would think of such a move, the count's delegate returned to tell his master that "Murphy would help."

So the young prince decided to leave Morocco, insisting, however, that he was going to Algiers not to organize any *coup,* but simply to answer a call from patriotic forces.

To travel through heavily controlled Allied territory a car would be needed and a permit with a false identity.

The car was provided by M. Pose's *Chef de Cabinet,* Marc Jacquet, the *laissez-passer* by General Monsabert, also a staunch royalist, who had been named head of the Corps Franc d'Afrique group of volunteers.

At dawn of December 8th into the car stepped the Abbé Cordier, Marc Jacquet, and a passenger called Boniface who, as assistant director for political affairs in Morocco, had been arrested with Béthouart and dismissed by Noguès because of his Allied sympathies. Boniface was to remain in Morocco and be replaced on the return journey by the pretender. At the wheel was a young musician, son of a poet, named Mario Faivre.

On December 10th they headed back for Algiers.

There, under the pseudonym of M. Robin, the pretender saw the chief notables of the High Commissariat and from conversations with them determined to his satisfaction that Giraud, Noguès, Boisson and Bergeret were in agreement to choose him as supreme chief in Africa in case Darlan should disappear.

In Algiers the plot thickened almost in broad daylight. In the Algeria, an apartment building on the boulevard de Télémly, day after day visitors would ring the bell at Jacquet's door and ask, "Is M. Robin in?"

At other times the count was in the home of the Princesse de Polignac, or in the white palace of the ancient Comtesse de Ligne— among its fountains and mosaics, all guarded by a retinue of Sudanese eunuchs in bright red pantaloons, carrying large curved scimitars—where Murphy was also a frequent guest.

Then came a contretemps—and one that was quite unexpected. Eisenhower, afraid that even a palace revolution might disturb "public order," refused to approve the scheme. Having shown no particular fondness for Darlan, who had caused him some severe problems, Eisenhower now refused point-blank to discuss any change whatsoever in the political situation which might endanger his efforts to mount a major attack in Tunisia. The French, he said, were to fight the Germans. If necessary, he would bring out his tanks in Algiers to keep things just as they were.

That same day the American government announced that the army Darlan wanted to build would receive its arms and supplies through a Lend-Lease arrangement, which, instead of being handled through civil authorities, would be a purely military transaction.

When the news of Eisenhower's reaction was brought to the young pretender, he is said to have hung his head and concluded, "Without Eisenhower's support, nothing is possible."

Gracefully he decided to retire to the coastal town of Sidi Ferruch.

The battle might be lost, but not the war.

His supporters, in any case, had no intention of giving in so easily. When the first plot failed, d'Astier immediately decided that another should be tried. Somehow Darlan must be eliminated to make way for the prince.

On December 20th, says Soustelle, the new plot was fixed. Excluded from it were Bergeret and Rigault, because, he says, they were too tied to the Darlan regime, and because toward Rigault the count "eprouvait la plus grande méfiance."

Lemaigre-Dubreuil was excluded, says Soustelle, because he was too close to Rigault, and anyway he was en route to the United States.

In London efforts were still being made to bring about a fusion of the forces of de Gaulle and Giraud. But a satisfactory go-between was lacking.

By accident, or design, two leaders of the Resistance arrived in London from underground France, one the head of "Liberation," d'Astier's brother Emmanuel.

Oddly, just a few days earlier, Churchill had hit upon that very person as a possible spokesman for de Gaulle in North Africa.*

On such a negotiator even Rigault was willing to agree, but Darlan refused. No representative of de Gaulle, he said, could come to Algiers. If there was to be any such meeting, it would have to take place in Gibraltar.

Nevertheless, on December 19th Murphy received a signal from London announcing the arrival in Algiers by plane of d'Astier de la Vigerie.

The person who arrived at Maison Blanche airport was indeed a d'Astier, but neither Emmanuel nor Henri. It was a third brother: General François, one of de Gaulle's principal coworkers in London, Deputy Commander of Free French Forces.†

Without British approval General François d'Astier could not have left England; nor could he have landed at Maison Blanche without the approval of AFHQ.

Butcher's explanation is that "Murphy . . . had overlooked mentioning to Darlan the prospective arrival of this Free Frenchman." He added, "When Darlan and his people heard of d'Astier's presence in Algiers, they wanted to arrest him."

---

* "You have," said the Prime Minister, "two heads of the resistance in London [Emmanuel d'Astier and Pierre Frenay]. The British government will put at their disposal the means for reaching Giraud in Algiers."

† Of the three brothers, all nephews of Cardinal d'Astier, François, the eldest, had been a general officer in the Air Force, with de Gaulle in London since 1940. Emmanuel, a journalist and author, had sold his possessions in France to finance an underground movement with leftist leanings. Henri, the third brother, a Gaullist in North Africa was, as we know, an original member of the Five.

To Darlan "the Allies seemed to have indulged in a puerile and not very courageous lie." Furious, he decided that the Gaullist general must not be allowed to see or talk to anyone of importance, and he put his police on the job.

But the Chief of Police was d'Astier's brother Henri!

Henri's position was certainly an odd one. The police in his charge obeyed partly his orders and partly those of the Minister of Interior, Rigault, as well as those of Bergeret, who, as a sort of vice-president, acted like a premier.

Some of Henri's police, says Soustelle (who was eventually to replace Henri in that job), were betraying him in favor of General Bergeret; others, "or the same ones, worked for Murphy, in an Algiers which seethed with agents and *indicateurs* of multiple and overlapping loyalties."

At Darlan's command, the police had just arrested a number of Gaullists and several members of the pro-Allied *coup* of the 8th, charged with having had posters placed on the walls of Algiers: WE WANT DE GAULLE. THE ADMIRAL TO THE SEA!

No sooner were General d'Astier and his aide-de-camp lodged at the Hotel Aletti than they found themselves virtual prisoners, caught in a net of police surveillance, "with [in the romantic words of Soustelle] an eye at every keyhole, an ear at every door, their telephone tapped, their every move shadowed, those to whom they spoke being immediately arrested."

But the hall porter, as is usual in such cases, immediately informed Achiary of General d'Astier's arrival, and he informed the other Gaullists. One of d'Astier's first visitors was his brother Henri.

And, says Soustelle, Robert Murphy was not long in making his appearance.

The evening of d'Astier's arrival, Murphy came to see him to "let him understand his game."

Murphy, says Soustelle, was backing Darlan, or rather, the Darlan-Bergeret team. His argument, says Soustelle, "showed how much importance he attached to Bergeret," whom Soustelle calls the "real cornerstone of the regime of Vichy II in Algeria."

Murphy also made it clear, says Soustelle, that he was "playing this game without Eisenhower's knowledge."

According to Soustelle, Murphy pleaded with d'Astier to go with him to see Bergeret, who was waiting for him at the High Commissariat at midnight. D'Astier refused.

Annoyed, Murphy threatened to force d'Astier to leave for Gibraltar the following morning without having a chance to see Eisenhower.

D'Astier held firm. He had come, he said, to see Eisenhower on military matters regarding General Jacques Le Clerc's Free French Forces in Southern Tunisia, and would do so; but he would not go to the High Commissariat with Murphy.

"The Irishman," says Soustelle, "went away somewhat dissatisfied."

As matters stood the night of the 19th, when General Bedell Smith went to see Eisenhower around 10 P.M. to give him a round-by-round account, "d'Astier," reports Butcher, "was refusing even to speak to the Darlan crowd."

"On Ike's authority," says Butcher, "Beetle had dispatched General McClure* and Mr. Murphy to do two things: 1) get Darlan not to arrest d'Astier; 2) get d'Astier to converse with Darlan."

D'Astier, who had gone to the Saint-Georges and left his card for Eisenhower, was invited to meet the Allied commander on the morrow.

This meeting took place at the Saint-Georges in the presence of Bedell Smith and Murphy and of the British Foreign Office representative, W. H. B. Mack, with Admiral Fenard speaking for Darlan.

During lunch, Butcher reports, Eisenhower said that d'Astier wanted *carte blanche* "and expected to have it from the Allied C-in-C, to visit and talk with de Gaullists all over French Africa, North and West. This was too much. Ike reviewed the whole cir-

* Brigadier General Robert A. McClure, formerly Eisenhower's G-2 in London, now at AFHQ to coordinate censorships, public relations, and psychological warfare.

cumstances, and arranged, after much parlez-vooing, that d'Astier talk unofficially with Darlan this afternoon." To which Butcher added an example of the buck-passing technique which had been brought to such perfection at AFHQ: "If d'Astier travels over Africa, this being French administration, it's up to Darlan."

Butcher then summed up the situation: "The possibilities of something that would lead to a reconciliation of the de Gaullists and Darlanists, out of d'Astier's mission, were almost smothered by the bad start."

Darlan, so reports his son Alain, sent the chief of his personal staff, Captain Hourcade, to see Murphy and draw his attention to "the consequences which the arrival of de Gaulle's emissary in Algiers threatened."

Again during the afternoon of the 20th toward 3 P.M. Murphy arrived at the Aletti to take d'Astier to see Darlan. Again d'Astier refused. His excuse was that he did not want to go under the sponsorship of Murphy (or the Americans).

Yet he intended, says Chamine, "to reap his Algerian report with the results of an interview with Darlan."

That night, after dark, the ubiquitous Fenard came to pick up d'Astier and drove him to his home, the Villa Arthur in Mustapha Supérieur. The patio of the villa was illuminated by no more than the light that filtered from the rooms giving onto the cloister. Through the windows d'Astier saw that the rooms were filled with naval officers and some sailors, fully armed. In the large salon Darlan was waiting for d'Astier, attended by Giraud, Bergeret and Rigault. Battet was also present.

Chamine reports that Darlan said to d'Astier, "I hope you have come to find grounds for an understanding. If that is so, I am here to listen."

But d'Astier completely ignored Darlan, "as if he were not even in the room," and began a conversation with Giraud, who "stood immobile, circumspect, and silent in the midst of the circle."

Darlan lost his patience. "Your behavior," said he, "is a bit gross. General Giraud and I are agreed on all points, and you cannot drive a wedge between us."

Ill at ease, d'Astier maintained that his mission was merely to regulate with the Algiers authorities the problems raised by Le Clerc's army (estimated at 1,800 men, of whom 300 were white).

"Despite several rumors," says Docteur, "nothing more was discussed."

Later that night Darlan and Giraud went to call on Eisenhower at his villa "to urge," says Butcher, "that d'Astier be sent out of Africa; they feared trouble."

Eisenhower "maintained this was a French problem and the French should work it out together."

They did. But in a manner to which Eisenhower was as yet unaccustomed.

On December 21st Giraud announced that he had seen d'Astier once more and that though he had finished his discussion about Le Clerc's army, d'Astier contemplated a stay of two or three weeks in North Africa including a visit to Oran and Casablanca. Darlan's reply was that he could not permit any such visits, that d'Astier, having arrived fraudulently, would now have to leave.

Meanwhile, d'Astier's antechamber in the Aletti had become, in the words of Chamine, the meeting place of all the opposition to Darlan in North Africa.

In the course of these meetings, General d'Astier decided to form a secret Gaullist triumvirate in Algeria with the responsibility for developing the Gaullist movement. The three heads were to be his brother Henri, René Capitant, and Louis Joxe.

But when Capitant, who was to bring General d'Astier a long and detailed report on the Algerian situation, tried to enter the Aletti, he found his passage barred by the police under orders from Rigault. Quickly alerted by Guy Cohen, the legal representative of the Aletti brothers managed to reach General d'Astier's room by the back stairs to deliver Capitant's report, adding to it his own picture of the situation with what Soustelle calls "his intimate knowledge of the Moslem and Jewish problems of which Darlan and Giraud were entirely ignorant."

Meanwhile, says Chamine, "Murphy multiplied his *démarches* between the two camps."

And all along the royalist plot continued. The Count of Paris also expressed a desire to see General d'Astier; so, "always anxious to obtain maximum information," says Soustelle, d'Astier had a brief interview with the count, limited to an exchange of courtesies, "in which the count did not unveil his plans."

General d'Astier then turned over to his brother Henri $38,000 in cash, ostensibly for Gaullist propaganda.

On December 23rd General François d'Astier left for London. "At this moment," says Admiral Docteur, "there is every reason to believe that the suppression of Darlan was decided."

Paradoxically the one person in North Africa who most wanted Darlan to stay at his job was General Eisenhower, convinced by now that Darlan, with hardly anywhere to turn, would be prepared to do almost anything requested of him by the Allies. Whether such an attitude meant an authentic change of heart or was just a short-term device to stay in power, Darlan's close collaboration was a welcome relief to Eisenhower, as it made his own task seem a great deal easier. In Murphy's words, "Eisenhower was understandably disposed to grant most of Darlan's requests after the Admiral did so much to hold together the various complex administrations in Africa."

On December 23rd Darlan gave a luncheon for Eisenhower, Clark, Murphy, and Admiral of the Fleet Sir Andrew Cunningham. Turning to Clark, Darlan said, "Tomorrow the Axis press will say I gave this luncheon because a gun was pointed at my head." To which Clark replied, "If the rest of the luncheons were as good as this, I would get my gun out every week."

A few moments later, while discussing with Mme. Darlan the desirability of sending their ailing son Alain to Warm Springs, Clark saw the chance of finding out Darlan's reaction to the possibility of his also being removed from the North African political scene. "I think," said Clark, "it could be arranged for the Admiral to go too if he chooses."

Darlan nodded and replied, "I would like to turn this over to General Giraud; he likes it here and I don't."

After lunch Darlan took Murphy into the privacy of his study and said to him, "You know there are four plots in existence to assassinate me. Suppose one of these plots is successful. What will you Americans do?'

Darlan then showed Murphy a list he had drawn up of possible successors, including de Gaulle, Giraud, Flandin, and former premiers Paul Reynaud and Édouard Herriot.

Darlan, says Murphy, seemed sincerely disturbed over the prospect, but as though he were talking about the death of someone else, not himself.

13

IN ALGIERS December 24 was a radiantly sunny day, the air crisp, the streets crowded with women shoppers looking for last-minute presents and toys for their children.

The morning papers carried suggestions that Algerians invite Allied soldiers to Christmas Eve dinner. Between 8 A.M. and noon the price of Algerian champagne, Mousse d'Islam, doubled.

It was an ideal day for a *coup d'état.*

The local garrison had been depleted by soldiers going on leave. During the festivities no courts were in session. Neither Eisenhower nor Giraud was in town.

In the spirit of Christmas, Eisenhower had gone off to the front to join British General Sir Kenneth A. N. Anderson for a study of the countryside over which to launch the most ambitious Allied attack against the Germans in Tunisia—scheduled for Christmas Day. At the front it was pouring rain.

On the rue Michelet the church bells of the small English chapel by the Palais d'Été struck 2:30 when a black Peuguot "402" drove up to the southern gate of the annex.

From it stepped a young man of twenty. Turning up the collar of his brown overcoat, he walked to the gated entrance to the low Moorish pavilion in which the officers of the High Commissariat were temporarily housed.

Admitted by a guard to a small waiting room, he signed the register and filled out a request to see M. Louis Joxe.

At that hour the building was almost empty. In the courtyard a detachment of native guards was idling somnolently in the winter sunshine.

The young man lit a cigarette and glanced along the somber corridor through which the admiral must return to his office.

Shortly after 3 P.M., a car drew up in the graveled churchyard. Admiral Darlan, followed by his aide Captain Hourcade, moved briskly down the corridor.

As they reached the antechamber to their offices, Hourcade was surprised that neither the sentry nor the doorkeeper was at his post. Passing a young man in the antechamber, he heard a shot. Turning, he heard a second shot and saw Admiral Darlan fall to the floor in the doorway to his office.

As the assassin leaped over the admiral's body, Hourcade caught him by the throat and one wrist. With a violent effort the young man tried to disengage himself, causing the two of them to spin. As they grappled, another shot grazed Hourcade's cheek; then the young man fell toward the corner of the room, opposite Darlan's office, and aimed at Hourcade's stomach.

Hourcade crouched and jumped. The bullet entered his thigh, causing him a violent pain in the lower abdomen.

Hourcade's last impression of the assassin was of tense, excited eyes, very blue, with the pupils dilated as if by a drug.

Falling, Hourcade bumped his head against the fireplace and retained only a vague idea of what followed, other than the sound of footsteps and blows as the young man cried out, "Don't kill me. Don't kill me."

As the assassin tried to escape through a window into the palace gardens, a Spahi cavalryman, attracted by the fracas, threw his regulation *chéchia* round the young man's neck like a lasso. Another guard hit the boy with a chair, knocking the gun from his hand.

The admiral lay very still, his eyes open, his mouth bleeding.

From their nearby offices came Saint-Hardouin and two other men. They lifted the admiral down to the courtyard. In the other corner of the room the guards still struggled with the boy.

In the courtyard the admiral's sagging body was placed in

Admiral Battet's car. A sailor took the wheel. A naval officer climbed in beside the prostrate Darlan and ordered the driver to the hospital in which Darlan's son was still lying ill with polio. No one suggested a nearby clinic.

On the way, though the admiral was still conscious, his wound prevented him from talking.

Meanwhile at the Palais d'Été, Bergeret had arrived in a staff car and heard a halting reconstruction of what had happened from the wounded Hourcade, who was still lying on the floor.

To his surprise, Bergeret saw M. Pose enter the room. Even Saint-Hardouin, says Chamine, was amazed at such a quick appearance "because his offices were six leagues away, and he seldom showed up at the Palais d'Été."

Odder still, neither Bergeret nor Rigault nor d'Astier was in his office at that particular moment of a regular working day. Their excuse was said to be that they were preparing to go to a special Christmas Eve Mass at 5 P.M.

Then Murphy and Clark arrived, much shaken. With Bergeret they left for the hospital, where they were joined by Mme. Darlan and Admiral Moreau.

After a longish wait, the surgeon came out and announced that the admiral's liver and intestines had been perforated, and that the admiral was dead. It remained a mystery whether he succumbed during an operation *in extremis* or was already dead on arrival.

On their way back to the Palais d'Été, Clark and Murphy asked Bergeret to withhold the news of the murder as long as possible so they could inform General Eisenhower, who was at the front, and have time to coordinate their next moves in case of possible repercussions.

Battet immediately took measures to prevent any possible troubles. He requested that both Eisenhower and Giraud return to organize a defense of the city against a possible *coup d'état*.

When Clark returned to the Saint-Georges, the French officers there begged him to summon Noguès from Morocco to take command.

"But I wanted Giraud," Clark said later. "And I wanted him

fast. I warned all those present that for the moment General Noguès was not even to be informed of the death of Darlan."

Clark then put a call through to Eisenhower at the headquarters of the British 5 Corps at Béja. When the call came through to him, Eisenhower was chatting with Juin, and so guarded was Clark, says Butcher, that Eisenhower could not be sure that Darlan had actually been shot; he nevertheless agreed to return right away.

Back at the Palais d'Été Bergeret spotted Rigault. In a corner of the still-disordered room where the murder had taken place, Bergeret whispered to Rigault, "The boy is not alone in this. We must find out who was behind him."

To which Rigault replied, "He's a child. He will talk."

To Police Commissioner Muscatelli, who had arrived on the scene, Bergeret gave orders to question the boy closely to discover his accomplices.

Muscatelli summoned Commissioner Garidacci, head of the 4th Garde Mobile brigade, and ordered him to interrogate the boy.

Garidacci, who was having Christmas Eve lunch with the journalist Alain de Sérigny, had just offered to drive the ladies to their Christmas shopping when he received the phone call and excused himself brusquely, saying he had a very serious matter to contend with.

Sérigny, by coincidence, also had an appointment that afternoon at the Palais d'Été with Saint-Hardouin, and likewise left the luncheon; but when Sérigny reached his destination he found the gate closed; a sentry, helmeted and bearing a carbine, would not let him by, explaining apologetically "that after what's happened you will understand."

Sérigny, not knowing what had happened, thought he meant the general trouble of the last few days, but was finally admitted and allowed to go to Saint-Hardouin's office. There he embarked on a discussion of Spanish politics with de la Tour du Pin, recently arrived from Madrid, and with de Witasse, a former French Minister to Tangier, then Chief of Protocol at the High Commissariat.

"We were having a fascinating discussion," says Sérigny, when the door opened suddenly and a navy lieutenant, very pale, announced, "The admiral is dead."

Sérigny jumped. "What admiral?"

"Darlan, *parbleu,*" said Saint-Hardouin. "A quarter of an hour ago a man fired on him."

"In absolute equanimity," says Sérigny, "the conversation went back to Spanish politics."

Outside, surrounded by policemen, the young assassin was being taken through the courtyard to a room in the basement to be questioned by Commissioner Garidacci.

As the cortege passed the line of official cars drawn up in the courtyard, one of the chauffeurs, seeing the prisoner, exclaimed, "But that's Bonnier de la Chapelle."

To the commissioner the boy insisted his name was Morand; he even exhibited a regulation identity card in that name. Shivering, white-lipped, his face bruised, his eyes to the ground, a tic of fatigue developing in his cheek, the boy kept repeating that he had acted alone, that he did not regret it.

Alain de Sérigny, now possessor of a scoop, rushed back to his paper, the *Écho d'Alger.* But a British censor informed him he would "not be allowed to write about the event for the next day's paper."

At the Central Commissariat, where Garidacci transferred the young assassin to question him more at his ease, it developed that the boy's identity card was perfectly valid, with the proper signature and cachet of the Service de la Sûreté Générale. The boy also possessed a passport in the name of Morand, also perfectly valid and duly registered with the police, complete with a valid visa for Spanish Morocco.

But there was no police dossier whatsoever in the main files under the name of Morand, nor any such address as appeared on the card.

Later that night Commissioner Esquerré took Garidacci aside to tell him that the assassin had been recognized as Fernand Bonnier de la Chapelle.

By the time Rigault arrived at the Commissariat, the boy had been placed in a cell where he had fallen asleep and Garidacci was out on the town following Esquerré's lead.

When Esquerré showed Rigault the dossier thus far, Rigault, as Minister of the Interior, considered it scandalously empty. "This is the report of a road accident," he commented acidly. "Tomorrow the Imperial Council is to meet. I want you to pursue the inquest all night if necessary. And wake me, no matter what the time, with any results."

By candlelight, half covered by a French tricolor, dressed in his full uniform, Darlan now lay in his hospital room, which had been turned into a *chapelle ardente,* his expression, in Murphy's words, "for the first time duly impressive."

PART FIVE

THE

MURDERER

14

ON CHRISTMAS DAY Darlan lay in state on a raised dais at Government House, in the great carpeted hall with its sumptuous hangings, its potted green plants, the air filled with the scent of flowers from the wreaths round the ritual catafalque.

Tirailleurs with bared halberds, Spahis with their red burnooses, and Darlan's own sailors in immaculate white puttees stood guard at the bier as a crowd of dignitaries filed slowly past.

In the city the struggle between contestants who wished to step into the admiral's shoes had become intense.

On the evening of the 24th Bergeret had received a visit from M. Alfred Pose, who came to ask him to receive the Count of Paris.

"The prince is in Algiers?" asked Bergeret in mock surprise.

"He arrives by plane tonight," said Pose with the straightest of faces.

Everyone knew quite well, says Chamine, that he had been in Algiers since December 10th.

On Christmas Day, according to Soustelle, the count had lunch with Bergeret and said he wished to place himself at the service of his country, not as a pretender but as a supra-political arbiter, to hold the position of High Commissioner only until victory, at which time he could solemnly return power to the people of France.

Would Bergeret, asked the count, report this to the Imperial Council and put forward the count's candidature? He explained that his installation could be accomplished by the simple process of nomination by the Imperial Council.

According to Chamine, Bergeret said yes but only meant that he would report the *démarche* to the Council.

By Christmas midday, says Soustelle, it looked as if the prince were on the point of coming to power, and that, as a result, the young murderer would be saved after a few days' inquest.

Meanwhile Bergeret had summoned Governor General Boisson, Noguès and Giraud to confer on the succession.

To sound out Bergeret, Murphy went to see him and discovered that his preference was for Noguès.

"The High Commissioner's function," said Bergeret, "is essentially a political one. General Noguès is both a civilian and a military administrator. He knows the whole country well. He has succeeded in several very delicate situations."

American public opinion, said Murphy, would no longer stand for Noguès as High Commissioner.

"And you?" queried Bergeret. "You have to stand for American public opinion?"

"Giraud," replied Murphy, "is very popular in the United States."

Bergeret grimaced. "He's a great soldier, no doubt. But he cares nothing for politics." Then he added with a shrug, "Still, I do not wish to prejudge the decision of the Council."

Murphy next went to see Saint-Hardouin to find out the sentiment among the Five.

"You know how I feel," said Saint-Hardouin. "It was in the

name of Giraud that the Allies were called to North Africa. It was with Giraud you signed the agreements as a preamble to the landings."

Then Giraud arrived from Tunisia, and his presence radically changed the picture.

Giraud's mind was full of the cold and muddy struggle being waged by the French along a 300-kilometer mountainous front with few arms and less equipment. Because of the rain and the sea of mud, Eisenhower's hoped-for Christmas Day attack had been canceled by General Anderson, who now faced the possibility of having to retreat from his exposed positions.

Giraud was in a hurry to get back to the front; terrified of anarchy or revolution, he was afraid that more attempts at assassination might be in the air. He had no desire for the job of High Commissioner.

Summoned to the Saint-Georges by Clark, he was to learn some distasteful news. Clark informed him that General Eisenhower "considered it necessary that he immediately take over the functions of High Commissioner."

"Giraud," says Clark, "wanted only a military command, but he quickly came around to our point of view and would second the plan."

So, just as everyone was discussing the relative chances of the prince and Noguès, says Soustelle, Giraud, "taken in hand by Clark, saw open before him the prospect of supreme power. Having refused it so long, he now changed his mind."

Eisenhower, having driven all night, also arrived in Algiers that afternoon, and, according to Butcher, "gave some discreet pushing to influence the selection of Giraud as the best man available."

Bergeret, scenting what was in the wind, decided to opt for Giraud.

As for Murphy, "after having encouraged the prince, he now found himself at odds with the American military, Clark and Eisenhower, and decided to ask instructions from Washington."

In his book *I Was There,* Admiral Leahy admits that on Christmas afternoon, after conferring with the President, he sent a cablegram to Eisenhower authorizing him "to appoint General Henri H. Giraud in charge of civil and military affairs in North Africa."

It is interesting to note in his *Crusade in Europe* how Eisenhower handled the incident: "While it was known, of course, that the person in the French Government I trusted most was General Giraud, my headquarters was still in no position to sponsor a puppet government. Such a resort to Nazi methods would have been a far more serious violation of the principles for which we were fighting than would the mere temporary acceptance of some individual whose past record was, from our viewpoint, distasteful. Moreover, in our inner councils we doubted Giraud's ability to establish himself firmly in the chief position—but no one else was both acceptable and immediately available."

Actually Noguès had automatically become High Commissioner pro tem, because by secret decree on December 2nd the Imperial Council had designated him to act in Darlan's stead in case of an emergency.

Butcher says that as soon as Noguès arrived in Algiers he went straight to the Saint-Georges and made it clear he did not want the job on a permanent basis—"possibly," says Butcher, "fearing a fate similar to Darlan's." When queried on the candidacy of the Count of Paris, Noguès is reported to have answered, "If it were his mother, I'd say yes right away."

Yet the Count of Paris was still optimistic, largely because there was no one kind enough to dissuade him.

Late that evening the count called in Rigault and Saint-Hardouin. Both told him that Giraud was likely to be elected.

"Do you mean," said the pretender, "that Giraud will not see it my way?"

"Indeed," they chorused.

"In that case," said the count, "I will go expose my views to Giraud. Please announce my visit."

"From this embarrassment," says Chamine, "they were saved by M. Pose, who offered to do so in their place."

Meanwhile a court-martial, ordered by Giraud, was due to convene at 6 P.M. to try Darlan's murderer. According to Achiary's testimony, an order had already been put through channels for a coffin for the boy.

By this time the police had established that the young man's name was in fact Fernand Eugène Bonnier de la Chapelle, that he was the twenty-year-old son of the law reporter of the *Dépêche Algérienne,* to whose name he had added that of his Italian mother (della Cappella) who lived in Venice, separated from her husband.

Brought up by an uncle in France, where he had studied at the École des Roches, in Algiers the boy had been a member of the Chantiers de la Jeunesse, and was now attached to the Corps Franc.

Standing before the court, Fernand Bonnier insisted once more that he had acted alone, without accomplices, and that all he had done was "to bring justice to a traitor who stood in the way of the union of France."

His defense lawyer, a Mr. Sansonetti, quickly hired by the boy's father, tried to argue that the inquest had been too short.

The court, presided over by a Garde Mobile colonel, declared itself to be sufficiently informed of the facts: as evidence they had the body of the late chief of government, found lying on the ground. Furthermore, the killer, with a weapon still hot in his hand, had duly acknowledged the crime, admitting to having premeditated it, and to being solely responsible.

Such a declaration, in time of war and under a state of siege, obliged them, said the judges, by the rules of military law, to rapid action.

After a short deliberation, the tribunal of the XIXth Military Region condemned Fernand Bonnier de la Chapelle to military degradation and to death, sentence to be carried out by shooting the following dawn at the *champ de tir* of Hussein-Dey.

Placed in a cell in the same building as the tribunal, Fernand Bonnier was more reserved when next questioned by Esquerré. He expressed the opinion that a mysterious hand would come that night to free him. He is reported to have said, "I am calm, London has been advised." During the night he asked his jailer if there was nothing unusual taking place in town: no troubles, no changes?

Romantically he spoke of a simulated execution like that of

Cavaradossi in *Tosca* before a firing squad with blank cartridges arranged by a modern Scarpia who would then allow him to slip away to Tangiers.

That night Saint-Hardouin had for dinner Pierre Bourdan (Maillaux), head of the French news agency in London, and some others, including Pierre Bret, head of the French news agency in Algiers. It was a funereal meal, says Chamine, as each phone call brought another dramatic twist to the story.

At the end of the meal Bret was called to the phone. It was Louis Joxe, in charge of press relations at the High Commissariat, who, *desolé,* was in possession of a short communiqué for the morning papers to announce the execution of the condemned prisoner.

Only one hope remained: a stay of execution from the chief of state.

By the laws of Vichy, this right was reserved to Marshal Pétain. But if Darlan's position as local chief of state had been the basis of recent legality, then the High Commissioner should be able to act in Pétain's stead.

Noguès, as pro-tem commissioner, insisted he had no such mandate to reprieve the boy.

To convince Noguès that at least he should stay the execution until a full-time commissioner had been appointed on the morrow, d'Astier went up to the Villa des Oliviers. But Noguès would not receive him.

"Sallow with fatigue," d'Astier and Pose returned to Saint-Hardouin and were silently given a drink.

D'Astier pleaded with Saint-Hardouin to accompany him on yet one more *démarche,* this time to Giraud. By virtue of the state of siege, Giraud, as supreme military commander of the French, held high hand as far as maintenance of order was concerned, and he alone could sign the order of execution.

But Giraud would not listen to them either. In a cold rage he answered Pose: "It's the law of the talion: an eye for an eye, a tooth for a tooth."

At midnight Giraud gave the order to General La Roubertie to have the execution carried out as planned.

From d'Astier's flat in rue Lafayette, the Abbé Cordier continued to try to muster support for the boy. Pose tried a new tactic by phoning Darlan's office in the Palais d'Été and warning his aide, Commandant de France, that if the execution were carried out it would bode ill for Giraud, and asking him to tell this to Bergeret.

De France answered, "Tell your friends we have a list of twenty or thirty people we can lock up. That is all we need to keep the peace."

As the dawn of December 26th was about to rise, a firing squad began its march toward Hussein-Dey. In the somber building of the military tribunal a chaplain entered Bonnier's cell.

In a last desperate attempt to save himself Bonnier pleaded for permission to write a note. But no one had any paper to give him. Fumbling through his pockets, he found a visiting card, not his own but that of his uncle in Paris, and addressing it to the Abbé Cordier, 2 rue Lafayette, he scribbled, "Please intervene immediately. I believe it is absolutely vital. I have full confidence in you, but you must act fast, very fast."

The chaplain promised to deliver the note.

A captain of gendarmes arrived at the cell with a picket of men.

In the streets the dawn had tinted the sky. On the balconies and rooftops of nearby buildings the black silhouettes of Gardes Mobiles men stood out against the skyline.

At Hussein-Dey the young prisoner—exactly twenty years and fifty-six days old—stood firmly before the firing post, and at precisely 7:45 he received the ritual *douze balles dans la peau*.

A few hours later his body was buried in an unmarked grave. Church bells tolled, but not for Bonnier. At almost the same moment the remains of Admiral Darlan were being quietly interred in a secret spot in the naval cemetery. Giraud, says Butcher, "knelt at the bier and shed a tear."

But as one reporter was to write, the members of the War Council, "composed of octagenarian reactionaries with no hope in the world but to hold on to their present positions," would quickly try to "bury the Admiral, bury the boy, and bury the story."

15

EARLY IN THE MORNING of the 26th, but not early enough, Alfred
Pose betook himself to the Palais d'Été in the company of M.
Robin. When Giraud saw the Economic Affairs Minister enter his
office he greeted him casually.

"Do you not know His Highness?" asked Pose in surprise.

"Ahaa," said Giraud, "but of course."

Immediately the count asked that Bonnier be spared, arguing
that he was a mere child, that he had acted out of pure patriotism.

"I regret," said Giraud, drawing himself up to his full 6 feet 4
inches, "to inform you that in conformity with the judgment of the
court, the admiral's assassin has been shot by a firing squad this
morning."

There was a long silence; then the count, says Chamine, proposed that Giraud support his candidacy for High Commissioner,
pointing out that it was only as political arbiter that he wished to
exercise power.

Whatever words Giraud may have used at the time, in his
memoirs he thus answered rhetorically, "A bundle of energy called
Henri de France does not easily camouflage the person of the pretender, and his designation as High Commissioner, whether he
likes it or not, would pass for a restoration."

At that moment Giraud must have been more diplomatic, for
the prince, says Soustelle, not only outlined his plan but listed the
ministers he proposed.

This, however, was too much for Giraud, who went into a rage
at the idea that the count could even think of surrounding himself
"with people of the Front Populaire" or of "opening the gates to
the Gaullists."

"*Non, monseigneur,*" was his recorded reply, "the monarchy
must be reactionary and of the church. *Laissez-moi essuyer les*

plâtres; go seek glory on the field of battle in Tunisia, and in three months you may be king."

On their way out, the prince turned to Pose: "Never," said he, "have I seen such a c. . . of a general. It's enough to make one turn republican!"

In the course of the morning, Murphy received the telegram from Leahy. The President wanted Giraud.

Yet Giraud dragged his feet.

In the end, when the Imperial Council met at noon, the prince's candidacy was not even put forward. Giraud boldly voted for himself. His election was unanimous.

As Soustelle summed it up, "Thanks to Mr. Roosevelt, Giraud was elected High Commissioner by the *gerarchs* of Vichy."

The nomination act started off equally boldly: "In the name of the impeded Chief of State [Pétain] and of the Government [Laval's], the Imperial Council . . ." etc., etc.

Taken suddenly ill, the Count of Paris retired from the scene to Sidi Ferruch.

Had he really given up? In his memoirs the count was to admit that though the *coup* planned by the royalists for the 18th had failed again on the 26th, there were to be more attempts, the next on either December 30th or 31st.

The election of Giraud and the burial of Darlan and Bonnier had not yet spelled the end of the story.

Several officers in the French Navy's Deuxième Bureau and some agents of the Securité Militaire were convinced that more trouble was to come. Among the first clues afforded the investigators were the recordings made by the censors of the various telephone conversations of the night before the execution. Rapidly the investigators deduced that several people seemed to have been aware that a murder was about to take place, even *before* it had happened. Coincidentally, these people turned out to be the ones who appeared most concerned about saving the boy from execution.

Pose's threat to Darlan's aide—that if the execution took place, *"certains milieux"* would make Giraud's life impossible—was considered by the investigators to be highly compromising.

From the growing police dossier it became clear that Bonnier had already been at the Palais d'Été on the morning of the crime, at which time he had asked to see not Joxe but de la Tour du Pin.

But how was it, asked the investigators, that the boy had known de la Tour du Pin was *not* at the Palais d'Été in the morning, and that in the afternoon it was Joxe who was out? Both Joxe and de la Tour du Pin, whose offices were a few feet down the hall from Darlan's, maintained they did not know the youth.

Next the police established that in the black Peugeot which had delivered Bonnier, three companions had waited till shortly after the murder, when, according to an eyewitness, "almost regretfully" they had put the car in gear and moved off before the sentries could stop them.

And why one of the windows in the antechamber had been left open *before* the murder, though it was a brisk December day, remained a mystery. Was it chance? Or had someone helped to plan an escape?

Another unsolved mystery was why both the sentry and the usher had chosen that particular moment to leave their posts for an unaccustomed walk in the garden.

The investigators now wanted to know: Who had been in the getaway car? What *milieux* did the young murderer frequent? Where had he obtained his weapon? Who had given him the false identity card and passport with a visa?

To their queries came some startling replies.

The killer, it developed, had been driven to the scene of the crime in a Peugeot belonging to an industrialist friend of Jacques Brunel; it was a car which Henri d'Astier, chief of the police, sometimes used, and which he often lent to others.

As for the occupants, one was none other than d'Astier's eldest son, Bernard; the driver turned out to be Mario Faivre, who had driven to Larache to fetch the Count of Paris, and had been an active conspirator in the *coup* of the 8th of November. The third member of the party, a Gilbert Sabatier, turned out to be a companion of Bonnier's in the Corps Franc, also devoted to d'Astier. AWOL from the corps, he had taken refuge after the murder,

interestingly enough, says Chamine, "with some English friends."
Coincidentally he had complained that his revolver had been stolen.

Up till this point the investigators, says Chamine, had thought
"they were looking into the past to establish the truth." Now it
dawned on them the real mystery might lie in a future "heavy with
suspended menace."

Undercover agents brought in similar reports.

On the 27th, at the Paris Restaurant, the Abbé Cordier was said
to have told an inspector of the Surveillance du Territoire that
there "will be more before the end of the year."

The next day, the 28th, again at the Paris, an officer was overheard to say, "Tomorrow there will be a *coup* with the Corps Franc
of boulevard Gambetta." The same day the *Chef de Cabinet* to
Bergeret received a call from a female friend warning him "to
guard his boss, Giraud, because some childhood friends of hers,
whom she would not name, were about to murder him."

Thus, says Chamine, developed the rumor that there was a vast
plot to gain power at the turn of the year by killing off Giraud,
Murphy, Chatel, etc., so that the conspirators could put their own
government into power.

Butcher duly noted the rumor in his diary: "Murphy, Bergeret
and Giraud are on the 'death list' of an assassin's ring here in
Algiers, according to the report of a trusted French agent who
gained the confidence of the conspirators. Murphy heads the
assassin's list. He is more than casually interested in the effort to
round up the ring."

Then came a bombshell in the form of a delayed report from two
Gardes Mobile men who had been assigned to duty with Bonnier the night before his execution.

During the course of his last night the boy had made several
confessions, but (says Darlan's son Alain) "these two officers did
not realize at the moment the capital importance of the declarations, and it was only during the course of the 26th, that is, after
the execution, that they drew up a detailed report of what transpired in the cell of the condemned boy on the night before his
execution."

This report, sent through military channels, only reached "competent authorities" three days later.

Toward 11 P.M. of the 25th, a Lieutenant Schilling of the Garde Mobile had entered Bonnier's cell, where he had found one Captain Gaulard already in conversation with the boy. Together they had stayed in the cell till 1 A.M. of the 26th.

The boy, said the officers, had first spoken almost gaily, quite sure that he would be freed. "Powerful personages," said the boy, "will get me out if I continue to say nothing."

Worried, the police officers kept looking and listening for signs of a coup to free him. But nothing extraordinary developed outside. The city of Algiers remained unusually calm for a Christmas night. Later, said the officers, as time was running short before the scheduled execution, the boy was suddenly overcome with panic and began to repeat, "I did what I promised. The promises which were made to me must now be kept."

Gaulard entered the boy's cell and heard from him the following confession, which he reported through channels:

"I killed Admiral Darlan because he was a traitor who was selling France to Germany for his own profit; I had in my hands the proof of his treason; it's the same as with Laval, they want power for themselves. I decided to kill the Admiral a few days ago. I learned that a certain person, who came from General de Gaulle, had asked to be received by the Admiral. The Admiral refused to receive General de Gaulle's envoy, showing he wished to keep for himself the power.

"Certain people spoke before me of this fruitlesss *démarche* and said: 'Darlan must disappear.' So I said to myself: 'Then I will undertake to make him disappear.'

"I came to the Palais d'Été on the morning of December 24th but could not accomplish the deed. When I reported this fruitless attempt I was told: 'Time is running short. Darlan must disappear.'

"So I went back in the afternoon. I did not kill the Admiral's adjutant; I could have easily done so if I had wanted to, as I had his head five centimeters from my pistol; it would have been silly. I had no reason for animosity against him. I shot at his legs to defend myself.

"The pistol was given to me. I had been given another, but either the ammunition was defective, or the pistol was no good: when I tried it out it would not work. I could have taken a submachine gun, but it was too bulky under my coat.

"I was told that after the deed I would be caught, condemned to death, and reprieved.

"However, they have tried me too fast. My friends needed two days in which to intervene.

"I know that my lawyer, M. Sansonetti, is trying hard.

"Furthermore, the Comte de Paris, whom I know, has been here for several days, twenty minutes from Algiers.

"I also know d'Astier de la Vigerie; they are several brothers, one of whom is with de Gaulle, another was with me in the Chantiers.

"In the end, if they do not reprieve me and shoot me tomorrow morning, it will be because my friends could do nothing. Henry IV said that Paris was worth a Mass; I say that France is worth my skin. For I know the Germans; that famous November 11 [1940] I was in Paris, on boulevard Saint-Michel; if the person for whom I made Darlan disappear did not take power, we would become Anglicized or Americanized; this, for France's sake, must not be.

"Though my name sounds royalist, I have only been so barely two months; and I am a good believer; I confessed before the murder and I told the priest I was going to kill; clearly the Ten Commandments forbid killing, but there are moments when one must go so fast that the death of one who stands in the way of the general good is a necessity. This is such a time. You cannot understand me because, despite my youth, I know a good deal.

"One thing worries me now. I was made to sign several papers; among them there was one which put some friends of mine *en cause;* I'm afraid that the person who made me sign it may use it, not to betray our cause, but to blackmail my friends.

"So, either I am reprieved and this will have no more meaning, or, if I am shot, my friends have let me down. But I don't think so.

"They went through my place and found some letters to me from my mother in Venice. This search was childish. I correspond with my mother. My parents are divorced.

"My trial was no trial, there was no inquest.

"They accuse me of killing a man. Well, on the 8th of November, General Noguès, in Morocco, had many killed for no reason, and Darlan did the same in Algiers . . ."

Several times during the course of the conversation, Captain Gaulard tried to find out who had furnished Bonnier the weapon, or who could have provided him with a machine gun; also who had told him that the disappearance of the Admiral was a necessity, and who were the people he hoped would come to power.

"Though my questions were direct," noted Gaulard, "I never got a precise answer."

"You will see soon enough" was the prisoner's answer.

The declarations of Gaulard and his colleague Lieutenant Schilling seem to have reached General La Roubertie late in the evening of December 29th. Giraud was awakened in the middle of the night and shown the dossier, to which had been added a list of suspects accused of plotting further murders: specifically Giraud's and Murphy's.

When Giraud saw the dossier he was skeptical, and could hardly believe that any such threat existed against him or Murphy; but when he saw the list of suspects he was "truly amazed." Everyone on the list had been involved in the *coup* of the 7th of November, designed to put Giraud in power.

Why, asked Giraud, would they now want to murder him?

But the connection with Darlan's murder and the reported imminence of further murders impressed him. He was worried on two counts: Like Eisenhower, he was afraid of disorder behind the lines and is said to have remarked, "I will put anyone in prison who interferes with the battle in Tunisia." Also he was worried about the possibility that at that moment a Franco-American incident "could have the most dreadful consequences"—not the least of which would be the termination of supplies for the units loyal to him.

Picking up a pencil, Giraud muttered, "Do what is necessary." The orders went immediately to Bergeret for action.

But with Rigault as Minister of Interior and d'Astier as chief of police, Bergeret would have had a hard time arresting those incriminated; they included not only members of the Five but partisans of the Allies who had aided the Allies in the seizure of Algiers.

Bergeret therefore decided to use a weapon left over from Vichy: "administrative interment" of persons whose activities could be considered damaging to the government.

North Africa was still in a state of siege; the military were responsible for order. Instead of making use of d'Astier's police, which he could not trust—especially as four top police commissioners were among those to be arrested—Bergeret decided to use the Gardes Mobile. To be sure that even the Garde members would not balk at his orders, Bergeret hit upon a Machiavellian ruse. Their orders were to read: "You will arrest certain German spies, extremely well armed and organized, who will fight dearly for their lives. You must seize them at any cost: dead or alive. Shoot at the slightest gesture."

At 26 rue Michelet they seized the grandchildren of Dr. Aboulker and terrorized them for half an hour, pointing submachine guns at them, trying to find out where their uncle José was hiding. Dr. Aboulker was dragged from his bed and made to stand in his pajamas on one leg (his brace had been removed for the night), his arms above his head, before being handcuffed.

Upstairs, in the apartment from which Colonel Jousse had made the final arrangement for neutralizing Algiers, the Garde men seized Jacques Brunel, son of the former mayor of Algiers.

Others were snared with more subtle ruses.

Dr. Fernand Morali, decorated with the Legion of Honor, in whose house *Combat* had been clandestinely edited, was roused in the middle of the night to come to the aid of a British officer who was reported to have fainted in the street. Grabbing his medical kit, the doctor had hardly crossed the threshold when he was forced into a car and spirited away.

Achiary, summoned on urgent police business to the headquarters of the XIX Corps, was arrested as he entered, then chained. When he asked to see the warrant for his arrest, he was told that it was not there but that one had been signed by "*Le Grand Chef*"—meaning Giraud.

When Achiary's former assistant, Bringard, who had been so helpful in tying up communications the night of the 7th, heard a violent banging at his door that sounded like the police, he presumed—as he had just been named director for the High Commissariat—that it was a gag. But having so many times been threatened with death by members of the SOL, he reached for his revolver.

Seeing a gun butt come through the door, Bringard put down his revolver—and wisely, for he might easily have been "liquidated" on the spot instead of being handcuffed and dragged away.

At Guyotville 25 Garde police surrounded the house of Raphaël Aboulker, then burst in and forced him to a car.

Only René Capitant, editor of *Combat,* managed to evade the Garde Mobile; he was hiding out (according to Renée Gossett) with some friends in British intelligence.

At Louis Joxe's office in the Palais d'Été, two Garde Mobile men arrived armed with a mobilization order and a car with which to dispatch him immediately to the Tunisian front.

And so it went. Lawyers, jurists, professors, doctors, police chiefs and industrialists—fifteen in all, though two were released because of their advanced age—were rounded up and carted away.

Soustelle maintains that by 6 P.M. on the 29th mysterious orders had reached the Caserne des Tagarins to arrest—as supposed Axis agents—the top Gaullists. These orders, says Soustelle, were issued by Bergeret, with the approval of Giraud.

Now, it is also a fact that this was the very day Giraud sent a message to de Gaulle in London in which he refused to discuss the establishment of a central provisional government in Algiers for the unification of all French forces—a refusal which Giraud was to repeat three times in the next ten days.

Meanwhile, according to Soustelle, during the evening of the 29th "Bergeret, Rigault and Chatel had clung to the phone, following the progress of the operation."

According to Esquer it was Bergeret, "in accord with Rigault, Chatel and the financiers, who devised the whole scheme of an imaginary plot to murder Giraud and Murphy." Chatel, says Esquer, was added "simply to provide him with a new virginity in the eyes of the Allies."

Renée Gossett elaborated by saying that some time later a secretary of Chatel's told her he had witnessed the scene and that Chatel had spent the night in his office at the Palais d'Été listening for the phone "and that each time it rang he would strike off a name from a list, heaving a sigh of relief."

"Who," asked Renée Gossett, "was at the other end of the wire?"

"Why, Rigault," said the secretary.

To which Gossett adds that those who had been involved in the *coup* of the 8th had built up a terrible dossier on Chatel and Mme. Chatel, compromising them not only for their very close relations with the German armistice commission, but for Chatel's colossal black-market operations via Spanish Morocco.

When Renée Gossett later approached Rigault and asked him point-blank why he had taken these measures against the Gaullists, he answered, "Because they bothered me. They agitated too much. They bothered even the Americans."

But by operating with the Garde Mobile instead of with Rigault's police, Bergeret was able to pretend the whole affair had nothing to do with the Ministry of the Interior—thus letting Rigault off the hook with his erstwhile friends. Because of Rigault's delicate position vis-à-vis d'Astier, Joxe, and Pose—who were officials at the High Commissariat—Bergeret personally struck their names from the list of those to be arrested.

But if it was Rigault who had prompted Bergeret and Giraud, who was behind Rigault? The answer, of course, was Lemaigre-Dubreuil.

On December 28th, in Washington, D.C., Cordell Hull received the visit of M. Lemaigre-Dubreuil, and after a pleasant chat the Secretary of State publicly expressed his satisfaction at Giraud's assumption of power in North Africa. Two days later Lemaigre

addressed a letter to Admiral Leahy in which he requested that
the Darlan-Clark accord be scrapped and that the Murphy-Giraud
agreements be made the base of Franco-American relations. Lemaigre also requested that Giraud's High Commissariat be allowed
to accredit diplomatic representatives abroad in lieu of Vichy. Far
from letting de Gaulle into Algiers, what Lemaigre sought was his
complete elimination from power in favor of Giraud.

Leahy's answer, and further conversations at State, fixed the
conditions under which Giraud, while leading the military action
of the French, would also represent and defend abroad French
interests, of which he was to become the trustee. The Murphy-
Giraud agreements would thus once more become the basis of relations between the Allies and French Africa.

Meanwhile, in London, Mr. Churchill was preparing quite a different deal with de Gaulle's Free French Committee, aimed at
bringing about a fusion of London and Algiers—rightly relying on
de Gaulle's superior political acumen to enable him to get the
better of Giraud.

A power struggle between Giraud and de Gaulle was inevitable.
How, then, could Giraud defend his position more effectively than
by eliminating all the principal supporters of de Gaulle in Algeria?

In chains, the prisoners were dragged off to the Caserne des
Tagarins, then taken to a concentration camp in Laghouat 200
miles into the Sahara. Thence they could be discreetly disposed of
3,000 miles across the desert to a sort of Guiana in Mauretania on
the Gold Coast, from which, as from Devil's Island, few were
likely to return.

But the pressure of American newspapermen and certain American officials, wrote Waverley Root, "was instrumental in prevent-
ing the Vichyites from revenging themselves on these men by giving
them a hasty and secret military trial and executing them."

To which Chamine adds: "The interventionists were the correspondents and eminent members of 'Psychological Warfare,' also
journalists by profession, who—with the exception of their chief,
Colonel Hazeltine, a career officer little affected by psychology—

were firmly persuaded of the superiority of the civil over the military, of citizens over functionaries."*

At noon on the 31st the foreign press correspondents were summoned to a press conference at the Palais d'Hiver where Giraud received them "with a stiff bow" and the opening remark that as a soldier he hated interviews. He then tried to explain away his action by saying he had ordered the arrests only because he had "absolute proof" there would be further assassinations, including, said he dramatically, that of Mr. Robert Murphy.

When Murphy was interrogated by the correspondents as to whether *he* had been shown any of this proof, he had to admit that he had not.

Giraud refused to reveal the names of the prisoners, intimating that some of them were Axis agents: an utterly preposterous charge. He then tried to say that his measure was purely in the interest of the French and of no concern to the Allies.

But the situation was now so embarrassing to Murphy that he had Rigault call a second press conference to mitigate the effect of the one given by Giraud.

The arrests, said Rigault, had no political overtones but were merely to clear up the circumstances of Darlan's murder and make sure that no more were planned. "As for the prisoners, they have simply been obliged temporarily to change residence." They could be released, he said, if they promised "not to take part in any future political agitation."

Rigault then made a bold stab at accomplishing his own scheme. Pretending to befriend the reporters, he suggested they "take good care not to reveal the truth—that the fourteen men arrested for implication in Darlan's assassination and 'plot' against Giraud and Murphy had Gaullist connections—as this would make a union of Frenchmen more difficult."

---

* For the sake of historical clarity let me add that it was in a secret code over a private radio link I had established between Algiers and New York that early in the morning of the 30th I advised the Deputy Director of Psychological Warfare of the secret arrests: my message, promptly relayed via Sherwood and Hopkins to F.D.R.'s desk, brought back a sizzler from Marshall to Eisenhower: "Tompkins says . . ." The cat was out of the bag.

In the North African press the entire affair was completely censored; no mention was even allowed of the fact that Giraud had given a press conference to members of the foreign press.

Yet Rigault's approach was to have its effect.

The next day Secretary of War Henry L. Stimson announced that those arrested must be "Vichyite or pro-Axis," and that he had been impressed by the "wisdom and loyalty" of Darlan.

As late as January 27, the Associated Press correspondent from Algiers was still reporting that "Some of those taken into custody claimed to have helped the Allied landings but most responsible authorities of the Allied force said they had never heard of them."

Then came a surprise in the story of Darlan's murder which was to lead to its unravelment.

On January 1st, Commissioner Garidacci, who for some strange reason had not been among the policemen arrested, went to see M. Temple, still the prefect of Algiers, to tell him that the four policemen sent to Laghouat were being falsely accused of having been involved in the murder of Darlan.

They had, said Garidacci, absolutely nothing to do with the murder. Of this he had proof, but would be risking too big a stake if he talked to anyone other than Giraud himself. Were Temple to promise to speak of the matter to Giraud alone, Garidacci would undertake to bring him within twenty-four hours the two persons responsible for plotting the assassination of Darlan, providing, of course, he was given the necessary freedom of action.

Also, said Garidacci, he would bring a confession from the person who had provided Bonnier with the gun.

Temple agreed, and promised to discuss the matter with Giraud alone.

On January 2nd Temple did see Giraud and told him what Garidacci had said. He added that the policeman was wary of Rigault.

But Giraud refused to receive Garidacci, or to hear his story, or even to have him received by any member of his staff. He suggested that Bergeret hear him and that in the meantime Temple try to pump him for more details.

In this Temple was successful to some extent. From Garidacci he learned that the person who had furnished Bonnier the gun was the Abbé Cordier, and that d'Astier de la Vigerie had been involved in the plot. Garidacci also spoke of a meeting at which several persons had learned of the murder immediately after it had happened, and as if it had been something they expected. Among those present, he said, had been de la Tour du Pin.

Immediately a search was instituted at d'Astier's house on rue Lafayette. There the searchers found the $38,000 brought from London by General François d'Astier, also the dummy front page of a newspaper announcing a *coup d'état*. On either side of a large photograph of the Count of Paris were those of Generals Giraud and de Gaulle. Under a three-column head was the following proclamation by the prince, justifying the change of regime:

"Called on by the representatives of the three departments of France still free, and by the will of the Army, I assume full power.

"Frenchmen: I come to you not as a partisan. I place myself beyond our old quarrels, above our ancient dissensions. I bear no other standard than that of our common fatherland, now beaten and wounded. I am here to unite all those who aspire to liberate her from the invader. . . . I am the denominator of all French energies, of all forms of French patriotism, of all aspirations to French grandeur. I recognize them all, I love them all equally. I unite them all in a solid *fascieau* for the resurrection of France. . . ."

Not a bad speech, especially after the inanities of Giraud and Darlan, spoiled perhaps by a clue to its real objective in the one word *fascieau*. Still, it ended in a rousing vein: "To me, then, soldiers of eternal France!"

The place for a banner headline had been left ominously vacant, clearly to announce the disappearance, in one way or another, of Admiral Darlan.

On the basis of this evidence the members of the Deuxième Bureau now felt they could go to work on the prisoners in Laghouat (who were still unaware that any steps had been taken to free them) to see what information could be extracted from them with the threat of banishment to the Gold Coast.

Cleverly, the jailers forbade the prisoners to gather together; but measures were taken to *"controller l'installation sanitaire,"* where their confidences could best be recorded.

Then Rigault went so far as to allow Murphy's "vice-consul" John Boyd to fly to Laghouat with soap, linen and cigarettes for the prisoners, as well as assurances that they would not be shot. Boyd even brought along Achiary's wife to visit him in jail.

The security men then produced a trump card in the form of a Commandant Paillole, who, says Chamine, had conveniently arrived from France on January 3rd, along with Generals Rivet and Ronin, former chiefs of security and counter-espionage for the Army of the Armistice in France, and who now took over the secret service of Giraud at the High Commissariat.

By coincidence Paillole had worked closely with Achiary in the past. "As technicians," says Chamine, "they understood each other well." By January 4th, Paillole had the story he wanted. All he needed was confirmation.

By January 9th a formal deposition could be drawn up for the Civil Tribunal of Algiers on the circumstances of the death of Admiral Darlan.

Signed by Achiary, it started off boldly: "I accuse two persons of being the direct instigators of the murder of Admiral Darlan: they are: the Abbé Cordier, and Henri d'Astier de la Vigerie, Assistant Secretary General for Political Affairs at the High Commissariat, both residing at number 2 rue Lafayette.

"These two persons had Admiral Darlan assassinated on behalf of the Count of Paris, who, according to a statement of M. Jacques Brunel, made to me at Laghouat on January 7th, urged them to be quick about carrying out the crime. The presence in Algiers of the Count of Paris at the time of the murder, which appeared to be fortuitous, as well as the luncheons and contacts he had with high personalities such as General Giraud, General Noguès, and M. Pose, constitute an element of proof to the above accusation, as the Count of Paris most certainly tried to have himself named High Commissioner in the place of Admiral Darlan.

"On this last point I can adduce the following personal testimony: the Count of Paris, counting on obtaining the post of High

Commissioner, had promised to M. d'Astier de la Vigerie the port-folio of the Interior. The latter sounded out my schoolmate M. Jacques Brunel to see if he would fill the role of head of the police in North Africa. The Saturday following the murder [December 26th], Brunel asked me to call on him to discuss a complete change of political life in the country as a result of the murder of Admiral Darlan.

"In the course of this conversation, which took place in M. Brunel's flat at 26 rue Michelet, the latter avowed to me that the Count of Paris was about to assume power and that d'Astier had offered him the job of police chief. Before accepting he wished to have my accord. I refused, categorically, and tried to show Brunel that he had been led on; I then gave him proof that d'Astier and his friends were actually maneuvering against his father, a known republican, who was then a candidate for the post of Governor General of Algiers.

"Jacques Brunel seemed shaken by my remarks, and when M. Luizet, ex sub-prefect of Tiaret, arrived on the scene he made the following remarks to me: 'I know who you are and esteem you, and would like to demonstrate to you that the Count of Paris can save the country.'

"Very violently I rebelled at this opinion, branding it as the at-titude of people who wanted to indulge in low politics when they should be thinking only of fighting the Germans. I must add, how-ever, that I believe in the absolute sincerity of M. Luizet in this affair. At the end of this conversation I insisted on giving my opinion directly, and in their presence, to M. d'Astier de la Vigerie, with whom I made an appointment for 1700 *chez* M. Langlois at 119 (*ter*) rue Michelet.

"There M. d'Astier confirmed that the Count of Paris was about to take power, and in the face of my refusal to collaborate, and the reproaches of Jacques Brunel with regard to his father, M. d'Astier seemed extremely ill-at-ease and expressed the desire im-mediately to return to the High Commissariat.

"That same Saturday afternoon, before seeing Jacques Brunel, I found the Abbé Cordier and expressed to him my feeling about the crime.

"On the day before Bonnier's execution I had a meeting first with Cordier and then with Cordier and d'Astier [at the Paris restaurant], where they confirmed to me that Bonnier was their envoy. They also affirmed they intended to get him out of his predicament and asked me to help in arranging an escape. I answered that this was absolutely impossible, that special police measures had most certainly been taken. It was then that Cordier asked me to take a piece of paper to the prisoner on which he had written his signature, saying 'with this piece of paper Bonnier de la Chapelle will understand that the bearer comes on my behalf.'

"I left them in front of the Paris restaurant and it was then that d'Astier said to me: 'The Count of Paris is here, everything will work out, don't worry.'

"If I did not report this conversation earlier it was for two reasons: Firstly, M. d'Astier de la Vigerie was still, in my eyes, the ardent combattant, and comrade, who had proved at my side that he had faith in a final victory of France and her Allies against the Germans. Also he was considered by all our friends as a sort of chief of the resistance movement against the Germans; secondly, he was the Chief of Police at the High Commissariat, and so considered; in all of what he did he gave the impression of acting in the name of the government.

"I must add that I violently reproached the Abbé Cordier for the criminal role he played, and in the face of my indignation he went away without saying a word.

"The same Saturday, at 1430, I went to the headquarters of the Corps Franc d'Afrique at the invitation of Captain Castaing, chief of its Deuxième Bureau. This officer and General Monsabert were afraid there might be suspicion about the Corps Franc because of Bonnier's belonging to it. In the course of the conversation, Captain Castaing told me he believed the weapon used in the crime had been obtained by Bonnier from another member named Sabatier, who had, I believe, reported the weapon as stolen."

Thus ended Achiary's deposition. On January 4th Sabatier was picked up for being AWOL from his unit.

At 6 A.M. of January 10th, Cordier and d'Astier were arrested. When Murphy heard the news, says Chamine, he was staggered.

Charges of plotting against the state were then brought against Alfred Pose, who was singled out as the leader of the plot with a preponderant influence on the others. He was accused of organizing the plot, of hiding the future chief of state while preparing the murder of the legal incumbent, and of trying to obtain the release of the murderer by the use of further threats. Marc Jacquet was also accused of plotting against the state because of his action as the key liaison man; Gilbert Sabatier was accused of plotting against the state and of furnishing the murder weapon.

Interrogated by the police, the Abbé Cordier admitted having known Bonnier for a short time after the formation of the Corps Franc, and that he had occasionally seen him at d'Astier's where the boy came in his capacity as a liaison officer.

Cordier also admitted having seen Bonnier on the morning of the crime at about 10 A.M. and of having heard his confession, saying that the boy had promised him the previous evening to put himself *en règle* from a religious point of view. The confession had taken place in an isolated street.

Cordier said he had learned of the murder only by chance, toward 8 P.M., from a chauffeur. That night he had been telephoned by Achiary, who asked to meet him in the street near the rue Lafayette. There, said Cordier, Achiary told him of the murder and it was then that he realized the assassin might be the young man he had confessed that morning. He therefore asked Achiary if something could be done for the boy, so long as he merited it.

When asked by the police why he took such an immediate interest in an assassin, to the extent of trying to prevent his just punishment, the Abbé answered that he had to admit he felt no severe affliction at the murder of Darlan, and believed that now that he was gone it would be easier to take up arms against the Germans.

Cordier admitted he was a monarchist but said that though he believed the Count of Paris would be called on to play a role, he doubted the monarchy could be established before the end of hostilities.

As for Bonnier, the Abbé said he did not believe the crime fell in the category of common law and he had therefore made several *démarches* to stay the execution, at least till the nomination of a new High Commissioner.

When asked how it was that he had given Achiary the piece of paper with his signature, the Abbé answered that he had forgotten to mention that he had made an arrangement that if the boy ever needed him and saw that signature he would know the Abbé was thinking of him.

The Abbé then refused to explain himself further, taking shelter behind the privilege of sacerdotal secrecy, saying he could not reveal what the boy had said during confession.

Thus the Abbé and d'Astier were jailed.

The next day, January 11th, Commissioner Garidacci was also arrested and it was then that he produced a missing link in the puzzle.

His own deposition also started off boldly: "I have acted during this affair in a flagrantly criminal manner."

It developed that during the course of the inquest he had withheld a true confession made by the assassin in which the boy had named his accomplices. In its place he had produced only a second confession in which the boy insisted he had acted alone.

The true confession ran as follows:

"In the year 1942 and the 24th of the month of December, before us, Garidacci, Commissioner of Police Mobile, officer of the P.J., M. Bonnier de la Chapelle, Fernand, student, 20 years old, resident at Alger, 56 rue Michelet, declares:

"I affirm having killed Admiral Darlan, High Commissioner in French Africa, after having told the Abbé Cordier I would do so in the form of a confession.

"It was M. Cordier who gave me the plan of offices at the Commissariat and of the office of the Admiral; it was through him that I was able to obtain the pistol and shells which I used to execute the mission I had assigned myself which was to dispose of the Admiral.

"When I joined the Corps Franc I recruited on my own initiative men of action from among the NCOs and troopers of whom M.

d'Astier might have need, though M. d'Astier was never informed of my personal actions.

"I know that Mssrs. Cordier and d'Astier have recently received the Count of Paris, as well as other personalities. Finally I have the impression that M. de la Vigerie is not on excellent terms with M. Rigault, whose activities for the Admiral are a hindrance to him and his friends.

"Signed: Bonnier de la Chapelle."

16

ON THE BASIS of these police reports and varied fragments of information it was possible to reconstruct the action.

On December 19th or 20th several young people—mostly veterans of the *coup* of November 7th—met at 7 rue de Charras in the office of the *Société des Carburants,* a regular meeting place in Algiers for members of the group known as the Corps Franc of Cap Matifou, put at their disposal by the same Aspirant Peauphilet who had surrounded Darlan at the Villa des Oliviers.

Immediately after the landings many of these young men—though predominantly Gaullist—had served as guards or couriers for General Giraud and his staff at Dar Mahieddine.

During all the jockeying that followed Clark's arrival, d'Astier had suggested that a proper group of actionists be reorganized because, as he put it, "If these gentlemen cannot make up their minds to govern, we may have to take power by force."

An appeal for volunteers placed in the *Écho d'Alger,* though it ran only once before being suppressed by Darlan's censors, produced a swarm of volunteers.

Among the first was young Gilbert Sabatier, who helped organize about 400 others. When these overflowed into the rue Charras, they were obliged to move to a property at Cap Matifou: hence their new name.

The Allies (actually the British) let it be known they would cover the organization with their authority providing it was kept a secret. The volunteers were then supplied with weapons, munitions, clothing and food.

When General Monsabert—like the officers who had aided the Allies, such as Mast, Béthouart and Jousse—found himself ostracized by Darlan, he agreed to head the volunteers.

They were formed into "commandos," and their training was so accelerated that by November 24th the first group of 80 men could be sent to Tabărka on the Tunisian front.

The next day, by Giraud's order No. 2 of November 25th, the unit was officially recognized by the French as the Corps Franc d'Afrique.

But ever since Darlan had "usurped" their victory on November 8th, most of these young men had been saying, "Darlan must go."

Whether because of Darlan's refusal to deal with de Gaulle's delegate General d'Astier, or because of Eisenhower's refusal to bring Giraud and de Gaulle together under the Count of Paris, December 19th seems to have been the day the decision was made that the time *had* come.

That night or the next, lots were drawn for the individual who should do the job. But the first young man to draw the short match refused when he realized what the plot would involve. A second drawing resulted in a second refusal.

At this point Fernand Bonnier de la Chapelle volunteered.

Bonnier, though a delicate and sensitive youth, was also impulsive. He was the offspring of divorced parents, and his schooling had been retarded by fragile health. In Paris, where he had completed his studies under the care of his father's brother, the boy had lived through the terrible days of the Fall of France and of the German occupation. On November 11, 1940, when Parisian students staged the first open demonstration against the Germans, Bonnier, then eighteen years old, was with them, says Soustelle, at the Arch of Triumph.

The mind of this natural rebel was fired by the romance of the Resistance and by working for British intelligence. Bonnier tried to escape to England and join de Gaulle, but having failed to make

Gibraltar, he decided to join his father in North Africa, where he signed up with the Chantiers de la Jeunesse.

Recruited for the pre-landing *coup,* he is believed to have been among the guards who surrounded the Villa des Oliviers.

In the Corps Franc, Bonnier found himself in his proper element. The morale was high, and the air breathed, says Chamine, was that of "fairy tales and glory, of sacrifice and poetry, in which all were predestined heroes."

Bonnier's job as liaison between Corps Franc headquarters and the romantic, dashing d'Astier de la Vigerie, hero of the 8th of November, boded well for Bonnier's advancement.

Then came a chance for action. His sufficient motivation, says Chamine, had been the shock not only of having seen his comrades such as Dreyfus and Pilafort cut down in cold blood, but of seeing their killers being decorated by Vichy under the patronage of Darlan with the support of Clark and Eisenhower.

When the time came, the details of the job were carefully worked out for the young volunteer. He was given a plan of the Palais d'Été and shown the location of Darlan's office; arrangements were made for him to escape through a window purposely left open so he could reach the getaway car at the gate; with excellent papers and a passport he could escape to Tangier—and who knows what adventures beyond.

To have weakened now would have been to destroy his whole self-image.

On December 23rd, all was ready. The Abbé Cordier, who had been d'Astier's right-hand man in the plotting, now reminded the youth that he must first put himself *"en règle avec le bon Dieu."*

They made a date for 10 A.M. on December 24th.

The meeting took place—as admitted by Cordier—in an isolated side street near the Abbé's lodgings on rue Lafayette. There, on the sidewalk, in a heavy whisper, the assassin-to-be, having confessed to the deed he was about to perform, was given absolution "before the crime."

This, says Chamine, amounted to a double precaution of safety:

spiritual for the boy, and temporal for the priest—who was thus protected by the secrecy of the confessional.

An hour later, shortly after 11 A.M. on a bright December day, Bonnier presented himself at the Palais d'Été to try to accomplish the deed, registering in the porter's lodge as Morand.

First he asked to see a certain M. Bourette, but as no one knew of any such person, he asked to see M. de la Tour du Pin.

By now it was close to midday. In the driveway wheels moved on the gravel. Looking out the window, Bonnier saw the admiral's car taking him away to lunch, and decided not to stay any longer.

For what happened during lunch there is the testimony of an anonymous witness as recorded in an article in *Le Figaro* of December 24th, 1945.

Three years earlier to the day, on December 24th of 1942, the anonymous witness was lunching at the Restaurant de Paris in Algiers with a friend. At a nearby table were lunching d'Astier and his son Bernard, as well as the Abbé Cordier and another young man.

A few days earlier, says the witness, the Abbé Cordier had asked his own luncheon companion if he could put him in touch with someone who was willing to assassinate Darlan.

If this seems hard to believe, Kenneth Pendar's testimony of the atmosphere of those days may be worth reporting:

"I would have found the inside story incredible myself," says Pendar, "if I had not sat in the Restaurant de Paris only a few weeks before, and heard some of our leading pre-landing collaborators blandly discussing past acts of violence of incredible and gruesome ferocity. It is hard but important for Americans to realize that the spirit of violence that lies deep in human beings, the spirit that broke out in our Ku Klux Klan, has been released on a really enormous scale in modern Europe. That release was, perhaps, the worst of Hitler's crimes. We saw it face to face in Algiers."

It is therefore not surprising that the witness at the fateful luncheon was unperturbed by the request for an assassin. Already he knew of a much larger plot, involving some hundred individuals, to attack Darlan openly in his car, shoot him down with machine guns, so as to enable the actual murderers to disperse in the resulting confusion.

But he need not have worried. By the end of the lunch the Abbé Cordier approached his friend again and told him that all was well, that he had found his man, that the deed would soon be accomplished. He then introduced to him Bonnier de la Chapelle, and asked if the friend could test Bonnier's pistol because it had a tendency to jam.

"We drove Bonnier," says the witness, "to the outskirts of Algiers, and tried out the pistol, which indeed did jam. But my friend had a pistol of his own, a Buby [sic] automatic 7.65 caliber which he lent to Bonnier."

If this person, as seems evident, was Mario Faivre, who had already been involved in fetching the Count of Paris from Larache, the casualness of Cordier's remarks and the cold-blooded testing of the pistols has an even more natural ring.

In any case, says the witness, they then drove Bonnier to the Palais d'Été: that is, Sabatier, d'Astier's son, and Mario Faivre.

This would also explain the disappearance of Sabatier immediately after the crime.

Meanwhile, according to Kammerer's account, the Abbé Cordier left the Paris about 2:30 P.M. and went to Saint-Augustin, where he heard confessions from 3 P.M. till dinner, which he took once more at the Paris in the company of d'Astier.

Summoned to the phone, he asked, *"De la part de qui?"*

"Ici Achiary. Do you know the news?"

"What news?"

"Quelle drôle d'affaire."

"You say that for the censors listening in."

"Would it not be best to meet right away?"

In a dark alley near the Paris Cordier met Achiary, and it was then that he learned how the murder had taken place.

Vainly Cordier pleaded with Achiary to intercede in favor of the boy. Achiary seemed to feel there was little hope of saving the boy.

Meanwhile Bonnier had been taken to Garidacci's office. There, for two hours, the boy repeated to Garidacci what he had told Esquerré when first seized: that he had acted alone, that he had needed no accomplice to do justice to a traitor who stood in the way of a union of Frenchmen. Only when taken to Garidacci's private office, where he was allowed to relax, had the boy begun to weaken. In the modest comfort of the Commissioner's office with its carpeted floor, its green shaded lamp, and a coal fire burning in the grate, the boy was more at his ease.

The commissioner pushed back his easy chair, joined his hands on the table, leaned forward, and in a soothing tone addressed the young murderer: "Now, my boy, just between you and me . . ."

It was the night before Christmas. Outside on the boulevards the tram bells were ringing. The footsteps of American soldiers could be heard on the sidewalk as they passed, whistling "White Christmas" on their way to being entertained in the houses of Algerians.

By 7 P.M. Garidacci had established that Morand was a false name, that no dossier existed under the pseudonym, and that the address the boy had given was also false.

About 7:15 the *juge d'instruction,* M. Rondreux, arrived and delegated to Garidacci any necessary investigative work.

Esquerré entered for a moment to tell Garidacci the boy's real name, which had been given him by someone from the base at Blida.

At last, breaking down, Bonnier admitted that Cordier and d'Astier had put him up to the murder and had provided him with the weapon.

Garidacci then drafted the text of a confession which he read aloud to the boy, and which the boy signed.

Later, when Garidacci was asked if he had told Bonnier that this deposition would *not* be put in his dossier for the trial, Garidacci denied this was so, affirming he had had every intention of placing the confession in the boy's dossier that night.

Garidacci also testified that when Bonnier signed the paper, he gave the impression of being calm and in full possession of his faculties. The declaration, said Garidacci, was in no way forced from him, nor obtained under the promise of immunity or a light sentence. It was just that the boy, said Garidacci, suddenly weakened, and Garidacci, in his role as a policeman, took advantage of the moment to draft a confession.

According to Garidacci, Esquerré was aware that a confession had been made, but had not read the text.

Toward 9 P.M. the boy was replaced in his cell and Garidacci went out to make a *pro forma* search of the boy's room in his father's apartment.

A little later that night Garidacci went back to the prisoner, alone; in the privacy of the cell he explained to the boy that if he wished to save his life and be free, it was essential for him to make a fresh declaration to the effect that he had acted entirely on his own accord, and without benefit of accomplices.

Now, one may ask, who had Garidacci seen since he had obtained the confession of complicity? Had someone made a promise to him in return for withholding the incriminating document and substituting another? Or was Garidacci merely paralyzed, afraid to reveal d'Astier's role in the murder because, in the morning, d'Astier might be the new Minister of Interior in a government formed by the Count of Paris; and equally afraid that were he prematurely to reveal d'Astier's role, d'Astier might *not* become Minister of the Interior?

Under oath, Garidacci later testified he had withheld the confession purely "in the interests of France," because he did not know whether at that time it would be "opportune" to reveal the real culprits. He also denied knowing personally either d'Astier or Cordier.

Back in Bonnier's cell, says Alain Darlan, Garidacci was apparently successful in making the boy believe he was an emissary of those who had encouraged him to commit the crime and had promised to save his life.

The boy therefore allowed himself to be persuaded to sign a second confession drafted by Garidacci, in which he declared he had acted alone.

The next day, when the *juge d'instruction,* M. Rondreux, came to Garidacci's office about 12:20 P.M. to pick up the dossier on

Bonnier, Garidacci said nothing to him about there being two confessions.

And at 3:30 when Rondreux came again, Garidacci still said nothing, but handed him the dossier with the second confession in which the boy inculpated only himself.

Glancing at the dossier, Rondreux remarked that it appeared to be an isolated crime: "the work of an intellectual, a Raskolnikov."

Meanwhile Bonnier's lawyer had obtained postponement of the trial till 6 P.M.

Waiting for it to start, Bonnier was left alone in an office in the courthouse building. There he drafted a note which he placed in an envelope and addressed to the Abbé Cordier. Whether or not he asked anyone to deliver it is not known.

Garidacci later testified that he had "found the envelope under the blotter," and that he did not know its contents but had placed it (along with the original confession) in a sealed envelope in a safe in his office.

Garidacci gave as his reason for not forwarding the envelope the excuse that by the time he came across it Bonnier had already been condemned to death and he had "some scruples about opening it."

At the court-martial, Bonnier played the role requested of him, and when condemned to death showed little or no emotion.

But during the night of the 25th and the 26th, as the hour of execution approached, and he could see no sign of anyone coming to help him, Bonnier became frightened and begged to be allowed to send a word to the Abbé Cordier.

As his panic mounted, he began to repeat spontaneously the truth about his accomplices. It was then that he made his declarations to Gaulard and Schilling, who, believing them to be no more than the ravings of a panic-stricken boy trying to build himself up by inculpating the chief of police and a Jesuit priest, did nothing about them.

And so he went to his death.

Garidacci too must have spent an uncomfortable night, knowing that with one phone call he could stay the execution, on the grounds that the prisoner had made another confession incriminating his accomplices.

Only when the boy had been shot, and when d'Astier had *not* become Minister of the Interior, did the dossier lose value. Then when Garidacci's colleagues, such as Esquerré, were arrested and accused of participation in the crime, the dossier began to recover its importance. Esquerré was aware that Garidacci knew the real culprits. So apparently did Commissioner Muscatelli. Yet Garidacci had not been arrested. Was this part of some deal devised during the interval between the drafting of the first and the second confessions? Why had Garidacci been so loath to discuss the matter with Rigault?

Though these questions remained unanswered, the military inquisitors considered that with the arrest of Garidacci they had uncovered enough of the story.

When Giraud had first heard of the crime, on December 24th, he had said, "I want light to be thrown on this matter."

Now, when the dossier was brought to him, he closed it quickly. In his own words: "I judged that circumstances required to let silence grow heavy on this affair."

He ordered the Commissioner of Government to classify the document.

What did Giraud see—or perhaps only glimpse—in the report? Chamine answers: "Some say a hand, some say a sleeve."

The French word *manche* can mean sleeve or Channel.

Even before the inquest was completed, says Alain Darlan, the rumor spread through Algiers that the murder of the High Commissioner had been organized by Allied Secret Services, and that two agents of the British intelligence responsible for it had actually been identified.

So convincing was the report, says Alain Darlan, that at the beginning of the inquest General Bergeret received a visit from the American General Bedell Smith, who declared to him that General Eisenhower wished that all efforts be made to determine if responsibility for the crime could be imputed to the British government, in any manner or degree. Were such a connection to be found and formally established, General Eisenhower had the intention of immediately resigning.

"But," says Alain, "the circumstances so favored covering up the job that General Eisenhower did not find himself in a position to have to or not abandon his post."

Darlan's son gave these reasons for blaming the British: "The accord between the Americans and Giraud may have seemed sufficiently inoffensive to the British for them to pretend to accept it. But an accord with a man of the stature and power of Darlan required rapid and radical measures. Darlan would have to go."

This possibility had already been envisaged by Darlan before his death, when he noted, "If one considers all the trouble the English have taken, and all the capital they have invested, to set up de Gaulle, it seems obvious they will be loath to see their efforts lost, and will probably try to do something about it."

Even before the landings, Darlan had confided in his notebook, "If ever I am called on to take command of the French Empire and launch it into the war, it will be in obedience to the permanent order given me by Marshal Pétain. . . . I would then become legitimate chief of all Frenchmen fighting the Axis, and de Gaulle's role will lose its meaning." At the same time Darlan doubted his chances of attaining that position: "Whatever attitude de Gaulle takes, the British will lose the handy instrument they have used till now . . . unless, of course, I retire from the scene or am retired."

As for the manner in which he might be retired, Darlan was specific enough in his notes: "If I survive to my natural death, it will prove only that those who pull the strings of the British policy have more scruples, or less means of action, than once upon a time."

At the time of d'Astier's arrest the proclaimed goal of the Gaullists was still to bring about an accord between de Gaulle and Giraud for the establishment in Algiers of a provisional republican government; but in a confidential bulletin circulated among their supporters, the Gaullists did not hide their feelings about Giraud:

"The entourage of General Giraud," ran the circular, "consists

largely of men of the extreme right, monarchists and Cagoulards.
. . . They are following a well-determined plan to maintain in North
Africa the institutions of the National Revolution. Behind the figure
of General Giraud a clique of *affairistes* and fanatics are attempting
to plot, just as they did in 1940 using the figure of Pétain, a cynical
exploitation of France's defeat. . . . Not only is Vichy not being
attacked, but its institutions are being revived, such as the Legion,
and the laws against Jews, secret societies, etc."

These feelings of the Gaullists were, of course, no secret to
Giraud and his henchmen. Nominally in political as well as military
control of French Africa, Giraud was having a hard enough time
with military affairs—in Tunisia matters were going from bad to
worse—so that he was obliged to leave the political side of his job
to the care of Bergeret and Rigault.

The result was a "reaction" against the Gaullists, even more
vehement; for the political existence of the Giraudists was now
directly at stake.

From Americans, both locally and in the United States, the
Giraudists received even stronger support.

Far from being removed, Murphy dug in his heels.

At a Cabinet meeting January 7th, President Roosevelt confirmed Eisenhower as the chief in North Africa and stipulated he
did not want him interfered with or undermined by anyone. To this
the President added that Robert Murphy, as State Department
representative, was in charge of civil affairs under General Eisenhower, adding that he wished to make it clear that by "under" he
meant "under."

But one of the first results of the disappearance of Darlan was
that Churchill requested of Roosevelt that he too be allowed to
have a personal political representative at Eisenhower's AFHQ. To
sweeten the pill, Churchill cabled Roosevelt: "He will be, I am
sure, a help. He is animated by the friendliest feelings toward the
United States, and his mother hails from Kentucky."

He was Harold Macmillan.

Political censorship in North Africa remained as stringent as
ever.

On January 11th Charles Collingwood did manage to get a broadcast through from Algiers in which for the first time the world learned about the royalist plot, and that the actual accomplices in the murder of Darlan had been arrested.

In the London press a clamor was raised. *The Spectator,* while acknowledging a debt to American broadcasters for their "wholesome candor," complained that "the mystery of Darlan's assassination remains a mystery; as does the series of arrests ordered by Giraud as soon as he had become High Commissioner."*

To the *New Statesman and Nation* Admiral Darlan's assassination left "a political cesspool whose stench not only infects the cause of the Western Allies, but threatens, unless there be plain speaking and better understanding, to poison Anglo-American relations."

No longer resolvable at the Murphy-Macmillan level, the conflict between Giraud and de Gaulle over the succession to Darlan now passed from AFHQ directly into the hands of the arbiters of Allied power: Churchill and Roosevelt.

17

AT THE 1943 New Year's Eve party in the White House, a movie was shown which caused Robert E. Sherwood to remark that there were "very few of those present who had any idea as to the significance of the selection."

The film, starring Humphrey Bogart and Ingrid Bergman, was called *Casablanca.*

A mile south of Casablanca atop a grass-covered hill stands a

---

* Amazingly, even twenty years after the fact, Murphy was to write in his memoirs: "The motive for the assassination of Darlan still remains a mystery. . . . Whoever influenced young de la Chapelle to commit the murder, supplying him with the pistol and apparently assuring him that he would be a national hero and would be fully protected from harm, never has been identified."

small pleasure resort of sparkling white villas round a modern hotel looking westward over the Atlantic. It is called Anfa.

During the second week in January Anfa's French and Moroccan inhabitants were ordered from their homes, the sick and aged were transported to clinics, the entire area was wired off, ringed with antiaircraft batteries, and patrolled by Patton's troops on "maximum security" orders.

What was a mystery to the rest of the world was, however, clear enough to Axis agents. Spanish spies radioed Berlin that Churchill was about to meet Roosevelt for a top-secret conference at Casablanca. But the German intelligence translator who handled the message rendered "Casablanca" literally into "White House"—a target too remote for the Germans to bomb—and so the conference was held undisturbed.

An early West African spring had touched the Anfa hilltop with color when the President flew in from the United States, via Brazil —the first time any American President in office had flown out of the country—on January 14, 1943.

Mr. Churchill had arrived the day before, equipped with a box of paints, and had already taken a walk by the sea, remarking with wonder on how anyone could have landed on such rocky coasts in the face of 20-foot breakers which burst into clouds of spray.

When Harry Hopkins came to bring Churchill the President's greeting, he found the Prime Minister in bed in the Villa Mirador, wrapped in a pink robe, enjoying a liter of wine for breakfast.

According to Eisenhower, the President too was in a holiday mood, and "seemed to experience a tremendous uplift at having slipped secretly away from Washington."

Roosevelt's two-story villa, Dar-es-Saada, had a living room 28 feet high, with French windows overlooking a beautiful garden and private swimming pool; the President's ground-floor suite, which belonged to the lady of the house, was adorned with a huge frilly bed and a sunken black bathtub.

The main purpose of the Allied conference was to decide where next to attack the Axis. The result was to be "Husky," a plan to invade Sicily as soon as North Africa could be cleared of the Axis.

But while the President and the Prime Minister were both on French territory, they hoped to resolve the annoying Giraud-de Gaulle rivalry.

Murphy—described by the President's son Elliott as "suave and smooth"—was among the first to call on Mr. Roosevelt, "anxious," adds Elliott, "to fill Father in on Giraud, how competent he would be as an administrator, how ideal a choice he was for the Americans to back."

Already, according to Root, the United States "was committed to make Giraud the leading figure in North Africa, regardless of the arrangements which might be made with de Gaulle." The first idea was to offer de Gaulle the ministry of war in a provisional government to be formed by Giraud.

On the 17th, Giraud arrived with Clark, and was received by the President that same evening. The President, says Elliott—who was witness to the scene—outlined to Giraud "the U.S. foreign policy as it regarded France during the war."

But as far as Giraud was concerned, "there was no such thing as a political problem. There was only the military question of war."

So intent was Giraud on his own plans, says Elliott, "that I doubt he perceived Father's negative reaction."

When the President asked Giraud for his assurance that he would at least sit down with de Gaulle to discuss the situation, Giraud answered, "That man! He is a self-seeker and a bad general. I need only support for the armies I can raise."

To the President—who immediately summed him up as "a very slender reed"—Giraud was a "vast disappointment," and as soon as he had left the villa, the President threw up his hands and pronounced a prophetic judgment: "This is the man that Bob Murphy said the French would rally around! He's a dud as an administrator, he'll be a dud as a leader!"

There was now "no question in Father's mind," says Elliott, "that somebody had erred, and erred seriously." From what he overheard, Elliott realized that Murphy's "governing concern seemed to lead in the direction of ensuring that any future government in France included—on a dominant level—the same men that had been among the principal 'appeasers' in the critical years before war broke out."

Yet the President would not dispose of Giraud then and there; and when Churchill, who was quick to learn how dissatisfied the President had become with Giraud, "returned once more, obliquely, to his contention that France's provisional government might be better left solely in the hands of de Gaulle," the President would not agree with him.

A remark of the President to his son gives an idea of the extent to which Roosevelt's attitude had been affected by anti-de Gaulle propaganda in Washington: "Elliott," said the President, "de Gaulle is out to achieve one-man government in France. I can't imagine a man I would distrust more. His whole Free French movement is honeycombed with police spies—he has agents spying on his own people. To him, freedom of speech means freedom from criticism—of him."

The President then hinted at the high-level problems which lay behind his attitude, by explaining to his son that it was his conviction that in the postwar world the British meant to hold onto their colonies and meant to help the French hold onto theirs and that the British "owned de Gaulle, body, soul and britches."

To the President, the problem of colonies and colonial markets "was the core of all chances for future peace."

"Exploit the resources of an India, a Burma, a Java," said the President, "take all the wealth out of those countries, but never put anything back into them, things like education, decent standards of living, minimum health requirements—all you're doing is storing up the kind of trouble that leads to war. All you're doing is negating the value of any kind of organizational structure for peace before it begins."

The whole conversation reflects the human frailty of a President trying to do his best, according to his conscience, on a humane and supranational basis—a sort of New Deal for the world—yet inexorably bound by the exigencies of "national interests" as viewed by the Army, Navy and State.

Of this the President was to give an almost comic example at

Anfa. After explaining to his son that "the colonial system means war," he excitedly set about trying to consummate with the Sultan of Morocco, over dinner, a deal for American exploitation of Moroccan oil.

At the same time he thus declaimed to his son: "Imperialists don't realize what they can do, what they can create! They've robbed this continent of billions, and all because they were too shortsighted to understand that their billions were pennies, compared to the possibilities! Possibilities that *must* include a better life for the people who inhabit this land. . . ."

All of which is germane in explaining the President's policy toward Giraud and de Gaulle.

It was the President's contention that France should be restored to world power, but given back her former colonies only on a trusteeship basis, bound each year to report on the progress of her stewardship, on how the literacy rate was improving, on how the death rate was declining, on how disease was being stamped out, etc.

When Elliott asked who would be doing the supervising, the President instantly responded, "The organization of the United Nations, when it's been set up."

This also gives a clue to the President's preference for Giraud and his aversion to de Gaulle. The former, being uninterested in politics, he believed would be more amenable to American policy.

Already it was rumored in London that when Gaullists had been approached by a negotiator representing himself as speaking for the United States Navy and certain American oil interests, demanding ninety-nine-year leases on certain French bases and colonial oil fields, de Gaulle was reported to have answered that he had no authority to make future commitments of this sort for France.

But Giraud was in no position to resist pressure from the Allies. There were even stories that he had made secret promises to Britain and the United States, that he had promised Great Britain a base at Bizerte, and America one at Dakar.

De Gaulle, on the other hand, considered himself committed to defend every scrap of prewar French interest throughout the world, at least till France was liberated and could choose a government of her own.

Oddly, though for different reasons, this was the declared objective of Lemaigre-Dubreuil, working through the amenable Giraud.

But once the President had seen Giraud, the dilemma, says Elliott, was thus defined in his mind: "a serious overestimation of Giraud's qualities of leadership and an ambiguous policy of cooperation with Vichyite French colonials made very difficult American opposition to the one-man British-backed government of Charles de Gaulle."

The President insisted that no provisional government could be left to one man, whether it be de Gaulle or Giraud, and asked Mr. Churchill to persuade de Gaulle to come to Morocco, adding to Elliott, "I have a strong sneaking suspicion that our friend de Gaulle hasn't come to Africa because our friend Winston hasn't chosen to bid him come yet."

In London de Gaulle insisted that before he would leave, Noguès must be jailed and held for trial as a collaborator.

The President therefore put pressure on Mr. Churchill to convince de Gaulle that he must come immediately—if necessary, cutting off his food supplies.

Mr. Churchill—who amused himself by complaining that "Of all the crosses I have to bear, the Cross of Lorraine is the heaviest," and who said of de Gaulle, "we call him Saint Joan and we're looking for some bishops to burn him"—duly applied some pressure.

After several refusals (which may or may not have been concerted with Churchill) de Gaulle finally put the problem to his full Committee: If they considered it useful to France, he would bow to the majority opinion.

The Committee voted its approval.

De Gaulle's arrival in Casablanca "was like heat lightning," wrote Elliott Roosevelt, "nevertheless clearing the air."

De Gaulle's first brush with the Americans was typical. Sensitive about being back on what he considered French territory, he refused to spend his first night in a house requisitioned from a Frenchman by "some foreign power."

Luckily the villa assigned to de Gaulle belonged to a neutral Swiss.

At the lunch arranged for de Gaulle by Giraud, host turned to guest and said, "Let me tell you about my escape from Koenigstein."

Cuttingly, de Gaulle replied, "First, *mon général,* why don't you tell me how it was that you were captured?"

As the meal continued in silence, de Gaulle remarked, "I see that your rations are strictly North American."

To which Giraud answered, "Do you consume only French products in London?"—missing the point that de Gaulle considered himself at home in French Morocco.

Later, when de Gaulle was to call on President Roosevelt alone, he arrived, according to Elliott, "with black clouds swirling around his high head," and "with very poor grace."

Not surprising, really, considering that everywhere de Gaulle moved in the compound he was requested to submit to security checks (new passes were issued every few hours), whereas Noguès, whom de Gaulle considered a traitor, was allowed to come and go as he pleased, with full military honors.

To add to this feeling of being treated in an unfriendly manner, during the course of de Gaulle's interview with the President, de-Gaulle noticed a Secret Service agent lurking behind a screen with a submachine gun, as if de Gaulle posed a threat to the person of the President. To make things worse, the President, who was in the habit of making his fellow Americans feel at ease by addressing them by their first names, proceeded to do so with de Gaulle, a liberty which no one in France would have dreamed of taking.

The interview turned icy. De Gaulle remained silently aloof, and the result was that the President cherished as little admiration for this aspiring French leader as he had for the other.

The President's first suggested compromise was to be a two-headed beast: a provisional government with Giraud and de Gaulle equally responsible for its composition and welfare, to run France until the country's liberation was complete.

This, however, meant playing right into the hands of de Gaulle, who, politically astute, could easily dominate the apolitical Giraud.

To save the situation Murphy turned up, as Elliott describes him, "like a well-oiled jack-in-the-box" with a Byzantine solution.

Both Root and Soustelle—whose sources were clearly Free French—report that Murphy's extraordinary scheme was to be a triumvirate power, consisting of Giraud, de Gaulle, and a third party.

When de Gaulle, says Root, put forward the inevitable question "Who will be the third?" Murphy was to answer that he could not be told.

From the reports he had received, de Gaulle first thought that "the American Minister had in mind the Comte de Paris," and remarked that though there were individual royalists in his group, "it was not monarchist but republican, and he could not accept participation in such a triumvirate."

But de Gaulle, says Root, may have been charitable in assuming Murphy's candidate was the Count of Paris. "There was reason to believe that Murphy had in mind another name, one so unbelievably impossible that it had never occurred to de Gaulle that it might seriously be presented to him. That was Jacques Lemaigre-Dubreuil."

To this de Gaulle would never have agreed.

The President's compromise was therefore to be accepted, when, at the last moment, the Giraud team was saved by Cordell Hull. In a conversation with Lemaigre-Dubreuil in Washington on January 16th, Mr. Hull suggested to Lemaigre that "it might be interesting for you to go back to North Africa, but, understand me, in a hurry."

Lemaigre understood and boarded the first plane for Algiers and Casablanca. Hurriedly turning up at Giraud's side at Anfa, Lemaigre sat up all night drafting a one-page memorandum for Giraud to present to President Roosevelt.

In the memo it was stipulated that the Giraud-Murphy accords should form the basis of future Franco-Allied relations, and that the United States and Great Britain should recognize as the trustee for all French interests, "military, economic, financial, and moral, the French Commander in Chief in Algiers"—meaning Giraud.

When the time came for Giraud to see the President again, Lemaigre insisted on accompanying the general, convinced that without his own subtle arguing, Giraud would never be able to put over such a coup on the President. But Giraud refused. Wringing his hands, Lemaigre was obliged to contemplate the prospect that all his hard work was once more about to go down the drain.

On his return from seeing the President, Giraud gave back to the stunned Lemaigre his memo, including a clause which fixed the dollar-franc rate of exchange at a liberal 1 to 50. The President had initialed the memo without change.

For Lemaigre this was a stupendous victory. Giraud was to be virtual dictator, with a huge army supplied by the United States, whereas de Gaulle was to be completely frozen out.

But Lemaigre had counted without Britain's Prime Minister. Churchill, with no intention of standing by such an accord (in which the President had casually included him), sensibly decided to keep silent until the President was safely back in the United States.

Meanwhile, something had to be done for appearances.

Around the compound there were a great many jokes about a shotgun wedding which were reflected in Roosevelt's jocose cable to Hull: "We produced the bridegroom, General Giraud, who cooperated very nicely on the proposed nuptials and was prepared to go through with it on our terms, I am sure. Our friends, however, could not produce de Gaulle, the temperamental bride. She has become quite high-hat about the whole affair and doesn't wish to see either of us, and shows no intention of getting into bed with Giraud."

From Algiers, without being told what was in store for them, the entire Anglo-American press corps was flown to Casablanca; but arriving too soon, they were rushed off to Rabat to visit the Sultan's zoo.

When the chiefs had finally got together on a communiqué, the press was brought down to Anfa, where, says Mr. Churchill, "they could scarcely believe their eyes; and when they were told we had been there for nearly a fortnight, their ears."

As the simplest way to convey to the world the story that Giraud and de Gaulle had met was to photograph them shaking hands, such a scene was contrived, but de Gaulle's expression was so dour that the performance had to be repeated; whereupon the two generals stalked away, trailed by Murphy and Macmillan, in the words of Drew Middleton, "exactly as nursemaids following wandering children."

Later, when the French rivals tried to concoct a purely domestic communiqué of their own, de Gaulle suggested an innocuous statement: "We met. We talked. We noted our complete accord on the goal to be achieved, which is the liberation of France and the triumph of democratic liberties. . . ."

But this was too much for Giraud who interrupted with a brusque "Never!"

"So be it," answered de Gaulle. "We shall write 'human liberties.' "

In the course of their discussions de Gaulle asked Giraud if he could outline for him his policy.

"My policy," answered Giraud, "is to make war."

"*Bien sûr,*" said de Gaulle. "But on the one hand you cannot always make war, and on the other you are not only military but civil commander in chief. At least that is what you have on your letterhead. You must, perforce, have some policy."

As Giraud refused to answer with anything but "I want to make war, I want to make war," de Gaulle coldly came to the point: "Of course you have a policy, and I'll tell you what it is. On May 4, 1942 you wrote to Marshal Pétain saying you were in agreement with him and his government and gave your word as an officer that you would never do anything to impede him in his action. That government was presided over by Laval. It is to this day. As I see it, you are in accord with them, in accord with the concentration camps, on racial measures, on millions of prisoners and deportees; in other words, on the regime of dictatorship and oppression actually reigning at Vichy; all of which we wish to have disappear as rapidly as possible. That is your policy, *mon général.*"

To which Giraud shouted back, "I hate Laval."

"And the marshal?" queried de Gaulle.

"Oh," said Giraud, "the marshal, that's different. He's a prisoner."

"And you imagine," said de Gaulle, "that the Fighting French have been struggling three years in order to come chanting *'Maréchal, nous voilà!'* If you do, you are wrong."

On January 26th the news of the meeting between Giraud and de Gaulle reached Algiers; but even well after it was common knowledge, Rigault, in charge of all information, still held a tight clamp on the news.

From his new offices in a girls' school, the Lycée Fromentin, he refused to allow the official communiqué to be published in the Algiers papers.

When Renée Gosset asked Rigault the reason for this anti-Gaullist attitude, he answered, "The Anglo-American communiqué carried the names of twenty-four Anglo-Saxon personalities who conferred for ten full days. At the end of this list two lines were added to the effect that during this conversation the opportunity was afforded for a de Gaulle-Giraud meeting. I find that in this historic meeting held on French soil, it is treating us a bit too negligently. I don't think it opportune to let the public note how we've been treated."

All that the French were allowed to print was that an inter-Allied council had been held at Casablanca between Roosevelt, Churchill and Giraud.

When the magazine *TAM* (for which Renée Gosset had now become a reporter) came out on January 26th, the issue—which had been made up well in advance—contained the photos of Roosevelt and Churchill with Giraud, and a large blank space the same size, censored at the last minute.

Not till 5 A.M. the next day did Rigault give in on the communiqué; then, for three more days, he still forbade any pictures of de Gaulle.

When Gosset challenged Rigault on this count, he answered, "I did not forbid them. I merely held them up a few days, for psychological reasons. After three years of frantic anti-Gaullism in which the only words used to qualify de Gaulle have been 'traitor,' 'felon,' and 'sold-out,' I thought we had better go in progressive steps with public opinion."

All of which was a poor excuse to cover up what was actually happening: a desperate stand by the anti-British, anti-Gaullist group to rally round Giraud and consolidate his position on the basis of Lemaigre's memorandum, and so smother the Gaullists that de Gaulle would not have the necessary popular support in North Africa with which to impinge on Giraud's dictatorship.

But despite the key positions held by Lemaigre's men, a stronger hand than Giraud's was needed to administer the restless, Gaullist-germinating Algerian caldron.

Even before the death of Darlan, a tough specialist in Vichy repression had been selected for the job: round, well-fed Marcel Peyrouton, who was in Argentina where he had resigned as Ambassador from Vichy.

In his *Crusade in Europe,* Eisenhower naïvely records: "In search for satisfactory individuals we decided to bring Marcel Peyrouton to Algiers." Then he adds quickly—though not so quickly at the time: "Bringing Peyrouton to Algeria as governor was a mistake, even though he was a vast improvement over his soft and vacillating predecessor [Chatel]."

But Peyrouton was too much to force down anyone's throat.

A former Vichy Minister of the Interior, who had developed the first Nazi-type concentration camps in France and North Africa, Peyrouton was a brother-in-law of the collaborationist Flandin, and son-in-law of Louis Malvy, the Interior Minister who was convicted in the First World War of contact with the Germans. As the Free French documented Peyrouton's past, another hue and cry was raised not only in the British but in the American press.

Even the conservative New York *Herald Tribune* editorialized: "What is going on in North Africa is an elaborate maneuver to preserve the men, the jobs, the reactionary institutions and anti-democratic philosophy of the Vichy *coup d'état* (it was nothing less than that) in a coming world in which the Western democracies and the Russians are triumphant. And the United States, embarrassed by our long history of pro-Vichy appeasement, is now witlessly involved in this enterprise in a particularly dangerous way. If it was a question only of North Africa, it might not matter. But it spreads its effects far beyond Algiers. . . . How can the oppressed Europeans believe in democracy if we give them the impression that we believe so little in it ourselves?"

Mr. Roosevelt's reaction to the sudden furor raised by the press was: "Oh, I don't care what Dotty Backer and the radical sheets are saying."

But when he was asked about the *Herald Tribune,* he looked up in amazement. "You mean to say the *Herald Tribune* doesn't approve?"

F.D.R.'s remedy, says Root, was to call in its editor, Wilbur Forrest, and "explain" American policy to him. "The personal intervention of the President, the application of his tremendous prestige, had its effect, and for some time thereafter, the *Herald Tribune* maintained an embarrassed silence as one blunder after another was exposed in North Africa. Finally the strain got to be too great, the power of the President's influence wore off, and the paper resumed its forthright and well-informed criticism of North African policy."

In North Africa, Giraud's response to this furor raised by the press was to announce on February 4th the abolition of the Imperial Council, which consisted of Peyrouton, Bergeret, Noguès, and Boisson, and its replacement by a War Committee, consisting of Peyrouton, Bergeret, Noguès and Boisson.

In London de Gaulle insisted that it was not a question of personalities, but of whether the collaborationists, the men of Vichy who had served the Germans, should be allowed to remain in power or be removed and brought to trial.

In a broadcast on February 4th, de Gaulle declared, "The French nation is determined to gain its freedom by blood and arms, helped by Allies whom it has helped in the past, whom it is still helping. It is determined to recover in due course all the liberties of which it was deprived either by the enemy or by an odious usurpatory regime. It intends to rebuild its house free from the pillars of cunning privilege and artificial power built on its misery by the high priests of disasters."

"Cunning privilege," "artificial power," "high priests of disaster": such epithets were not chosen by de Gaulle for the mere resonance of oratory, but to indicate to the unsophisticated that France was indeed locked in a monstrous civil war between those who yearned to revive the moribund republic and those who wished only to see it buried.

His words appeared to be hermetic because the story of treachery and corruption which led to the Fall of France and to the conspiracy in North Africa was too incredible, too jesuitical, too shameless, to be absorbed by a world of innocent doubters.

To counter Vichy's powerful lobbies in London and Washington the Gaullist publicists constantly hammered home their message: that the Vichy regime was not the mere result of an honorable and inevitable defeat of the French Army in the field at the hands of overwhelmingly superior German forces; that such a defeat had instead been plotted by certain of the vanquished in collusion with the victors, so as to dispose once and for all of the Third Republic, replacing it with an authoritarian state; that when these Frenchmen realized the Allies might defeat the Germans, they quickly tried to salvage their position by endearing themselves to the Allies through the offer of helping them into Africa and Europe.

To support their theme the Gaullists adduced a great deal of evidence—plus the gospel that only with de Gaulle could the record be straightened.

As the drama approached its inevitable denouement, the underlying motivation of the various protagonists was to become apparent, their true features more clearly discernible beneath the innumerable masks of conspiracy.

PART SIX

THE

CONSPIRACY

18

FROM THE MOMENT Lemaigre-Dubreuil first emerged on the scene, it was plain that the aim of French collaborators was to salvage what they could of their position in Europe by acting as intermediaries between the major belligerents. What was at first less evident was the link between the collaborationist Frenchmen of Vichy and certain powerful Germans, who hoped to salvage what *they* could of their own position in Europe through a negotiated peace with the West.

Even a cursory study of Lemaigre's prewar career and contacts should have been enough to reveal the nature of his basic role. Apart from his clandestine operations in extreme right-wing and fascist organizations, Lemaigre's most overt political job before the war had been as head of the Taxpayers' League, a group which had a strong hold on Cabinet ministers by virtue of the large number of

244 THE MURDER OF ADMIRAL DARLAN

voters and legislators which supported the League. Known as a cover for "armed mobs organized for street fighting," it was held by many to be one of the moving forces behind the 1934 riots at the place de la Concorde in which 20 were killed and 2,000 hurt.

In January of 1937, at the time of the Cagoulard plot to take over France, Lemaigre launched a political and social weekly, *L'Insurgé,* with the open intent of influencing French workers along national-syndicalist and corporative lines. Designed for fascist activists, it was anti-Semitic, antidemocratic and xenophobic, declaring openly that it would fight the existing French government "on all grounds, by all means, with all weapons."

Shortly before the war Lemaigre acquired controlling interest in *Le Jour,* then an extreme right-wing daily, sometimes described as the Chicago *Tribune* of France.*

But it was as one of the fifteen governors of the Bank of France, who held seats on the boards of some 250 companies—including thirty-one private banks, two railroad companies, six public utilities, eight mining, twelve chemical and eight insurance companies —that Lemaigre was linked to many of those who were to figure in the history of the Vichy government.

At the same time Lemaigre, as a brother-in-law of the owner of one of Paris's largest department stores, Le Printemps, was deeply involved in antilabor lobbying and organizing department store owners to fight legislation which threatened their special interests, such as labor laws designed to improve the lot of employees.

Among Lemaigre's secret activities, the Gaullists charged that he distributed large sums to all sorts of fascist organizations and publications, that he was involved in the fascist *coup* of February 6, 1934, which aimed at installing a totalitarian regime in France by constitutional methods, and that when that plot failed, Lemaigre took part in the 1937 *coup* to seize power by insurrection with the

---

* As an indication of the importance attached by the extreme right wing to controlling the press, it is worth noting that the conservative *Temps,* considered the equivalent of the London or New York *Times,* and whose editorials, inspired by the Foreign Ministry under all governments, were considered semiofficial, was influenced by the Comité des Forges, the giant of French metallurgy.

use of the secret revolutionary organization of the Cagoule and parts of the army.

Sworn testimony linking Lemaigre to the Cagoule was not easy to obtain, but on June 6, 1945, a deposition was made to the director of the Sûreté Nationale by one Fernand Ladislas Jakubiez who admitted having belonged to the Action Française since 1928 and having acted during 1936 as a receptionist in the Cagoule offices on rue de Caumartin, as well as driver for the Cagoule chief, Eugène Deloncle, who was also on the board of several shipbuilding and financial enterprises.

Jakubiez testified that in his capacity as chauffeur he had been called on to drive Deloncle to the offices of Lemaigre-Dubreuil at the Taxpayers' League, and that on one occasion Lemaigre had delivered to Deloncle the sum of one million francs.

As for the role of the Cagoule, whose members, like the Mau Mau, were sworn to secrecy on pain of death, for ten years every effort was made to hush it up; but the truth was finally revealed that it had been a secret paramilitary revolutionary organization bent on overthrowing republican government by force of arms.

Recruiting its members from among army veterans and such right-wing organizations as the Croix de Feu, the Cagoule had built up a secret military force, complete with first, second, third and fourth *bureaux,* numbering some seven brigades (about 12,000 men in Paris and some 30,000 more around the country), uniformed in brown helmets, black leather jackets with crossed blue bandoliers, and riding breeches, and armed with the latest Italian and German automatic weapons (as yet unavailable to the French Army or police).

Gradually it was established that these automatic weapons had been smuggled into France and were hidden in caches, along with hand grenades, bombs and explosives, in private villas, in doctors' offices, and in special concrete cellars, which doubled as private jails and torture chambers.

The weapons were to be used for a lightning *coup* to paralyze the city long enough for the Army to take over and install a fascist regime on the trumped-up excuse (as with the burning of the Reichstag) that they were scotching a Communist take-over. As part of the 1937 plot (which came within a hair of succeeding), the Cagoulards had reconnoitered and marked the way through Paris's estimated 30 kilometers of medieval sewers so as to be able to arrive unmolested at the various ministries, key government buildings, radio and telegraph stations, and even the private dwellings of government officials.

But the plot failed, and through the indiscretions of one Cagoulard (who was later condemned to death by the Cagoule), many of the codes of the secret organization were deciphered, including the name "Marie" for the overt leader Deloncle, in whose house 4,000 other names were discovered, along with the interesting clue that the codes were based on lines from such books as *Reading in Money and Banking* by Chester Arthur Philips.

However, a thorough police investigation led so high among the notables of France that the government shrank from exposing the real military leaders—which included generals and marshals—let alone the political and financial higher-ups behind them, for fear of starting a civil war in the country. Instead, the dossiers were classified and secreted in the Ministry of Justice.

Arrested Cagoulards were not even brought to trial for their treasonous attempt to overthrow the government and most were released on one pretext or another. Some managed to escape to safety in totalitarian countries, later to turn up in Pétain's Vichy government after the Fall of France. One of these was Henri du Moulin de la Barthète, who fled to Italy only to return as head of Pétain's civil Cabinet.

Pétain's government went to great lengths to hide the incriminating documents about the Cagoule and its directive body, known as CSAR (or Secret Committee for Revolutionary Action), and the one man still in the know—the Socialist Minister of Interior of the Third Republic at the time of the police inquiry, Marx Dormoy—was prevented from revealing the truth by a favorite method of the Cagoule: an explosive charge placed in his hotel bedroom by a pretty blond agent, which splattered Dormoy's brains across the ceiling.

The incriminating documents were then carefully hidden and might have been lost forever had it not been for a tip from the wife of the concierge at the Bordeaux tribunal, which enabled Free French officers to discover them behind a secret partition, after which a parliamentary inquiry revealed the truth.

Even more sensational revelations—about the organization of the higher-ups into a hierarchy of even more secret groups behind the Cagoule—were revealed by a *louche* character with "fakir" eyes by the name of Dr. Henri Martin.

Once head of the Cagoule's Deuxième Bureau, he too had fled to Italy before the police could arrest him for preparing germ cultures in his laboratory with which to dispatch embarrassing politicians; later he returned to Vichy to be a collaborator of Laval, in charge of a special branch of the supplementary police, but he turned against Laval. Then, either because he knew no better, or did not care, Martin attempted to expose the secret organization behind the Cagoule by circulating a "Confidential Report on the Secret Polytechnic Society known as the Mouvement Synarchique d'Empire."

Though much had already been bruited about this higher secret society, the facts had for a long time been available only in the secret reports in the archives of various Allied intelligence agencies, such as the "*Memoire* on the action of the CSAR from 1919 to date [1941]," which dealt with the disintegration of republican institutions in France, of the treason, defeat and enslavement of the French people involved in the Fall of France.

That same year, another basic document on the higher conspiracy behind the CSAR was found in Lyon, in the house of a M. Chevillon, Grand Master of the Martinist order, who was murdered in 1944. At that time, shortly after the liberation of Rome, a very well-documented study—known as the Chavin report—turned up in a car abandoned by the Germans, along with other documents revealing the longtime relation between the CSAR and Italian fascists.

Ironically, Chavin, who was Vichy's *Inspecteur de Securité Nationale,* had first turned over his report to the then Minister of the Interior, Pierre Pucheu, unaware that Pucheu was a secret member of the organization which Chavin was so carefully exposing. The result was that Chavin found himself suddenly exiled to the provinces.

In these various reports, which eventually formed the basis for a detailed study on the synarchic movement by Geoffroy de Charnay, the conspiracy was defined as an international organization "born after the Versailles Treaty, financed and directed by certain groups of financiers of high international banking circles." Its purpose: "to overthrow parliamentary regimes wherever they existed, on the grounds that they were too hard to handle by virtue of the number of individuals that had to be controlled."

Dr. Martin's report revealed that the technique of the Synarchists had been the long-range placing in key governmental positions, and especially within the permanent civil service, of their own secret adherents recruited mostly from among the Inspectors of Finance, the École Polytechnique, the École Centrale and the École Normale Supérieure.*

The immediate reaction to Dr. Martin's revelations of the existence of the Mouvement Synarchique d'Empire was to be all sorts of guffaws and denials by Vichy ministers: it was precisely they who were to be identified as members of this secret society.

The various secret reports on synarchy agree that in its modern guise the movement took root in the West soon after the Russian Revolution of 1917 destroyed the Russian governing class, flowering into an international organization with branches in Germany, France, Italy, Spain, Portugal, the Argentine, Mexico and the United States—"to cut the ground out from under the large parties

---

* The Inspectors of Finance formed a sort of closed corporation of government officials who had been through special training to qualify them for high functions in the Treasury. Their job was to "see to it that the economic and financial laws of the country were being properly carried out." By tradition, the sons of influential families were groomed for this particular service. "They had," says Root, "little compunction about using their offices in support of the economic theories they favored, and the actual government was helpless if they desired to sabotage its own economic plans, which was what happened in the case of the Popular Front. The technical . . . nature of their work and their knowledge of detail made it difficult to replace them *en masse,* so they constituted a sort of state within the state with the continuity of civil servants, self-selected and trained."

of the extreme left, especially the communists, by voluntarily realizing, without revolution, an economic system analogous to that in Russia of the Bolsheviks, but to the advantage of a *bourgeois équipe* prepared and selected from among the *anciens cadres.*"

In France, the main conspiratorial society was the Mouvement Synarchique d'Empire, run by a more restricted group, the Comité Synarchique Central, which, in turn, was but the French branch of a worldwide international organization.

In the course of the 1920s the MSE contrived to place its members in key government positions, especially the civil service, the Inspectors of Finance, and the high ranks of the Army and Navy. In this way they were able to control policy through the offices of each Cabinet minister, irrespective of the incumbent, their plan being first to discredit, then to paralyze, democratic government.

Not subject to dismissal with each change of Cabinet, such offices as the Conseils d'État, the Cour des Comtes, the Army, Navy and the Ministry of Finance could operate with impunity, and perpetuate themselves by virtue of being able to select and train their own cadres.

By 1933 the MSE apparently considered it had so thoroughly infiltrated France that it could seize power constitutionally; hence the *coup* of February 6, 1934, when it attempted to unite the two chambers into a National Assembly in Versailles, but failed.

After the collapse of the 1937 attempt to seize power by insurrection with the use of the Cagoule, it was realized that the only way to topple the republican government was by means of outside pressure—by losing a rigged war against the Germans.

Lilian Mowrer wrote that by 1940, cabinet ministers, generals, and admirals had become more or less conscious participants in a giant conspiracy, organized in anticipation of German victory, which they accepted as the prelude to coming to power and prosperity in a fascist world. They did not want or envisage a long war. Once in power, their ostensible leader, Pétain, was to negotiate on terms favorable to an authoritarian France.

That Pétain was involved in such a plot for a long time before the Fall of France was abundantly documented at his trial.

The act of accusal against Pétain before the High Court revealed his "relations with members of the Synarchic Pact, the goal of which was to make of the professional organization the cadre for a hierarchical authoritarian state, dear to Pétain, of which the Law of 16 August 1940 forms the first step."

This law, which created the Comités d'Organization, described by Langer as the financiers of the SOL and PPF, enabled Pétain to place at the head of all French activity "those who had prepared the war, organized the defeat, and were to profit from the debacle and ruin."

The law, which was to cap the Bank Reform Law of July 6th that had put all financial transactions into their hands, permitted the Synarchists to assume control of every industrial enterprise in France. A ruthless censorship was imposed on the press, radio and films. Freedom of assembly was virtually suppressed. No one could write about public affairs or even discuss them. The authorities were empowered to arrest and imprison without trial any person they considered suspect, and there was no appeal. Nazi-style concentration camps were instituted—by Pucheu.

According to the French journalist Philippe Barrès, the men of Vichy were not feeble personalities who succumbed to German force under the pressure of defeat, but responsible proponents of a well-considered plan which long antedated the German victory. They were partisans of a complete political, economic, military and intellectual system: men of a plan, not victims of an accident.

Their enterprise was nothing less than the complete subordination of France to Germany through a series of measures: the fusion of the heavy industries of the two countries, the exploitation of the colonial empire by mixed Franco-German corporations, a preferential French tariff for German products, cooperation between the banks and the industries of the two countries, so close that it would force the eviction of all American and English banks, a military alliance, and, finally, for the French, the re-orientation of education to make this vassalage acceptable.

As Paul Winkler, a solitary prophet writing at the time, was to point out, "German economic agencies follow closely on the heels of armies of occupation, and endeavor to transform the temporary hold on conquered countries into a permanent economic control."

In Paris an army of German accountants and auditors followed the army of soldiers, to draw up inventories of all important French enterprises. "After these inventories were drawn up," wrote Winkler, "German officials and delegates of private industry called upon the various enterprises to secure for themselves absolute and quite legal control of these firms by the aid of political pressures of every sort, and especially by means of the aid lent by the collaborators within the French government."

Those who tried to resist were forced to retire, one way or another. As occupiers, and with Vichy to make the laws, the Germans could easily enforce their interests. Vichy banks could withhold credit on the say-so of the Germans. By stringent regulations and the withholding of raw materials they could convince owners to sell a controlling interest to Germans or their French proxies.

Sometimes the Germans would combine a whole French industry into one great trust, then buy a majority of the shares of the central holding company for the equivalent German trust. And, most important, these so-called purchases cost the Germans nothing; the funds were provided by what the Germans charged the French for the costs of occupation: about 300 million francs a day.

Gradually all of France became German property: factories, mines, communications, insurance companies, public services, everything of importance. Yet the annexation of French business was not the Germans' chief aim. Their major object was to harness the heavy industry of France, which was the next-greatest industrial power on the continent of Europe, second only to Germany.

As Root points out, cooperation between French and German industry had begun at least before the turn of the century: "Its fruits appeared in the first war in the mutual sparing of armaments factories whose ownership was divided on both sides of the warring fronts."

These early arrangements were probably largely commercial, the interest of both sides being largely the business advantage they could obtain from the establishment of cartels and elimination of competition. But the game became uneven with the advent of the totalitarian Third Reich, at which time German members became instruments of the state, to be used for the subjugation of France.

As a result, the French had to become willing junior partners in a Franco-German heavy-industry combine which would dominate all of Europe, even if in the process of acquiring that domination their own country had to be defeated in battle.

It was in the years 1929 and 1930 that Hjalmar Schacht laid the foundation stones for a German war economy; and it was in the Cologne banking house of Baron Kurt von Schroeder, financier of Germany heavy industry and head of a group of private banks, that Hitler first gave sufficient assurances for Franz von Papen to persuade his friends, the Junkers and industrialists, to place their bets on Hitler.

Schroeder's role in later developments in France and North Africa was to prove especially interesting. Just as German military subjugation was prepared by introducing spies disguised as tourists, so was their economic absorption of a country. In dealing with a prospective victim the Germans habitually selected some local private bank or banks as their exclusive agent.

In France the representative of the Schroeder bank was the Paris banking house of Worms et Cie., which had extensive interests in other banks, notably the Bank of Indochina, the Banque Nationale de Crédit, and the Banque de Paris et des Pays-Bas, as well as in coal, shipping and foreign enterprises, particularly railroads.

"The Worms bank and its members," says Root, "appeared in the financing of all pre-war activities hostile to the Third Republic, notably the Cagoulard plot, and . . . it was the center of the transfer of France's businesses to German ownership."

With the formation of the Vichy government, as if by some legerdemain, virtually the entire board of the Worms bank turned up as ministers in Pétain's Cabinet.

As Emmanuel d'Astier de la Vigerie was to remark, the Vichy government came to look like a subsidiary of the Worms bank.

And who should have been elected a board member of the Worms bank but M. Lemaigre-Dubreuil?

"The Banque Worms," says Root, "was the leading spirit in the plundering of France for Germany's benefit; and gradually, the conviction grew in the minds of those who studied this process that it was Lemaigre-Dubreuil who represented the Banque Worms with the Bank of France, and thus helped make its activities possible."

It will now be seen why one of the reasons the Gaullists had such a hard time convincing the world of the existence of a major conspiracy was the very dimension of the conspiracy. Could Pétain's Cabinet really consist almost entirely of members of a German banking subsidiary? Yet such were the facts.

In 1944 the OSS (through the efforts of its more dispassionate investigators in the Research & Analysis Branch) had already drawn up from the carefully screened data of various intelligence sources, a comprehensive list of top Vichy personnel. In this document, which was kept secret for almost twenty years, and which is still very hard to come by, the OSS revealed the links between members of the Banque Worms and Pétain's successive cabinets.

According to this report, Paul Baudoin, Pétain's Foreign Minister, was a board member, and acted as link between the Worms bank and the Bank of Indochina, of which he was also general manager.

Pétain's Secretary of State for Industrial Production and National Equipment, François Lehideux, as well as being a member of the Worms bank, was the son of Jacques Lehideux, head of the banking firm of Lehideux et Cie., financial representatives of French Catholic officials; he was also married to the daughter of Louis Renault, the automobile manufacturer, who was among the first pro-German collaborators. François's sister married Henri du Moulin de la Barthète, the Cagoulard, also a member of the Worms bank, who, as a former Inspector of Finances, was to become head of Pétain's civil Cabinet.

Another Inspector of Finances, and a board member of the Worms bank, was Jacques Barnaud. A financial adviser to the Comité des Forges, he became Pétain's Delegate General for Franco-German Relations in 1942.

Yet another Inspector of Finances and budget director under Laval was Yves Bouthillier, a member of Worms et Cie., who was to become Pétain's first Minister of National Economy and Finance.

The Secretary General for Industry and Domestic Commerce under Pétain was Jean Bichelonne, a specialist in exchange of French and German and Belgian ores, and an ardent admirer and collaborator of the Germans; he too was a member of the Worms bank.

The board of the Worms bank could even boast of the services of a professional labor leader, René Belin, and of a working journalist, Jacques Benoît-Mechin, who became Pétain's Secretary of State in charge of French manpower in Germany.

Most interesting in terms of the North African adventure was Pierre Pucheu, another Worms member and organizer of the Franco-German steel cartel, who became Pétain's Minister of the Interior, and was smuggled by Giraud to Algiers via Spain and Portugal.

The OSS's conclusion that board members of the Worms bank should become the government of Vichy, responsible for turning over to Germany the bulk of French economy, is extraordinary enough. Even more extraordinary is the fact that these men were also suspected of being members of the Mouvement Synarchique d'Empire. Again the evidence is abundant. It also serves to unravel the complex conspiracy between Vichy and the Allied landings in North Africa.

A secret document entitled "*La dissidence Giraud et la Synarchie*," which was forwarded to the British War Office through a Resistance network in 1943, specified that the Giraud dissidence had been organized in France as of January, 1942, without Giraud's knowledge, and that its Synarchist organizers were directing their efforts not against the Reich but against the dissident groups around de Gaulle as well as against the British and the Russians.

By the time of Darlan's murder this was common knowledge in the French underground, and *Je Suis Partout* complained publicly that a "*dissidence truquée*" in North Africa had been organized by "*les grand chefs cagoulards*" and by "members of the Mouvement Synarchique d'Empire, with the aid of the Vichy government and the toleration of the occupying authorities."

Up till the end of 1941, the Synarchists' scheme for Franco-German control of Europe had run like clockwork. Then the United States entered the war. For those in a position to know—those who understood the economic realities of war—Hitler's failure to reach the Soviet oil fields plus the weight of American production made it clear that the Germans could eventually lose the war.

In France, the powers behind the scenes became worried. A British victory, and the return of de Gaulle, would mean punishment for all those who had collaborated in the defeat.

A substitute leader (for both Pétain and de Gaulle) would have to be found, reliable enough to insure their own position behind the scenes, but able to muster sufficient popular support to remain in office and guarantee their immunity no matter what happened.

Their first choice was Weygand. Before the war he had been on the board of directors of several of the larger French enterprises, and such international ones as the Suez Canal Company. The Church would support him, and so would the Army. Though considered anti-British, he was *persona grata* with the Americans.

But Weygand, on the excuse that he was too old a dog to be learning new tricks, begged off.

It was a blow to many, including Lemaigre-Dubreuil. But it was at this point that Lemaigre himself became important. The moment Weygand backed out, someone was needed to make clandestine contact with the Allies so as to pave the way for the transfer of collaborationist interests from the German camp to that of the Allies.

North Africa was the natural spot for building up contacts with the Allies: arms and agents could more easily be smuggled there than into France, and it was ideal for an Allied landing. Paradoxically, the fact that North Africa's key personnel had been carefully selected, with Vichyites to replace Gaullists, made it all the more attractive. With censorship and police repression, it would be that much easier to keep out de Gaulle, hoodwink the Allies, and prevent the Gaullists from telling the world what was happening.

Lemaigre maintained that by virtue of his extensive business connections in North Africa he could operate there with impunity and sufficient cover to arouse suspicion from neither side. Still, a leader for the North African venture was absolutely essential. Lemaigre's first choice was Édouard Herriot, the democratic leader of the Radical Socialist Party, pro-American, anti-German, and a steadfast opponent of collaborationists and of the Vichy government. With this name Lamaigre went to the British, who turned him down. And in any event, Herriot, who knew Lemaigre-Dubreuil and what was behind his scheme, refused to serve.

Shortly after Pearl Harbor, Lemaigre approached the Americans, first in Vichy and then in North Africa, and they listened to him readily.

But when a substitute for de Gaulle was mentioned, they too insisted on Herriot.

Again Herriot refused.

It was then that Lemaigre, in desperation, conjured up Giraud. Like so many of his army colleagues, Giraud had the right political background, and his record with Vichy was clean—if only because he had been a prisoner of the Germans since 1940. As a curious coincidence, Lemaigre had also been a captain on Giraud's staff during the "*drôle de guerre*."

But what of Darlan? How did he enter the picture?

By his own testimony, Darlan had been working parallel to Lemaigre—of whose activities and relations with the Americans he claimed to be thoroughly informed.

There is evidence that the Synarchists might well have preferred Darlan in the role of Giraud from the beginning, but dared not impose such a figure on the Americans after he had offered his services to Hitler at Berchtesgaden in May of 1941.

Fundamentally anti-British, Darlan had rallied to the Germans when offered the dauphinate of France by Pétain, and command of the New Order Navy by Hitler.

But at the beginning of 1942, Darlan was obliged to change his mind when he saw a report from his own chief of naval intelligence which showed comparative statistics on United States and Russian production of coal, steel, oil and shipping, against that of the Third Reich and its dependencies. Darlan's first step appears to have been to get in touch with the French underground and offer his services to sway France to the side of the Allies. But the underground refused to have anything to do with him. Darlan then put out feelers, as confirmed by his son, to test the reactions of the Americans. No doubt he discussed his designs with his fellow naval officer, Admiral Leahy, our Ambassador to Vichy, for there are references in Leahy's still-secret diaries referring to a prospective deal with "Popeye," as he was known in the private code of the State Department.

After Leahy's recall, Darlan kept in touch with Murphy through Fenard, Chrétien and Dorange.

Darlan's overall plan, like Giraud's, was to be climaxed by an anti-Hitler general's *coup* in Germany, to be supported by the West in time to stave off the menace of the Russians.

But whom was Darlan dealing with among the Germans? According to the testimony at Nürnberg of the Austrian-born General Erwin Lahousen—who was an aide of the chief of the German Abwehr intelligence service, Admiral Canaris—Darlan was in touch with Canaris during 1942, through none other than Deloncle, former head of the Cagoule and now in German uniform as head of a brigade of French anti-Bolshevik volunteers in the Reichswehr. Deloncle, who was in constant touch with Darlan through one of the latter's private secretaries, acted as one of Darlan's top intelligence agents, in close touch with the Abwehr officers who were planning to save Germany by ditching Hitler.

After Darlan's murder, Canaris furnished Deloncle with a false passport to go to Spain to get in touch with Ambassador Sir Samuel Hoare and Allied agents to sound them out on a compromise peace; and while he was there, Deloncle insistently begged Giraud for an appointment.

Back in Paris, Deloncle was surprised in his flat by the Gestapo, and shot when he tried to resist.

Ironically, it was because Darlan was willing to be *more* pro-German even than Laval that he had first replaced Laval in Pétain's government. As the German counselor in Paris summed it up: "When you ask Laval for a chicken, he gives you an egg and a smile; when you ask Darlan for an egg, he gives you a chicken." Laval, in his curious way, though a close collaborator with the Germans, could not see turning over to them the entire economy of France. Laval had wanted France to play a bigger role in the New Order and had been planning a revolution of his own along the lines of Mussolini and Hitler: "a dictatorship, but which eliminated every intermediate authority between dictator and people, with war on the Trusts and Cartels."

When Laval balked at enacting the legislation considered essential by the Synarchists, he was replaced by Darlan.

Darlan did not hesitate to sanction the decrees which enabled the MSE to gain a stranglehold on French industry and banking, and announced a "new era in collaboration, the transformation of French economy." He even agreed with Otto Abetz, German Ambassador to Vichy, to establish joint Franco-German staff conversations as a step toward bringing Vichy into the war against Britain on the side of the Germans.

Darlan then began filling every important military and civilian post in North Africa with officials (mostly of the Navy) whom he could count on as loyal to himself and to Vichy, causing Cardinal Liennart of Lille, during a grave illness, to joke: "I don't dare die now. They would replace me with an admiral." It was, as Renée Gosset remarked, a great period for admirals: they were everywhere but at sea.

At his trial for treason in Algiers in March 1944, Pierre Pucheu testified that it was he who tipped off Darlan concerning the Anglo-American landings. And it was then that Darlan hurried to Algiers. Flandin also joined him shortly before the landings, and Pucheu came along later, after a stay in Spain.

They were not, as was first supposed, "rats fleeing a sinking ship," but rather, as Paul Winkler was to report in *The Nation* the day after Darlan's murder, "engaged in carrying out an important mission intrusted to them by certain French financial circles which, in full agreement with German industrial groups, plan a joint control of the European economy—an association in which the Germans are to have the leading role and the French must content themselves with that of junior partners."

It was Root's contention, well supported by evidence, that certain Germans also knew that something was going to happen in North Africa, and took advantage of the information.

There were several massive transfers of capital from France to French North Africa, especially by the two largest Franco-African companies—one of them a chemical concern owned by the Franco-German combine of which Germany's I. G. Farbenindustrie held 51 per cent of the stock. The other, the Trans-Africa Company, under majority control of the Deutsche Bank and several German industrial firms.*

Not only were these sums—which were moved from France to North Africa in obvious expectation of the invasion—controlled to a large extent by firms collaborating with or owned by the Germans, but all monetary transfers of this kind required German permission before they could be carried out. The Germans were thus instrumental in bringing about the shift of capital, whose details were handled in many cases through Lemaigre-Dubreuil.

In an article in *The Protestant* of February 1943, an anonymous writer, giving as his source Swiss banking circles, unfolds a play-by-play account of the steps taken: "Lemaigre-Dubreuil," says the author, "informed his good friend and superior in the French business hierarchy, Pierre Pucheu. . . . Pucheu approached one of his colleagues, M. Bréart de Boisanger, a bank director, who served as Vichy's contact man to German industry. . . . Pucheu informed Boisanger of the British and American plans to occupy North

* The Trans-Africa Company, in which both Lemaigre-Dubreuil and Charles Bedaux had a large hand, was based on plans for a railway from the Mediterranean all the way across the Sahara to Dakar and Nigeria to open up West Africa and develop it as a jumping-off base for operations in South America, and eventually the United States. A pet project of the Synarchists, it was revived by Darlan and Pucheu, who underwrote it with a huge government bond issue.

Africa in the near future and asked him to pass this information on to . . . representatives of German industry and finance. The meeting between Pucheu and the Vichy contact man to German industry took place in Geneva to avoid rousing comment or suspicion. Boisanger, as permanent delegate to the Bank of International Settlements, lived in Basel.

"By convenient chance, Baron von Schroeder . . . was vacationing at the time in Switzerland. Boisanger got in touch with Baron von Schroeder, who immediately . . . hurried back to Germany." Some days later, the two big German-French North African trusts, whose headquarters were in Paris, were ordered to transfer all money available to the subsidiaries of the Banque de Paris (probably, says Root, the Banque de Paris et des Pays-Bas, which, with the Union Parisienne, was associated with the Trans-Africa Company; the Deutsche Bank controlled both of these French houses) and the Union Parisienne in Morocco and Algiers.

At almost the same moment other French industries in which there was considerable German capital began transferring huge sums to enterprises in North Africa. Root estimated that in the last three weeks before the landings French financiers brought altogether about 9 billion francs out of France, for deposit in the French banking houses in North Africa.

On the free market, French francs could easily be obtained at the rate of 150 or more to the dollar, although the official rate was to be 50. Before Anfa, American authorities had proposed to peg the franc at 75, which was generous enough. But the Lemaigre crowd urged the Americans to give them an even more favorable rate of 50, on what Root calls "the totally fallacious pretext that this would increase the purchasing power of the North African population."

Thus the time came to cash in the large amounts of capital which Franco-German enterprises had transferred to North Africa before the invasion. They had moved francs with which they could buy dollars by paying 150 for each dollar received; now they were able to get a dollar with only 50 francs. By the arrangement they tripled their money.

Unfortunately there were just not enough dollars in North Africa to permit the full conversion. So representatives of the Banque Nationale pour le Commerce et l'Industrie, North African representative for the Worms bank, persuaded the representative of a group of three American banks to grant a loan of 50 million dollars to the Giraud administration.

To the Americans it looked like an easy way to earn a good interest rate, especially as the American banks would not even have to provide the money—only exchange it—since the loan was to be subscribed in North Africa. All the Americans had to do was "underwrite" it—which meant handing over 50 million dollars for the equivalent in francs at the favorable rate (to the French capitalists) of 50 francs to the dollar, which Lemaigre had talked the United States into granting.

And who should have been the key figure in North Africa to handle the transaction with the Allies? Kammerer reports that it was none other than M. Alfred Pose, ex-Inspector of Finance, and director of the Banque Nationale pour le Commerce et l'Industrie.

To sum up: The conspirators hoped to take out insurance against any eventuality. If Hitler won, the Schroeder bank would protect them. If he lost, *their* man, Lemaigre-Dubreuil, would have the ear of the Allies.

That the Axis was in a sorry condition was by now no secret to its leaders. Just before Anfa, Mussolini's son-in-law Count Ciano was to record in his diary: "Military forces are scarce. Africa, Russia, the Balkans, the occupied countries, everywhere, new and greater forces are needed. I have the impression at times that the Axis is like a man trying to cover himself with a blanket that's too small. If he warms his feet his head is cold. His feet will freeze if he tries to keep his head warm."

It is Root's contention that Peyrouton's arrival in North Africa in the very midst of the Anfa conference could only be explained if he was the bearer of a German-negotiated peace offer, supplied to him via the German Embassy in Buenos Aires, in which the German economic group offered a great number of concessions in the political field, for the purpose of stabilizing the German economic empire throughout Europe—with or without the Nazis.

That such a move might have been successful was indicated by Field Marshal Sir John Dill, British representative to the Combined Chiefs of Staff in Washington, when he reported to Churchill that there were powerful forces in the United States which still considered that a negotiated peace with the Germans was the best that could be hoped for.

But something happened at Anfa which resulted in the adoption of a policy, summed up in the phrase "Unconditional Surrender," that was to spell the immediate defeat of Lemaigre-Dubreuil (and the forces behind him), the eventual defeat of Giraud, and the triumph of de Gaulle.

PART SEVEN

AFTERMATH

19

SHORTLY AFTER Anfa, during the first week of February, on a penetratingly cold day with but brief patches of sunlight, a distinguished visitor paid a secret visit to Algiers, arriving from the airfield in a bulletproof car and establishing himself in a villa not far from the Saint-Georges, heavily guarded and surrounded by barbed wire.

Summoned thither, Mr. Murphy was told that one of the items in the Anfa memorandum drawn up by Lemaigre and initialed by Roosevelt was unsatisfactory as it stood and would have to be amended. The text, said the visitor, had obviously been drawn up in a hurry, and the item about the trustee for French interests would have to be rewritten.

There were two French chiefs. The text would have to be made applicable to both or to neither. Could not a matter so simple, asked the distinguished visitor, be settled then and there, while he was still in Algiers?

The visitor, of course, was Mr. Churchill, on his way back to London from Ankara. He wanted to undo, with a minimum of excitement, what Lemaigre had achieved for Giraud at Anfa, thus bringing de Gaulle back into the picture.

In the very elegant villa in Algiers to which Murphy had moved his residence, there took place an odd scene between Lemaigre-Dubreuil and Murphy in the presence of Colonel Julius Holmes.

"I'm surprised," said Holmes, addressing Lemaigre, "that you have the nerve to call on Mr. Murphy after having lied to him."

"Me? Lie?" answered Lemaigre. "That's a disagreeable word. When? Where? How?"

"On your way home from Washington," specified Holmes, "did you not ask me for a military priority on a plane to Casablanca, saying you wished to go see your family? Instead, you went to see General Giraud and injected yourself into the Anfa conference. If I obtained for you that place, it was after phoning Murphy that you had promised to retire from politics and rejoin your family. You lied. And you have betrayed Murphy's friendship."

Lemaigre turned to Murphy: "Surely after all the struggles we have been through together these last two years you have something to say to such a charge, made in your own house!"

Murphy hung his head, then suggested that Lemaigre go to London, to work for a union with the Free French.

To Lemaigre this was tantamount to asking him to step into the lion's cage. If he went to London, he saw the prospect of being "quickly neutralized, perhaps by the quiet hand of some secret service."

The next day Murphy paid a visit to Giraud and put Churchill's suggestion to the apolitical French executive, giving it his full support.

"Well," said Giraud good-humoredly, "if they have it so much at heart, I accept the revision."

When he heard the news, Lemaigre could but gasp: "It was like severing his own head." Immediately he appealed to Giraud to "defend the interests of France" and spelled out to him the meaning of the revision: "This wipes out all I painfully achieved in Washington, and all you obtained at Anfa."

In a halfhearted attempt to salvage some of the lost ground, Giraud addressed a letter to Murphy on February 10th; but by the 19th Murphy officially confirmed Mr. Roosevelt's retraction of the agreement at Anfa.

The way was now open to de Gaulle.

Two days later, on February 21st, Jean Rigault lost his job as Secretary for Information and Propaganda. It went to General René Chambe, described as a "military officer without pro-Vichy inclinations."

Within a few days the Gaullist *Combat* was allowed to appear legally on the streets of Algiers, though it was six more weeks— April 10th, to be exact—before it could publish any criticism of the "Father of the National Revolution," the venerable Marshal Pétain. And it was to be several months yet before an effective freedom of the press could be established by the abolition of all censorship of political and diplomatic matters.

From London General Georges Catroux arrived in North Africa to represent General de Gaulle. His job was to find an effective way to implement the union between the two rival forces. Several formulas were explored. Catroux suggested that Giraud be named Lieutenant General of the Republic, a sort of chief of state, and at the same time Supreme Commander of French Forces, and that de Gaulle be Prime Minister of the political body, the National Committee.

Next it was suggested that Giraud and de Gaulle be joint presidents of a new Committee, directing it together, and jointly signing all decisions. As a condition for this compromise, de Gaulle insisted on the abolition first of all Vichy legislation, repudiation of the armistice, and the elimination of all persons implicated in the capitulation of June 22, 1940.

In de Gaulle's own words, "The nation intends that on every inch of liberated soil the caricature of Fascism with which Vichy has disfigured it be instantly swept away . . . never in all its history has France more ardently resolved to be master in its own house."

In his approach to the problem de Gaulle had already received the enthusiastic support of the underground movements in France.

Giraud, afraid of further Gaullist demonstrations for his rival, insisted on meeting him only in some remote spot such as Marrakech, away from a politically organized population, where de Gaulle would be cut off from access to the press and public opinion.

Finally Giraud was obliged to agree to meet in Algiers, but just as de Gaulle was boarding his plane, word came from Eisenhower and Murphy that de Gaulle could not come, ostensibly because of the impending battle for Tunis.

With a liberated Tunisia, and the support of a victorious Eisenhower, Giraud felt his position solid enough to withstand the arrival of de Gaulle, though he was careful to take precautions against any demonstration of welcome for his rival.

On June 1st de Gaulle's plane was brought in at Blida airfield, an hour from Algiers, on a Sunday morning, far from any possible well-wishers. Only Giraud was there to greet him with *"Bon jour,* de Gaulle." Then they left in separate cars.

The local press was forbidden to announce de Gaulle's arrival, and the general was placed in a small villa called Wisteria near the Palais d'Été where he had to operate from a "small, stuffy bourgeois salon."

To welcome de Gaulle, members of *Combat* organized a demonstration at the foot of the war memorial, where de Gaulle placed a wreath; the news of his arrival was spread by word of mouth.

At 5 P.M. de Gaulle received both the foreign and the French press at his residence. It was a golden spring evening, the garden bustling with dashing Free French veterans in their Western Desert shorts. De Gaulle's first demand was for the immediate removal of Noguès, Boisson, and Peyrouton to show that France had repudiated Vichy.

Giraud, in a fury, refused.

On June 2nd the city of Algiers appeared to be in a state of siege: armored units were concentrated in the gardens of the Palais d'Été, all meetings and parades were forbidden, military and police units blocked the exits to the city and the adjacent airfields. General Eisenhower considered it prudent to strap on an Army automatic.

That evening Winston Burdett of CBS revealed the plans for an underground *coup* to arrest de Gaulle and his principal supporters, and to suppress all Gaullist activity in the city. To defend Algiers against the Gaullists, Admiral Émile Muselier, appointed prefect by Giraud, brought in the 7th Regiment of Chasseurs d'Afrique. But their commander turned out to be Colonel Van Ecke, who sided with de Gaulle. At the last minute, Admiral Muselier, who was to have given the order to arrest de Gaulle, dared not do so, fearing that the local police was too pro-Gaullist for the *coup* to succeed. "It would mean civil war," the admiral warned, "were I to try to enforce the plan."

"Who," asked Burdett rhetorically, "was behind the *putsch?*" Then he answered that it was a last desperate stand by Lemaigre-Dubreuil and Rigault.

The next day Giraud ceded and announced that Noguès, Bergeret, Peyrouton and Mendigal had been dismissed.

In their stead a French Committee of National Liberation was set up to act as provisional authority for France and its empire. Its Secretary General was to be Louis Joxe.

As Giraud's official adviser, Lemaigre resigned. Jean Rigault was ordered deported to Morocco.

But even with the top Vichyites out of the way, it was hard for de Gaulle to get cooperation from Giraud.

"The smallest question, which should be settled in a few moments and be immediately executed, takes up endless discussions," wrote de Gaulle. As one French observer remarked: The two generals indulged in such table pounding that they besplattered each other with ink.

When de Gaulle brought in Soustelle as his information chief,

Giraud complained of his presence at conferences because he was a civilian.

"*Si cela vous gêne,*" answered de Gaulle, "we can always dress him up as a general."

Giraud then tried to control the situation by ingratiating himself at the source of power, with the Americans, where he could count on the support of Eisenhower, "who had little use for de Gaulle's superior intelligence."

Also, certain American members of the OSS, in their attempt to rival the British, were happy to support Giraud agents against de Gaulle.

To counter his rival's influence, Giraud, as Commander in Chief of the French Armed Forces, organized his own intelligence service with the object of building up in occupied France a separate resistance movement.

There, a secret army was to prepare the way for Giraud to assume power, quite possibly "not in the name of Pétain, but with Pétain at the top."

But de Gaulle was implacable.

On August 14 Pucheu was arrested, tried and convicted of having turned over French hostages to be shot by the Germans.*

Placed before a firing squad at Hussein-Dey, Pucheu calmly insisted on shaking hands with each member, then giving the order to fire. Admiral Michelier was retired from the Navy and forbidden to live near a port. Admiral Derrien was jailed, and died in prison. Bergeret was arrested, charged with arbitrary sequestration and fomenting a royalist plot; he ended up in a jail cell next to Flandin and Boisson. Peyrouton was taken to Laghouat and charged with treason, for which he was to spend five years in jail. In October a law was passed by the Gaullist provisional Assembly on repression of trading with the enemy, aimed at those who had financial relations or clandestine commerce with the Germans. Lemaigre-Dubreuil, about to be arrested by order of the Committee of National Liberation, escaped with Rigault to Spanish Morocco, and thence to Spain.

* As of 1943 an estimated 25,000 Frenchmen had been executed as hostages in France.

In a parting letter to de Gaulle, Lemaigre explained his action: "They will say I have gone over to the Germans, to collaboration. It will, however, be difficult to make the world believe that having fought against Germany uninterruptedly and at times when everything seemed to presage a German victory, I should change camps at the very moment when everyone is proclaiming, you included, that Germany's defeat is assured."

For "German" read "Nazi" and the sophistry is patent.

Harold Callender, reporting from Algeria, wrote to *The New York Times* that Lemaigre and Rigault were believed to be on their way to Madrid to meet Noguès and Chatel, who wished to get in touch with the Allies "in the interest of Vichy and those who backed Vichy."

"The theory," wrote Callender, "is that the reactionary capitalists who had put their money on Marshal Henri Philippe Pétain are now busily seeking an alternative front that would enable them to shift to the winning side and collaborate with the Allies as they have collaborated with Germany. Any 'front' would do, it is argued here, if it frustrated General de Gaulle and his social program and enabled extreme French conservatives to join like-minded groups in Britain and the United States at the eleventh hour."

Meanwhile from Algiers, unknown to de Gaulle or to the French agency responsible, the OSS dropped into France for Giraud an agent who went straight to Marshal Pétain to sound him out on the chances of a return of Giraud at the head of French forces. Pétain, says Soustelle, gave his accord, "with the proviso that there remained to be gotten the approval of the Germans, or certain Germans."

At this point the agent's secret radio for signaling to Algiers went dead and the conspirators were obliged to communicate via Noguès in Lisbon, whereupon Heinrich Himmler got wind of the plot.

As an illustration of the appalling political naïveté of Giraud in such matters, Soustelle cites the case of a Captain Larribere who admitted to Soustelle that, without de Gaulle's knowledge, Giraud had him parachuted into France to get in touch with the Resistance in the Midi. Having duly made contact with several military organizations, Larribere, on orders from Giraud, gave them certain coded conventional phrases which were to be broadcast by Radio Alger two or three days before the Allied landings in France to indicate the time and place.

When Soustelle checked on Larribere he found him to be an active Communist. (He was later Communist senator from Oran.)

Had Giraud's plan been put into effect, it would have enabled the Communists to be at the points where the Allies landed and put themselves at an admirable advantage with leaders of the Resistance.

To cap this political naïveté, Giraud proceeded, of his own accord, to vote against himself in the council of the French Committee, thus ceasing to be a joint head of it.

Though Eisenhower continued to insist that Giraud keep command of the Army, de Gaulle pointed out to Eisenhower that such a choice was now hardly the prerogative of the Allies.

Refusing any further functions offered him, Giraud retired to a villa near Mostaganem to wait out the war and a turn of fortune. There he narrowly avoided being felled by an assassin's bullet which struck him in the jaw. Since he was politically bankrupt, would the Gaullists have bothered to kill him? Or was someone afraid he had learned too much of the plot that had been built up behind him? As it was, Giraud survived the liberation of France, then went quietly to his grave in the Invalides where his remains lie buried next to Foch's.

Meanwhile, at the grave of Darlan's murderer, homage was paid to young Bonnier de la Chapelle on the anniversary of his execution. As the Associated Press reported the scene: "A group of about 50 persons, the majority of whom fill official positions under the orders of General de Gaulle, celebrated the anniversary of the death of Fernand Eugène Bonnier de la Chapelle, who assassinated Admiral Darlan, by placing a wreath on his tomb and observing a minute of silence.

"Among the personalities was Emmanuel d'Astier de la Vigerie, Secretary for the Interior."

Later, an Algerian Court of Appeals annulled the sentence against the young assassin, citing in part as its reasons "documents found after the liberation of France which showed conclusively that Admiral Darlan had been acting against the interests of France and that Bonnier's act had been accomplished in the interests of the liberation of France."

Now that he was legally and morally rehabilitated, Bonnier's crime disappeared from the record. As a consequence, so did that of any accomplices.

In September of 1943, only three months after de Gaulle's arrival in Algiers, Giraud rendered a *"non-lieu"* in favor of Henri d'Astier, Cordier, and Garidacci, who were then released.

The day he got out of jail, d'Astier received the *Croix de guerre* with palms from Giraud, and the following day the Medal of the Resistance from de Gaulle. Two days later he was named a member of the Consultative Assembly.

Cordier was awarded the *Croix de guerre*.

Garidacci was fired.

Of the twelve who had been arrested for conspiracy in the murder of Darlan, Muscatelli became Prefect of Algiers, Jacques Brunel Prefect of Police—with José Aboulker as his *chef de cabinet*—Bringard the Chief of Police of Algiers, Achiary Assistant Prefect of Batna. Of the other conspirators some went even further: Capitant became a minister in de Gaulle's Cabinet and Louis Joxe became Ambassador to Moscow.

As for Rigault and Lemaigre-Dubreuil, after the liberation of France they slipped across the border from Spain and were promptly arrested on charges of having "negotiated with a foreign power."

Murphy, now an Ambassador, and special political adviser to Eisenhower for most of Europe, brought pressure for their release, and though *Combat* and *Franc-Tireur* raised a cry about the interference of an American official in a matter of French justice, the case against both defendants was dropped.

Rigault set about recording with the aid of a female friend from Algiers—Mme. Geneviève Dumais—a two-volume history of the events which had transpired in North Africa, to which was assigned the pseudonym of "Chamine." By 1955 he was back with Pierre Étienne Flandin and René Belin, editing a financial sheet called *Le Bulletin de Paris* which later changed its name to *Capital*.

As for Lemaigre-Dubreuil, on July 12th of 1955, shortly after he had acquired controlling interest in the *Maroc Presse,* he was shot to death by unknown assailants on the doorstep of his Casablanca house.

The Minister of Moroccan Affairs, Pierre July, announced that Lemaigre had been "the victim of counter-terrorists."

And so it goes. No doubt many of the Vichy protagonists believed that what they were doing was right, that they were defending the values of Western Christianity against the atheism and apostasy of Communism.

But as de Gaulle kept pointing out, by their behavior and activities they seemed to be creating more Communists than Lenin and Stalin could proselytize in a whole generation.

To de Gaulle, the Allied penchant for dealing with "men who have destroyed all freedom in France and who seek to model their regime on fascism or a caricature of it is the equivalent of introducing into politics the principles of the poor simpleton who, for fear of getting wet in the rain, threw himself into the sea."

BIBLIOGRAPHY

ABOULKER, MARCEL, *Alger et ses complots*. Les Documents Nuit et Jour, Paris, 1945.

ANDERSON, LT. GEN. SIR KENNETH A. N., "Report to the War Office" in *London Gazette*, Nov. 5, 1946.

ARMSTRONG, HAMILTON FISH, *When There Is No Peace*. The Macmillan Company, New York, 1939.

ARON, ROBERT, *Le Piège où nous a pris l'histoire*. Michel, Paris, 1950.

ASTIER DE LA VIGERIE, EMMANUEL D', *Sept fois sept jours*. La Guilde du livre, Lausanne, 1956.

AUPHAN, GABRIEL A. J. P., *L'histoire de mes "trahisons."* Plon, Paris, 1951.

BARJOT, PIERRE, *Le Débarquement du 8 novembre 1942 en Afrique du Nord*. J. de Gigord, Paris, 1946.

BARRÉ, GEORGES, *Tunisie, 1942–1943*. Éditions Berger-Levrault, Paris, 1950.

BAUDOIN, PAUL, *Neuf mois au gouvernement*. Éditions de la Table ronde, Paris, 1948.

BAYET, ALBERT, *Pétain et la cinquième colonne*. Société des éditions de Franc-tireur, Paris, 1944.

BENOIST-MÉCHIN, JACQUES G. P. M., *Sixty Days That Shook the West: the Fall of France,* tr. by Peter Wiles. G. P. Putnam's Sons, New York, 1963.

BÉTHOUART, MARIE ÉMILE, *Le Procès Pucheu*. Amiot-Dumont, Paris, 1947.

BOIS, ÉLIE J., *Truth on the Tragedy of France,* tr. by N. Scarlyn Wilson. Hodder & Stoughton, Ltd., London, 1941.

BOURGET, PIERRE ANDRÉ, *Témoignages interdits sur le Maréchal Pétain*. A. Fayard, Paris, 1960.

BOUTHILLIER, YVES, *Le Drame de Vichy*. Plon, Paris, 1950.

BRADLEY, OMAR NELSON, *A Soldier's Story*. Henry Holt and Company, Inc., New York, 1951.

BRET, PAUL-LOUIS, *Au Feu des événements*. Plon, Paris, 1959.

BRUGÉRE, RAYMOND, *Veni, vidi Vichy . . . et la suite, témoignages (1940–1945)*. Deux rives, Paris, 1953.

BUTCHER, HARRY C., *My Three Years with Eisenhower*. Simon and Schuster, Inc., New York, 1946.

CAPITANT, RENÉ (editor), *Combat*.

CARTIER, RAYMOND, *Les Secrets de la guerre, dévoilés par Nuremberg*. A. Fayard, Paris, 1947.

CATROUX, GEORGES, *Dans la bataille de la Méditerranée: Égypte, Levant, Afrique du Nord, 1940–1944*. Juilliard, Paris, 1949.

CHAMINE (pseud.), *La Conjuration d'Alger*. A. Michel, Paris, 1946.

———, *La Querelle des généraux,* A. Michel, Paris, 1952.

CHARNAY, GEOFFREY DE, *Synarchie*. Éditions Médicis, Paris, 1946.

CHILDS, MARQUIS W., *Eisenhower, Captive Hero*. Harcourt, Brace & Company, Inc., New York, 1958.

CLARK, MARK WAYNE, *Calculated Risk*. Harper & Brothers, New York, 1950.

CLIFFORD, ALEXANDER, *Conquest of North Africa, 1940–1943*. Little, Brown & Company, Boston, 1943.

COT, PIERRE, *Triumph of Treason*, tr. by Sybille and Milton Crane. Ziff-Davis Publishing Company, New York, 1944.

CRAS, HERVÉ, *La bataille de Casablanca*. Plon, Paris, 1952.

DARLAN, ALAIN, *L'Amiral Darlan parle*. Librairie Académique Perrin, Paris, 1953.

DARLAN, FRANÇOIS, *Messages aux Français*. F. Sorlot, Clermont, 1941.

DASHIELL, SAMUEL, *Victory Through Africa*. Smith & Durrell, Inc., New York, 1943.

DE MONTMORENCY, ALEC, *The Enigma of Admiral Darlan*. E. P. Dutton & Co., Inc., New York, 1943.

DÉSERT, JOSEPH, *Toute la Vérité sur la cagoule*. Librairie des Sciences et des Arts, Paris, 1946.

DEWAVRIN, ANDRÉ (pseud.: Colonel Passy), *Souvenirs*. R. Solar, Monte Carlo, 1947.

DHERS, PIERRE, *Le maréchal Pétain et le débarquement africain*. Flammarion, Paris, 1958.

DOCTEUR, JULES T., *Darlan, amiral de la flotte, la grande énigme de la guerre*. Éditions de la Couronne, Paris, 1949.

DU MOULIN DE LABARTHÈTE, HENRI, *Le Temps des illusions: souvenirs (juillet 1940–avril 1942)*, Les Éditions du Cheval ailé, Genève, 1946.

DUPAYS, P., *Débarquement allié en A.F.N., chronique historique: libération, 8 novembre–décembre 1942*. Éditions de la Critique, Paris, 1953.

———, *Renaissance de l'A.F.N., chronique historique: la vie reprend, janvier–avril 1943*. Éditions de la Critique, Paris, 1953.

———, *Vie nouvelle en A.F.N., chronique historique: août–décembre 1943*. Éditions de la Critique, Paris, 1953.

EISENHOWER, DWIGHT D., *Crusade in Europe*. Doubleday & Company, Inc., New York, 1948.

ESQUER, GABRIEL, *8 novembre 1942, jour premier de la libération*. Éditions Charlot, Paris, 1946.

FARAGO, LADISLAS, *Patton—Ordeal and Triumph*. Ivan Obolensky, Inc., New York, 1964.

FARRERE, C., *François Darlan, amiral de France et sa flotte*. Flammarion, Paris, 1939.

FLANNER, JANET, *Pétain: The Old Man of France*. Simon and Schuster, Inc., New York, 1944.

FONROY, J. H., *La Bataille des Services Secrets*. Éditions du milieu du monde, Paris, 1958.

FONTENAY, FERNAND, *La cagoule contre la France*. Éditions sociales internationales, Paris, 1938.

FOOT, MICHAEL, *La Vérité sur l'affaire Pétain*. Éditions du milieu du monde, Genève, 1945.

GALLAGHER, WESLEY, *Back Door to Berlin: The Full Story of the American Coup in North Africa*. Doubleday & Company, Inc., New York, 1943.

GAULLE, CHARLES DE, *Le Fil de l'épée*. Éditions Berger-Levrault, Paris, 1932.

———, *War Memoirs*, 5 vols. Simon and Schuster, New York, 1960.

GÉRARD, ANDRÉ, *The Gravediggers of France*. Doubleday, Doran & Co., Inc., Garden City, 1944.

GIRARD, LOUIS DOMINIQUE, *Montoire, Verdun Diplomatique*. A. Bonne, Paris, 1948.

GIRAUD, HENRI HONORÉ, *Un Seul but, la victoire, Alger 1942–1944*. R. Juilliard, Paris, 1949.

GOOCH, ROBERT KENT, *The Pétain Government and the Vichy Régime*. Carnegie Endowment for International Peace, New York. 1940.

GOSSET, RENÉE, *Le Coup d'Alger*. Les Éditions de la Revue moderne, Montréal, 1944.

———, *Expédients provisoires*. Fasquelle, Paris, 1945.

GUEDALLA, PHILIP, *The Two Marshals: Bazaine, Pétain.* Hodder & Stoughton, Ltd., London, 1943.

HATCH, ALDEN, *General Ike: A Biography of Dwight D. Eisenhower.* Henry Holt & Company, Inc., New York, 1944.

HERRIOT, ÉDOUARD, *Épisodes, 1940–1944.* Flammarion, Paris, 1950.

HERMANN, LAZAR, *The Darkest Hour: Adventures and Escapes,* tr. by Ralph Marlowe. Houghton Mifflin Company, Boston, 1941.

HOWE, GEORGE FREDERICK, *Northwest Africa: Seizing the Initiative in the West.* U.S. Military History Office, Washington, 1957.

HULL, CORDELL (assisted by Andrew Berding), *Memoirs,* 2 vols. The Macmillan Company, New York, 1948.

ICHAC, PIERRE, *Nous marchions vers la France.* Amiot-Dumont, Paris, 1954.

JEWELL, NORMAN L. A., *Secret Mission Submarine,* as told to Cecil Carnes. Ziff-Davis Publishing Company, New York, 1945.

JOESTEN, JOACHIM, *The Red Hand: The Sinister Account of the Terrorist Arm of the French Right-Wing Ultras in Algeria and on the Continent.* Abelard-Schuman, Inc., New York, 1962.

KAMMERER, ALBERT, *Du débarquement africain au meurtre de Darlan.* Flammarion, Paris, 1949.

———, *La Vérité sur l'armistice.* Éditions Médicis, Paris, 1945.

KÉRILLIS, HENRI DE, *De Gaulle, dictateur: une grande mystification de l'histoire.* Éditions Beauchemin, Montréal, 1945.

LANGER, WILLIAM L., *Our Vichy Gamble.* Alfred A. Knopf, Inc., New York, 1947.

——— and GLEASON, S. EVERETT, *The Undeclared War, 1940–1941.* Published for the Council on Foreign Relations by Harper & Brothers, New York, 1953.

LAVAL, PIERRE, *Laval parle.* Diffusion du livre, Paris, 1948.

LAZAREFF, PIERRE, *Deadline: the behind-the-scenes story of the last decade in France,* tr. by David Partridge. Random House, Inc., New York, 1942.

———, *De Munich à Vichy.* Brentano's, Inc., New York, 1944.

LEAHY, WILLIAM D., *I Was There.* McGraw-Hill Book Company, Inc., New York, 1950.

LEMAIGRE-DUBREUIL, JACQUES, *Les relations franco-américaine et la politique des généraux.* Publications Élysées, Paris, 1949.

——— (pseud.: Crusoe), *Vissicitudes d'une victoire.* Editions de l'ame francaise, Paris, 1946.

LIDDEL HART, B. H., *The Other Side of the Hill: Germany's Generals, Their Rise and Fall.* Cassell & Co., Ltd., London, 1948.

LOUSTAUNAU-LACAU, GEORGES A. A., *Mémoires d'un Francais rebelle, 1914–48.* R. Laffont, Paris, 1948.

MACVANE, JOHN, *Journey into War: War and Diplomacy in North Africa.* Appleton-Century-Crofts, Inc., New York, 1943.

MANSTEIN, FRITZ ERICH VON, *Lost Victories,* tr. by Anthony G. Powell. Henry Regnery Co. Publishers, Chicago, 1958.

MARTIN DU GARD, MAURICE, *La Chronique de Vichy, 1940–1944.* Flammarion, Paris, 1948.

MATTHEWS, HERBERT L., *Two Wars and More to Come.* Carrick & Evans, Inc., New York, 1938.

MICHEL, A., "Procès du maréchal Pétain" (stenographic account, Paris).

MIKES, GEORGE, *Darlan, a Study.* Constable & Co., Ltd., London, 1943.

MORISON, SAMUEL ELIOT, *History of United States Naval Operations in World War II,* 15 vols. Little, Brown & Company, Boston, 1947–62.

———, *Strategy and Compro-*

mise. Little, Brown & Co., Ltd., Toronto, 1958.

MURPHY, ROBERT D., *Diplomat Among Warriors*. Doubleday & Company, Inc., New York, 1964.

OLIVEIRA, MAURICIO DE, *Pound & Darlan*. Parceria A. M. Pereira, Lisbon, 1940.

PATTON, GEORGE S., Jr., *War As I Knew It*. Houghton Mifflin Company, Boston, 1947.

PENDAR, KENNETH W., *Adventure in Diplomacy: Our French Dilemma*. Dodd, Mead & Company, Inc., New York, 1945.

PÉTAIN, HENRI PHILIPPE, *La Politique sociale de la France*. Introduction by Jacques Bardouse. F. Sorlot, Paris, 1941.

PEYROUTON, BERNARD MARCEL, *Du service public à la prison commune*. Plon, Paris, 1950.

POL, HEINZ, *Suicide of a Democracy*, tr. by Heinz and Ruth Norden. Reynal & Hitchcock, Inc., New York, 1940.

POZZO DI BORGO, LOUIS, *Algérie d'hier et d'aujourd'hui*. Éditions du Conquistador, Paris, 1957.

PRICE, G. WARD, *Giraud and the African Scene*. The Macmillan Company, New York, 1944.

REIBEL, CHARLES, *Pourquoi et comment fut décidée la demande d'armistice*. Vanves (Seine) Imprimerie Kapp, Paris, 1940.

——, *La Vérité sur les origines du débarquement Allié en Afrique du Nord*. Les Presses Alpha, Paris, 1946.

RICHARD, RENÉ, and SERIGNY, ALAIN DE, *L'Enigme d'Alger*. A. Fayard, Paris, 1947.

ROOSEVELT, ELLIOTT, *As He Saw It*. Duell, Sloan & Pearce, New York, 1946.

ROOT, WAVERLEY, *Are You Ready for World War III?* Committee for a Democratic Foreign Policy, New York, 1944.

——, *The Secret History of the War*. Charles Scribner's Sons, New York, 1945–1946.

ROUGIER, LOUIS A. P., *Les Accords secrets franco-britanniques de l'automne 1940*. B. Grasset, Paris, 1954.

——, *Mission secrète à Londres: les accords Pétain-Churchill*. Éditions du Cheval ailé, Paris, 1948.

——, *Les Mystiques èconomiques: comment l'on passe des démocraties libérales aux états totalitaires*. Librairie de Médicis, Paris, 1938.

SAINT-YVES D'ALVEYDRE, JOSEPH, ALEXANDRE, MARQUIS DE, *Les Clefs de l'Orient*. Édité par Librairie Hermétique, 1910.

——, *Mission de l'Inde en Europe*. Dorbon aîné, Paris, 1949.

——, *Mission des Juifs*. Dorbon aîné, Paris, 1928.

——, *Mission des Souverains*. Nord-sud, Paris, 1948.

SHAPIRO, LIONEL, *They Left the Back Door Open: A Chronicle of the Allied Campaign in Sicily and Italy*. Jarrolds Publishers, Ltd., London, 1945.

SHERWOOD, ROBERT E., *Roosevelt and Hopkins*. Harper & Brothers, New York, 1948.

SIMON, O. K., *J'Accuse! The Man Who Betrayed France*. The Dial Press, Inc., New York, 1940.

SMITH, WALTER BEDELL, *Ike's Six Great Decisions: Europe, 1944–45*. Longmans, Green & Co., New York, 1956.

SOLANO, RAMON, *Un Crimen en Las Sombras: la muerte de Darlan*. Madrid, (Editorial Page) 1944.

SOUPIRON, PAUL, *Petain, Laval, Abetz and Mutinies of CPO*. Éditions Gutenberg, Lyon, 1946.

SOUSTELLE, JACQUES, *De Londres à Alger*. R. Laffont, Paris, 1947.

SULZBERGER, CYRUS L., *The Test: De Gaulle and Algeria*. Harcourt, Brace and World, Inc., New York, 1962.

TOURNOUX, JEAN RAYMOND, *Secrets d'état*. Plon, Paris, 1960.

WARBURG, JAMES P., *Unwritten Treaty*. Harcourt, Brace & Company, Inc., New York, 1946.

WELCH, GALBRAITH, *North African Prelude, the First Seven Thousand Years*. William Morrow & Company, Inc., New York, 1949.

WELLES, SUMNER, *The Time for for Decision*. Harper & Brothers, New York, 1944.

WEYGAND, MAXIME, *Rappelé au service*. Flammarion, Paris, 1950.

WINKLER, PAUL, *Les sources mystiques de concepts moraux de l'occident*. Éditions de Trevise, Paris, 1957.

———, *The Thousand-Year Conspiracy: Secret Germany Behind the Mask*. Charles Scribner's Sons, New York, 1943.

WORDELL, MALCOLM T., and SEILER, E.N., *Wildcats over Casablanca*, as told to Keith Ayling. Little, Brown & Company, Boston, 1943.

INDEX